Football, Community and Social Inclusion

This book addresses the complex reality of English community football organisations, including Football in the Community (FitC) schemes, which have been attending to social agendas, such as social inclusion and health promotion. The positioning of football as a key agent of change for this diverse range of social issues has resulted in an increase in funding support. Despite the increased availability of funding and the (apparent) willingness of football clubs to adopt such an altruistic position within society, there remains limited empirical evidence to substantiate football's ability to deliver results.

This book explores the current role of football clubs in supporting and delivering social inclusion and health promotion to its community and seeks to examine the philosophical, political, environmental and practical challenges of this work. The power and subsequent lure of a football club and its brand is an ideal vehicle to entice and capture populations that (normally) ignore or turn away from positive social and/or health behaviours. The foundations of such a belief are examined, outlining key recommendations and considerations for both researchers and practitioners attending to these social and health issues through the vehicle of football.

This book was originally published as a special issue of *Soccer & Society*.

Daniel Parnell is a Senior Lecturer in Sport Business Management at Leeds Beckett University, UK. His primary research interests are in sport, health and management, and his current projects concern the role of sport as a vehicle for social change, health improvement evaluation and organisational development, with a specific focus on football. He has worked with a range of Premier League and Football League Clubs.

David Richardson is the Director of the School of Sport and Exercise Science at Liverpool John Moores University, UK. His research tends to be qualitative in nature (including interviews, ethnographic techniques, action research) and represented through the utilisation of traditional qualitative analysis and/or exploring the use of creative non-fiction narratives to capture and illuminate observations of culture and associated applied practice.

SPORT IN THE GLOBAL SOCIETY – CONTEMPORARY PERSPECTIVES

Series Editor: Boria Majumdar

The social, cultural (including media) and political study of sport is an expanding area of scholarship and related research. While this area has been well served by the *Sport in the Global Society* series, the surge in quality scholarship over the last few years has necessitated the creation of *Sport in the Global Society: Contemporary Perspectives*. The series will publish the work of leading scholars in fields as diverse as sociology, cultural studies, media studies, gender studies, cultural geography and history, political science and political economy. If the social and cultural study of sport is to receive the scholarly attention and readership it warrants, a cross-disciplinary series dedicated to taking sport beyond the narrow confines of physical education and sport science academic domains is necessary. *Sport in the Global Society: Contemporary Perspectives* will answer this need.

Titles in the Series

Australian Sport
Antipodean Waves of Change
Edited by Kristine Toohey and Tracy Taylor

Australia's Asian Sporting Context
1920s and 1930s
Edited by Sean Brawley and Nick Guoth

Bearing Light: Flame Relays and the Struggle for the Olympic Movement
Edited by John J. MacAloon

'Critical Support' for Sport
Bruce Kidd

Disability in the Global Sport Arena
A Sporting Chance
Edited by Jill M. Clair

Diversity, Equity and Inclusion in Sport and Leisure
Edited by Katherine Dashper and Thomas Fletcher

Documenting the Beijing Olympics
Edited by D. P. Martinez and Kevin Latham

Ethnicity and Race in Association Football
Case Study analyses in Europe, Africa and the USA
Edited by David Hassan

Exploring the cultural, ideological and economic legacies of Euro 2012
Edited by Peter Kennedy and Christos Kassimeris

Fan Culture in European Football and the Influence of Left Wing Ideology
Edited by Peter Kennedy and David Kennedy

Football, Community and Social Inclusion
Edited by Daniel Parnell and David Richardson

Football in Asia
History, Culture and Business
Edited by Younghan Cho

Football in Southeastern Europe
From Ethnic Homogenization to Reconciliation
Edited by John Hughson and Fiona Skillen

Football Supporters and the Commercialisation of Football
Comparative Responses across Europe
Edited by Peter Kennedy and David Kennedy

Forty Years of Sport and Social Change, 1968-2008
"To Remember is to Resist"
Edited by Russell Field and Bruce Kidd

Global Perspectives on Football in Africa
Visualising the Game
Edited by Susann Baller, Giorgio Miescher and Ciraj Rassool

Global Sport Business
Community Impacts of Commercial Sport
Edited by Hans Westerbeek

Governance, Citizenship and the New European Football Championships
The European Spectacle
Edited by Wolfram Manzenreiter and Georg Spitaler

Indigenous People, Race Relations and Australian Sport
Edited by Christopher J. Hallinan and Barry Judd

Modern Sports in Asia
Cultural Perspectives
Edited by Younghan Cho and Charles Leary

Moral Panic in Physical Education and Coaching
Edited by Heather Piper, Dean Garratt and Bill Taylor

Olympic Reform Ten Years Later
Edited by Heather Dichter and Bruce Kidd

Reflections on Process Sociology and Sport
'Walking the Line'
Joseph Maguire

Security and Sport Mega Events
A Complex Relation
Edited by Diamantis Mastrogiannakis

Soccer in Brazil
Edited by Martin Curi

Soccer in the Middle East
Edited by Alon Raab and Issam Khalidi

South Africa and the Global Game
Football, Apartheid and Beyond
Edited by Peter Alegi and Chris Bolsmann

Sport – Race, Ethnicity and Identity
Building Global Understanding
Edited by Daryl Adair

Sport and Citizenship
Edited by Matthew Guschwan

Sport and Communities
Edited by David Hassan and Sean Brown

Sport, Culture and Identity in the State of Israel
Edited by Yair Galily and Amir Ben-Porat

Sport in Australian National Identity
Kicking Goals
Tony Ward

Sport in the City
Cultural Connections
Edited by Michael Sam and John E. Hughson

Sport, Memory and Nationhood in Japan
Remembering the Glory Days
Edited by Andreas Niehaus and Christian Tagsold

Sport, Music, Identities
Edited by Anthony Bateman

Sport, Race and Ethnicity
The Scope of Belonging?
Edited by Katie Liston and Paddy Dolan

The Changing Face of Cricket
From Imperial to Global Game
Edited by Dominic Malcolm, Jon Gemmell and Nalin Mehta

The Consumption and Representation of Lifestyle Sports
Edited by Belinda Wheaton

The Containment of Soccer in Australia
Fencing Off the World Game
Edited by Christopher J. Hallinan and John E. Hughson

The History of Motor Sport
A Case Study Analysis
Edited by David Hassan

The Making of Sporting Cultures
John E. Hughson

The Olympic Movement and the Sport of Peacemaking
Edited by Ramón Spaaij and Cindy Burleson

The Olympic Games: Meeting New Challenges
Edited by David Hassan and Shakya Mitra

The Other Sport Mega-Event: Rugby World Cup 2011
Edited by Steven J. Jackson

The Politics of Sport
Community, Mobility, Identity
Edited by Paul Gilchrist and Russell Holden

The Politics of Sport in South Asia
Edited by Subhas Ranjan Chakraborty, Shantanu Chakrabarti and Kingshuk Chatterjee

The Social Impact of Sport
Edited by Ramón Spaaij

The Social Science of Sport
A Critical Analysis
Edited by Bo Carlsson and Susanna Hedenborg

Towards a Social Science of Drugs in Sport
Edited by Jason Mazanov

Twenty20 and the Future of Cricket
Edited by Chris Rumford

Who Owns Football?
The Governance and Management of the Club Game Worldwide
Edited by David Hassan and Sean Hamil

Why Minorities Play or Don't Play Soccer
A Global Exploration
Edited by Kausik Bandyopadhyay

Women's Football in the UK
Continuing with Gender Analyses
Edited by Jayne Caudwell

Women's Sport in Africa
Edited by Michelle Sikes and John Bale

Football, Community and Social Inclusion

Edited by
Daniel Parnell and David Richardson

LONDON AND NEW YORK

First published 2015
by Routledge
2 Park Square, Milton Park, Abingdon, Oxon, OX14 4RN, UK

and by Routledge
711 Third Avenue, New York, NY 10017, USA

Routledge is an imprint of the Taylor & Francis Group, an informa business

© 2015 Taylor & Francis

All rights reserved. No part of this book may be reprinted or reproduced or utilised in any form or by any electronic, mechanical, or other means, now known or hereafter invented, including photocopying and recording, or in any information storage or retrieval system, without permission in writing from the publishers.

Trademark notice: Product or corporate names may be trademarks or registered trademarks, and are used only for identification and explanation without intent to infringe.

British Library Cataloguing in Publication Data
A catalogue record for this book is available from the British Library

ISBN13: 978-1-138-85591-5

Typeset in Times
by RefineCatch Limited, Bungay, Suffolk

Publisher's Note
The publisher accepts responsibility for any inconsistencies that may have arisen during the conversion of this book from journal articles to book chapters, namely the possible inclusion of journal terminology.

Disclaimer
Every effort has been made to contact copyright holders for their permission to reprint material in this book. The publishers would be grateful to hear from any copyright holder who is not here acknowledged and will undertake to rectify any errors or omissions in future editions of this book.

Contents

Citation Information ix
Notes on Contributors xi

1. Introduction 1
   Daniel Parnell and David Richardson

2. Corporate social responsibility and social partnerships in professional football 6
   Geoff Walters and Mark Panton

3. Little United and the Big Society: negotiating the gaps between football, community and the politics of inclusion 25
   Annabel Kiernan and Chris Porter

4. Growing the football game: the increasing economic and social relevance of older fans and those with disabilities in the European football industry 42
   Juan Luis Paramio Salcines, John Grady and Phil Downs

5. Fit Fans: perspectives of a practitioner and understanding participant health needs within a health promotion programme for older men delivered within an English Premier League Football Club 61
   Daniel David Bingham, Daniel Parnell, Kathryn Curran, Roger Jones and Dave Richardson

6. Effect of a health-improvement pilot programme for older adults delivered by a professional football club: the Burton Albion case study 80
   Andy Pringle, Daniel Parnell, Stephen Zwolinsky, Jackie Hargreaves and Jim McKenna

7. 'I just want to watch the match': a practitioner's reflective account of men's health themed match day events at an English Premier League football club 97
   Kathryn Curran, Barry Drust and Dave Richardson

8. Ethnographic engagement from within a Football in the Community programme at an English Premier League football club 112
   Kathryn Curran, Daniel David Bingham, David Richardson and Daniel Parnell

CONTENTS

9. 'Motivate': the effect of a Football in the Community delivered weight loss programme on over 35-year old men and women's cardiovascular risk factors 129
   Zoe Rutherford, Brendan Gough, Sarah Seymour-Smith, Christopher R Matthews, John Wilcox, Dan Parnell and Andy Pringle

10. Assessing the impact of football-based health improvement programmes: stay onside, avoid own goals and score with the evaluation! 148
    Andy Pringle, Jackie Hargreaves, Lorena Lozano, Jim McKenna and Stephen Zwolinsky

Index 167

Citation Information

The chapters in this book were originally published in *Soccer & Society*, volume 15, issue 6 (November 2014). When citing this material, please use the original page numbering for each article, as follows:

Chapter 1
Introduction
Daniel Parnell and David Richardson
Soccer & Society, volume 15, issue 6 (November 2014) pp. 823–827

Chapter 2
Corporate social responsibility and social partnerships in professional football
Geoff Walters and Mark Panton
Soccer & Society, volume 15, issue 6 (November 2014) pp. 828–846

Chapter 3
Little United and the Big Society: negotiating the gaps between football, community and the politics of inclusion
Annabel Kiernan and Chris Porter
Soccer & Society, volume 15, issue 6 (November 2014) pp. 847–863

Chapter 4
Growing the football game: the increasing economic and social relevance of older fans and those with disabilities in the European football industry
Juan Luis Paramio Salcines, John Grady and Phil Downs
Soccer & Society, volume 15, issue 6 (November 2014) pp. 864–882

Chapter 5
Fit Fans: perspectives of a practitioner and understanding participant health needs within a health promotion programme for older men delivered within an English Premier League Football Club
Daniel David Bingham, Daniel Parnell, Kathryn Curran, Roger Jones and Dave Richardson
Soccer & Society, volume 15, issue 6 (November 2014) pp. 883–901

CITATION INFORMATION

Chapter 6
Effect of a health-improvement pilot programme for older adults delivered by a professional football club: the Burton Albion case study
Andy Pringle, Daniel Parnell, Stephen Zwolinsky, Jackie Hargreaves and Jim McKenna
Soccer & Society, volume 15, issue 6 (November 2014) pp. 902–918

Chapter 7
'I just want to watch the match': a practitioner's reflective account of men's health themed match day events at an English Premier League football club
Kathryn Curran, Barry Drust and Dave Richardson
Soccer & Society, volume 15, issue 6 (November 2014) pp. 919–933

Chapter 8
Ethnographic engagement from within a Football in the Community programme at an English Premier League football club
Kathryn Curran, Daniel David Bingham, David Richardson and Daniel Parnell
Soccer & Society, volume 15, issue 6 (November 2014) pp. 934–950

Chapter 9
'Motivate': the effect of a Football in the Community delivered weight loss programme on over 35-year old men and women's cardiovascular risk factors
Zoe Rutherford, Brendan Gough, Sarah Seymour-Smith, Christopher R Matthews, John Wilcox, Dan Parnell and Andy Pringle
Soccer & Society, volume 15, issue 6 (November 2014) pp. 951–969

Chapter 10
Assessing the impact of football-based health improvement programmes: stay onside, avoid own goals and score with the evaluation!
Andy Pringle, Jackie Hargreaves, Lorena Lozano, Jim McKenna and
Stephen Zwolinsky
Soccer & Society, volume 15, issue 6 (November 2014) pp. 970–987

Please direct any queries you may have about the citations to
clsuk.permissions@cengage.com

Notes on Contributors

Daniel David Bingham is a PhD student in the School of Sport, Exercise and Health Science at the University of Loughborough, UK. His main focus is the correlates of early years physical activity.

Kathryn Curran is Lecturer in Sport Development and Coaching at the University of Bolton, UK. Her work and research using football as a vehicle for physical activity and health engagement with socially disadvantaged men has been championed by the World Health Organization as an example of best practice.

Phil Downs is Secretary and Disability Liaison Officer of the Manchester United Disabled Supporter's Association, Manchester, UK.

Barry Drust is Professor in the School of Sport and Exercise Science at Liverpool John Moores University, Liverpool, UK. His specialist research area is the physiology of intermittent exercise, with a particular interest in football.

Brendan Gough is Professor of Social Psychology and a Core Member of the Institute for Health and Well-Being at Leeds Beckett University, Leeds, UK. His work enables commissioners, care providers, specialist voluntary sector bodies, businesses, and enterprises to have a greater insight into people's behaviour, with a particular focus on masculinity and lifestyle challenges.

John Grady is Associate Professor of Sport and Entertainment at the University of South Carolina, Columbia, South Carolina, USA. His research interests focus primarily on the legal aspects of the business of sport.

Jackie Hargreaves is completing her PhD at Leeds Beckett University, Leeds, UK, focusing on physical activity and quality of life in people with psychosis. Her specific interest lies in exploring how physical activity can be beneficial for mental health and mental illness.

Roger Jones is National Manager at the National Older Men's Network, Liverpool, UK.

Annabel Kiernan is Director of the Centre for the Study of Football at Manchester Metropolitan University, Manchester, UK. Her research interests cover public sector reform and the role of football in local service delivery and community identity.

Lorena Lozano is a PhD student in Sport, Physical Activity and Health at Leeds Beckett University, Leeds, UK. Her research focuses on men's experiences of weight management, using a longitudinal qualitative study which draws upon ethnographic and narrative approaches to research.

Christopher R. Matthews is a Faculty Member in the School of Sport and Service Management, University of Brighton, UK. His research interests include gender, sexuality, class, violence, and combat sports.

NOTES ON CONTRIBUTORS

Jim McKenna is Professor of Physical Activity and Health at Leeds Beckett University, Leeds, UK. He is Head of the Active Lifestyles research centre, where the main focus is on identifying outcomes resulting from physical activity and ways of optimising the promotion of physical activity.

Mark Panton is a PhD student in the Sport Business Centre at Birkbeck, University of London, UK. His research interests include the work of football community schemes and the use of sport in urban regeneration.

Juan Luis Paramio Salcines is a Researcher in the Department of Physical Education at the Universidad Autónoma de Madrid, Spain.

Daniel Parnell is a Senior Lecturer in Sport Business Management at Leeds Beckett University, Leeds, UK. His primary research interests are in sport, health and management, and his current projects concern the role of sport as a vehicle for social change, health improvement evaluation and organisational development, with a specific focus on football. He has worked with a range of Premier League and Football League Clubs.

Chris Porter is Director of the Centre for the Study of Football at Manchester Metropolitan University, Manchester, UK. His research interests include the links between football fandom and politics, consumption, popular culture, class-consciousness, neoliberal ideology and globalisation.

Andy Pringle is Reader in Physical Activity and Public Health, he is based at the Institute of Sport, Physical Activity and Leisure at Leeds Beckett University, Leeds, UK. Andy undertakes research into the impact of physical activity and health interventions including those in football-led settings.

David Richardson is the Director of the School of Sport and Exercise Science at Liverpool John Moores University, UK. His research tends to be qualitative in nature (including interviews, ethnographic techniques, action research) and represented through the utilisation of traditional qualitative analysis and/or exploring the use of creative non-fiction narratives to capture and illuminate observations of culture and associated applied practice.

Zoe Rutherford is Senior Lecturer in Physical Activity, Exercise and Health at Leeds Beckett University, Leeds, UK. Her research is based around the promotion of healthy living.

Sarah Seymour-Smith is Senior Lecturer in the College of Business Law and Social Sciences at Nottingham Trent University, Nottingham, UK. Her research focuses on masculinities, primarily the study of a range of men's health issues, but also incorporating issues of fatherhood and male sex offenders.

Geoff Walters is a Lecturer in Management at Birkbeck, University of London, UK. He is a Director of the Birkbeck Sport Business Centre.

John Wilcox is Public Health Development Manager at NHS Nottingham City, UK.

Stephen Zwolinsky is a PhD student at Leeds Beckett University, Leeds, UK. He is also a Research Officer in the Centre for Active Lifestyles. His current research focuses on men's health and lifestyles. He has been working with colleagues from the Carnegie Faculty on an evaluation study, Premier League Health, which is being run in partnership with 16 English Premier League and Championship football clubs.

Introduction

Daniel Parnell[a] and David Richardson[b]

[a]Centre for Active Lifestyles, Carnegie Faculty, Leeds Metropolitan University, Leeds, UK; [b]The Football Exchange, Research Institute for Sport and Exercise Sciences, Liverpool John Moores University, Liverpool, UK

In the year of the World Cup in Brazil 2014, the sheer mass of content across multiple sources in both the media and research outputs suggests that football is a world game. Estimates of viewing figures for the most recent Football World Cup Finals range from 250 million actual viewers (i.e. those that watched the final game) to 700 million viewers who consumed 'some part' of the game (i.e. the reach) (see FIFA, No. 1 Sports Event). FIFA also reported that the cumulative television viewing figures for each of the 2006 and 2010 World Cups in Germany and South Africa was an incredible 26.29 billion.[1] Significantly, it is the ability of football to 'reach' so many people that makes it a true game for all, irrespective of gender, age, ethnicity, religious belief, disability, socio-economic or health status. Brazil is the heart of creative and attractive football and the home of carnivals and sunshine. The business world readied itself to capitalize on the exposure that any alignment or presence at the World Cup could bring global awareness to their brands. However, it would seem that those who seek to encourage and foster social good through football have been slow to capitalize on such intrigue and interest in order to capture and connect with all who have some propensity to consume football or to be reached by and through football. Most notably, the limited attention to social good or social welfare campaigns aligned to the World Cup was arguably the biggest miss of the whole tournament. This volume explores the power of football and its role in engaging and including its 'populous' in positive social and behavioural activity. Specifically, this volume highlights a range of approaches that have been adopted and actioned by researchers, practitioners and organizations in order to stimulate, create and influence social good through football.

The notions of inclusion and inclusivity require a coherent alignment to high accessibility, low costs and involvement of all. The social roots of football have long been established. Across the globe, football's culture, heritage and identity are entrenched within its respective local communities. As such, the relationship between the football club and the community has been inextricably linked. It is this relationship that ensures that, in order for football to continue to flourish, or even exist, it will forever be indebted to its communities. It is the synergy between football's local and global appeal, its reach and subsequent responsibility and indebtedness to its communities that we must capitalize on, in order to ensure that football can act as a vehicle for the promotion of social good for all. Given

England's global football brand and its long established football-based community outreach programmes viewed by many as models of 'best practice', this volume (mainly) focuses on activity occurring in football clubs in England. Within the England, the link between football clubs and the community has been actively nourished through the development of the national Football in the Community (FitC) programme.

Football clubs in England have a relatively long history of engaging in community-based work. The late 70s saw the first moves to formalize a 'Football and the Community' programme. These early schemes were backed by the then Labour Government and the Sports Council.[2] The mid-80s saw the Sports Council pass governance of the programmes to other agencies which included the Football League and the Professional Footballers' Association through the Footballers' Further Education and Vocational Training Scheme.[3] During this time, the reputation of football was in steep decline as a consequence of emerging social issues (i.e. hooliganism, gangs and firms). Concerns over the increasingly fractured relationship between football and its communities demanded government intervention in order to re-establish the interconnected and mutually beneficial relationship. For many years, FitC schemes across the country were positioned as deliverers of community engagement.[4] This delivery, typically involved encouraging more children to play, watch and support their respective football teams. Whilst the presence of the football club in its communities was more visible, questions remained as to the exact purpose of the football club's community programme. Whilst football in England began to experience increasing commercialization, the relationship between football clubs and its communities remained strained and distant. In essence, people began to ask whether, given the apparent commercial growth of the football club, they (the clubs) could do more for their communities.[5] In essence, the continuing commercialization and 'Sky-ification' of football further contributed to this divide and the subsequent questioning of the moral obligation of football to its communities.[6] As such, stakeholders within and external to the 'game' called for football clubs to display a greater level of corporate social responsibility (CSR), with a view to reconsidering and re-establishing their relationships with their communities.[7]

The continuing appeal of football, the subsequent television deals and the apparently unabated rewards for clubs have intensified the pressure on football to 'genuinely' consider its social role. Indeed, the presence, and examination, of CSR practices within football is becoming increasingly scrutinized.[8] Such scrutiny has been reported to be affiliated to New Labours' election win in 1997 and the evolving welfare reform, as part of their 'Third Way' ideology, which in essence asserted that business was required to consider a more socially responsible approach to their operations. Football was not, and is not, immune from such scrutiny. The Football Task Force (FTF) emerged with a remit to monitor the social responsibility of the football sector.[9] Football stadia were identified as key arenas for encouraging and engaging fans in the development of positive health messages,[10] covering all aspects of stadia functions and the football clubs were positioned as vehicles to deliver on a range of key policy objectives including health, education, community cohesion, employment, regeneration and crime reduction[11] Despite this, very little is known of the day-to-day existence and impact of such work. Some success has been reported through the engagement of men in health-related behaviours with 'raised health awareness' being reported as a consequence of delivering health messages at football clubs, a place where men feel comfortable.[12] Further findings included positive health changes, increases in physical activity levels, improved weight status and a reduction in alcohol consumption. This research coupled with a recent study in the Lancet, which evidences successful weight loss in men via the Fit Fans in Training programme delivered across Scottish Premier League Clubs, suggests that mixing football and health promotion can work. Whilst the latter of these studies was costly to deliver, the positive impact of this work suggests that football can play a key role as part of the wider Public Health Service delivery.[13]

With football clubs being asked to deliver so much (i.e. monitored and evaluated health-related programmes), we are left with a skills shortage within and across practitioners working in football and the community programmes.[14] Despite the apparent success of such ongoing and developing cases, we are in an age of public spending austerity and as such the existing practitioners are being asked to deliver on ever increasing and expanding agendas that (technically) require an accumulation of many more skills than just coaching. Such skills, including physical and physiological awareness, dietary and health advice, counselling, welfare and well-being alongside research, evaluation and monitoring techniques, require training and investment. Moreover, such practitioners require elevation to, alignment with, and/or consideration of inclusion in the Health and Care Professions Council (HCPC) which includes areas such as social workers, psychologists and dieticians. Such a shift in the professional status and recognition of the FitC coach will better enable the coach and football industry to deliver to these expanding health and care agendas.[15]

Never has it been more important to adopt a genuine and inclusive approach to engaging with our local and global communities. As we reflect on the overwhelming media hype of the World Cup, and admire the way in which the business and commercial world has capitalized on such an iconic platform to accrue further global recognition, we must ask whether football and its populous have genuinely benefited from and/or capitalized on this phenomenon. The excellent examples of social good and positive individual and organizational behaviour change highlighted in this volume only scratch the surface of potential. We and football have the power to change lives. We can all do more …

It is beyond the scope of this introductory preamble to provide a summary of discussion of the articles; the abstracts offer ample insight into the excellent work that has been undertaken and collated here. Suffice to say that the ambition of the volume, when the original call for contributions was made, was to locate likeminded researchers who have a shared interest in football and inclusivity. The papers draw on sociological, political and economic perspectives from a breadth of contexts concerning the inclusivity, societal good, positive behaviour change, governance and practice of football clubs. The special edition also lends from an array of methodological lens that allows you, the reader, to see what is possible to achieve when working, and collaborating, with and alongside industry partners. To this end, we are satisfied that the journal offers a truly holistic, contextual and real understanding of the joys and complexities associated with working within football in the community programmes whilst trying to make a difference to peoples' lives through football.

We hope that the collective nature of the papers offered in this journal will encourage football-governing bodies and football CEOs to recognize that inclusion, inclusivity and social welfare make sound moral and business sense. This special issue champions the business case for inclusivity through the integration and mutual alignment of economic, social and health factors. We believe that it is time to stop asking football to cure, solve and eradicate societal ills through ad hoc, short-term and short-sighted investments and begin to gather real critical mass behind a long-term strategic plan to engage, include, utilize and measure football's power in engaging the masses in positive social good and social welfare practices. Football can change lives but it needs to better understand its reach, its fan base and their subsequent indebtedness to positively impact their local and global communities. In the spirit of inclusivity, we believe that it is the responsibility of all levels of the football industry, including football-governing bodies, football CEOs, practitioners and the perspectives of the participants or people genuinely affected by and/or reached by football, to make this happen.

Collaboratively, the authors offer both research and applied insight and perspectives with a genuine desire to capitalize and optimize the social role of football. As such, the authors represent a growing interest including Manchester Metropolitan's Football and its Communities research group and the critical mass of researchers representing the Leeds Metropolitan University Carnegie Faculty of Sport and their collaboration with the Football Exchange at Liverpool John Moores University. The editors would like to formally thank and compliment all of the contributors for their novel research, time and effort in making a genuine contribution to the literature and applied working practice. This work represents the work undertaken by those with applied experience and insight, alongside their academic duties. As such those working in football and aligned stakeholders including policy-makers, commissioners, project managers, health professional, community practitioners and coaches should find this special issue a pertinent, informative, timely and moreover a rally call to embrace a more holistic approach to tackling issues of inclusivity through football with a long-term strategic investment in making change and improving lives.

Acknowledgements

This special issue has benefited from the support from both the Higher Education Innovation Fund (Leeds Metropolitan University) and the Carnegie School of Sport, New Researcher Fund (Leeds Metropolitan University).

Notes

1. Viewing figures for World Cups 2006 and 2010.
2. Mellor, 'The "Janus-faced sport"'.
3. Walters and Chadwick, 'Corporate Citizenship in Football', 60.
4. Parnell et al., 'Football in the Community Schemes: Exploring the Effectiveness of an Intervention in Promoting Positive Healthful Behaviour Change'.
5. Brown et al., *Football and its Communities*.
6. Taylor, 'Multi-paradigmatic Research Design Spaces for Cultural Studies Researchers Embodying Postcolonial Theorising' and Anagnostopoulos and Shilbury, 'Implementing Corporate Social Responsibility in English Football'.
7. Taylor, 'Multi-paradigmatic Research Design Spaces for Cultural Studies Researchers Embodying Postcolonial Theorising'.
8. Walters and Chadwick, 'Corporate Citizenship in Football', 60; Anagnostopoulos and Shilbury, 'Implementing Corporate Social Responsibility in English Football' and Breitbarth, and Harris, 'The Role of Corporate Social Responsibility in the Football Business. Towards the Development of a Conceptual Model'.
9. Mellor, 'The "Janus-faced Sport"'.
10. See latest EU Healthy Stadia report.

11. Mellor, 'The "Janus-faced Sport"'; Parnell et al., 'Football in the Community Schemes: Exploring the Effectiveness of an Intervention in Promoting Positive Healthful Behaviour Change'.
12. Pringle et al., 'Effect of a National Programme of Men's Health Delivered in English Premier League Football Clubs'.
13. Hunt et al., 'A Gender-sensitised Weight Loss and Healthy Living Programme for Overweight and Obese Men Delivered by Scottish Premier League Football Clubs (FFIT): A Pragmatic Randomised Controlled Trial'.
14. Mellor, 'The "Janus-faced Sport"'; Parnell et al., 'Football in the Community Schemes: Exploring the Effectiveness of an Intervention in Promoting Positive Healthful Behaviour Change'; 'Implementing Monitoring and Evaluation Techniques within a Premier League Football in the Community Programme: A Case Study Involving Everton in the Community'.
15. Parnell et al., 'Football in the Community Schemes: Exploring the Effectiveness of an Intervention in Promoting Positive Healthful Behaviour Change'; "Implementing Monitoring and Evaluation Techniques within a Premier League Football in the Community Programme: A Case Study Involving Everton in the Community'.

References

Anagnostopoulos, C., and D. Shilbury. 'Implementing Corporate Social Responsibility in English Football: Towards Multi-theoretical Integration'. *Sport, Business and Management: An International Journal* 3, no. 4 (2013): 268–84.
Breitbarth, T., and P. Harris. 'The Role of Corporate Social Responsibility in the Football Business: Towards the Development of a Conceptual Model'. *European Sport Management Quarterly* 8, no. 2 (2008): 179–206.
Brown, A., T. Crabbe, G. Mellor, T. Blackshaw, and C. Stone. *Football and Its Communities: Final Report*. London: The Football Foundation, 2006.
FFIFA, No 1 Sports Event, FIFA.com. 2014. http://www.fifa.com/ (accessed January 10, 2014).
Health Stadia. *European Healthy Stadia Programme – Evaluation Report 2012*. http://www.healthystadia.eu/resource-library/eu-healthy-stadia-pilot-documents.html (accessed January 20, 2014).
Hunt, K., S. Wyke, C.M. Gray, A.S. Andersen, A. Brady, C. Bunn, P.T. Donnan, et al. 'A Gender-sensitised Weight Loss and Healthy Living Programme for Overweight and Obese Men Delivered by Scottish Premier League Football Clubs (FFIT): A Pragmatic Randomised Controlled Trial'. *Lancet* 383 (2014): 1211–21.
Mellor, G. 'The "Janus-Faced Sport": English Football, Community and the Legacy of the "Third Way"'. *Soccer & Society* 9, no. 3 (2008): 313–24.
Parnell, D., G. Stratton, B. Drust, and D. Richardson. 'Football in the Community Schemes: Exploring the Effectiveness of an Intervention in Promoting Healthful Behaviour Change'. *Soccer & Society* 14 (2013): 35–51.
Parnell, D.G., G. Stratton, B. Drust, and D. Richardson. 'Implementing Monitoring and Evaluation Techniques within a Premier League Football in the Community Programme: A Case Study Involving Everton in the Community'. In *The Routledge Handbook of Sport and Corporate Social Responsibility*, ed. J. Salcines, K. Babiak, and G. Walters, 328–43. London: Routledge, 2013.
Pringle, A., S. Zwolinsky, J. McKenna, A. Daly-Smith, S. Robertson, and A. White. 'Effect of a National Programme of Men's Health Delivered in English Premier League Football Clubs'. *Public Health* 127 (2013): 18–26.
Taylor, N. 'Giving Something Back: Can Football Clubs and their Communities Co-exist?' In *British Football and Social Exclusion*, ed. S. Wagg, 47–66. London: Routledge, 2004.
Walters, G., and S. Chadwick. 'Corporate Citizenship in Football: Delivering Strategic Benefits through Stakeholder Engagement'. *Management Decision* 47, no. 1 (2009): 51–66.

Corporate social responsibility and social partnerships in professional football

Geoff Walters and Mark Panton

Birkbeck, University of London, London, UK

> Within the professional football industry one of the most prominent ways to address corporate social responsibility is through a social partnership involving a range of organizations such as a Community Sports Trust (CST), a professional football club, business organizations and local authorities. These partnerships are responsible for the delivery of community initiatives around a range of social issues. This article seeks to understand the managerial aspects of this type of social partnership, and in particular the objectives and motivations for partnering, by drawing on three analytical platforms that take into account how differences between sectors affect social partnerships. Based on a series of interviews, it is shown that organizations get involved in social partnerships for different reasons and perceive the partnerships in different ways; that from an individual organizational perspective it is difficult to perceive a social partnership entirely in the context of one of the theoretical platforms; and that despite what would appear to be a strong sense of homogenization of organizational form across the sector there are significant differences between social partnerships. The article concludes by arguing that further research is needed to better understand the differences between social partnerships.

Introduction

Corporate social responsibility (CSR) has been a prominent management trend since the 1990s with business organizations under pressure to address not only economic imperatives but also to consider the social and environmental impact of business operations. The ubiquitous nature of CSR suggests that it can be considered as a taken-for-granted concept within western society.[1] As Brammer et al., argue, 'CSR itself has become a strongly institutionalized feature of the contemporary landscape in advanced industrialized economies'.[2] One of the key ways in which organizations address the issue of CSR is through the formation of a social partnership.[3] A social partnership is where two or more organizations from different economic sectors collaborate to address a social issue and where there is a shared understanding of responsibilities and a commitment of resources.[4] These partnerships form in part because addressing social issues can be overly challenging for an individual organization and requires collaboration with multiple actors that bring different skills to the partnership.[5] There are four types of social partnership: business and non-profit partnerships; non-profit and government partnerships; business and government partnerships; and tripartite partnerships between all three sectors.[6] These reflect a change in the roles and responsibilities between government, business and the civil sector.[7]

Within the professional football industry (and the professional sport sector more broadly), one of the more prominent ways in which CSR is addressed is through a social partnership involving a range of partner organizations including a Community Sports Trust (CST), a professional football club, business organizations, local authorities and other organizations. In this type of social partnership, the CST is a charitable organization that acts as the delivery vehicle for a range of community programmes that address social issues such as inclusion, education, health and crime reduction, and draws on funding and other support from the partners. This type of social partnership originally emerged in the 1980s through the Football in the Community (FiTC) schemes partly to counteract some of the more negative aspects associated with the industry, such as hooliganism and a lack of community engagement.[8] However, at this point in time, the FiTC departments were internal to a football club; more recently, there has been a separation between the clubs and the schemes with the vast majority now constituted as independent charitable organizations. This can be explained in part by institutional pressures; the perceived success of the conversion to this model by early adopters encouraged imitation across the sector, whilst more recently coercive pressures exist due to the fact that this form of organizational structure is required in order to receive central funding from the Premier League or the Football League.[9] At present, almost all professional football clubs in the Premier League and Football League partner with a CST operating under the names of community trusts, foundations and community education and sporting trusts (89 out of 92 clubs).

This article seeks to explore the managerial aspects of this type of social partnership[10] and in particular the objectives and motivations for partnering. Research has shown that managing partnerships is complex and inadequately understood.[11] At the same time, the concept of shared responsibilities and a commitment of resources underpinning social partnerships raise questions about the motivations underpinning social partnerships.[12] Whilst there has been a growing body of literature that looks at the CST model in the UK only recently has the nature of the social partnership been the subject of focus.[13] For example, it has been shown that the partnership between a football club and CST can be close, with the CST often drawing on resources (both financial and in-kind) that the football club provides and having football club representation on the board of trustees.[14] However, Anagnostopoulos and Shilbury found there to be a 'dysfunctional affiliation' between football clubs and CST managers.[15] What this demonstrates is that despite the development of a social partnership, there can be differences in the way that the social partnership is perceived, the motivations and objectives, and therefore, potential implications on the success and longevity of the partnership.

This article builds on previous research by seeking to understand social partnerships in professional football through three analytical platforms that take into account how differences between sectors affect social partnerships; an area that Selsky and Parker[16] argue is an emerging area of research within organization studies. These platforms – social issues; societal sector; and resource dependence – are argued to exist independently. This article uses these platforms as a model or framework with which to study the social partnerships in professional football although it looks primarily at the perspective of those involved in CSTs as they are the key partner in these social partnerships. The article begins by briefly reviewing literature on social partnerships and setting out the three partnership platforms and five characteristics/dimensions underpinning each identified that form the framework for this article. It then details the methods used for this study, presents the findings and discussion, before a brief conclusion is made.

CSR, social partnerships and three underlying analytic platforms

Social partnerships have become increasingly prominent and it has been argued that they offer an interesting area for research on CSR.[17] Indeed, Seitanidi and Ryan[18] argued that partnerships are 'one of the most exciting and challenging ways that organizations have been implementing CSR in recent years'. A key question surrounding the emergence of social partnerships to address CSR-related issues relates to the underlying reasons for their development and therefore their underpinning motivations. For this reason, it is useful to draw on the work of Selsky and Parker[19] who identify three theoretical platforms that underpin social partnerships; these platforms are termed social issues, societal-sector and resource dependence platforms. They contend that the three social partnership platforms take into account differences in the underlying cognitive frames held by those involved in managing these partnerships and are essentially 'sensemaking devices that managers use to envision a partnership project, frame it, and make it meaningful and sensible'.[20] In this sense, depending on how an individual perceives a particular social partnership will play a role in determining what they expect to achieve and their motivations and objectives for the partnership.

Table 1 from Selksy and Parker[21] illustrates the three social issues platforms and defines them in relation to five dimensions. The first platform is termed the social issues platform in which a social partnership exists primarily to address a particular social concern.[22] In this type of partnership, it is the *issue* that assumes the prominent reason for organizational collaboration. In this type of partnership, a normative imperative is the prevailing justification for the development of the partnership. The organizations involved in the partnership are therefore motivated by the desire to

Table 1. Social partnership platforms.

Dimension	Platform		
	Social issues	societal sector	Resource dependence
Primary interest	Mandated or designed around a social problem	Mixed self- and social interest	Voluntary, based largely on self-interest with secondary interest in the social issue
Contextual factors	Pressure for CSR	Pressure for adaptation to complexity, turbulence	Pressure for mission related performance
Source of problem definition	Externally defined by existing interest groups and public issues	Envisioned or emergent public issues; constructed over time	Each organization brings its definition to the partnership
Dependencies	Manage/segment interdependencies	Integrate interdependencies	Retain autonomy
Time-frame	Finite or indefinite depending on the social need/issue	Long term and open ended to enhance learning	Finite, delimited to meet organizational needs

Note: This table is taken from Selsky and Parker, 'Platforms for Cross-sector Social partnerships', 30.

address a particular social concern in recognition of the obligation to be a good citizen and adhere to ethical values. The partnership can be seen as a responsive approach to CSR[23] in which the partnership is seen as a source of social progress whereby stakeholders are seen as an end in themselves rather than simply a means to an end.[24] This aligns with Donaldson and Preston's[25] argument that behaviour towards stakeholders is considered as pure philanthropic behaviour which benefits the recipient only and demonstrates the donor's social conscience (i.e. that it is normatively motivated). Selsky and Parker[26] note that social issues evolve over time citing the example of environmentalism and how addressing it has become an institutionalized feature within organizations. This demonstrates the importance of cognitive frames and sensemaking by those involved in the partnerships and how this can impact upon the nature of the social issue.

The societal sector platform is the second analytical platform and this is based on the notion that the lines between government, business and civil society have become blurred due to a variety of factors such as the rise in governmental and non-governmental organizations; a reduction in government funding meaning more competition for resources; privatization and the increasing reliance on business and the third sector to deliver services; and the increasing concern for business organizations to be more accountable and to contribute to addressing societal problems.[27] In the UK, the value of contracts to the third sector between 1982 and 1992 rose from £1.85 billion to £42 billion,[28] facilitating the development of the sector (and consequently social partnerships) as a legitimate sector that was able to address market and state failures. More recently social partnerships were central to New Labour policy in the UK with the continued recognition of the voluntary sector and collaboration across sectors to address welfare and social inclusion issues.[29] This leads organizations naturally to seek to collaborate across sectors to address social issues, although the nature of the issues within each sector can impact upon the development of partnerships between sectors. CSR is one such example; instances of corporate misbehaviour may lead business organizations to partner with trusted non-profit organizations in order to gain legitimacy.[30]

In partnerships between businesses and non-profit organizations, the issues that are often selected are chosen for strategic benefit. In such circumstances, the partnership can be viewed through the resource dependence platform. The underlying principle of this third platform is that organizations partner firstly for self-interest and secondly to address a social concern. As Selsky and Parker[31] state, 'social partnerships here are conceived in a narrow, instrumental, and short-term way; they are viewed as a way to address organizational needs with the added benefit of addressing a social need'. Viewed through a resource dependence lens, a social partnership can be a way to enhance reputation, to gain legitimacy, to improve corporate image and competitive advantage, and to manage reputational risk.[32] The partnership may be a way to develop constructive stakeholder relationships that may benefit an organization in a particular way, for example, by contributing towards the 'reservoir of goodwill'.[33]

The resource dependence approach has been discussed in other work on CSR: for example, Graafland and van de Ven[34] set out the positive strategic view of CSR, in which it is seen that CSR leads to financial success, as opposed to the positive moral view in which CSR is seen as a moral duty of the firm. Similarly, Scherer and Palazzo[35] consider that the majority of research and understanding of CSR takes a positivist, instrumental approach that aligns with an economic theory of the firm, rather than what they term post-positivist CSR in which it is justified on normative grounds. This third type of partnership therefore is reflective of the move towards CSR implementation based on an instrumental, performance-oriented motivation.[36] However, this perspective overlooks concerns surrounding the supposed compatibility of CSR and the market logic.[37] For example, Brammer et al.[38] argue that the market logic adopts a limited view of the corporation as simply profit-driven and the idea that CSR is a strategic tool neglects a focus on more societal aspects. Much of the academic research that looks at how CSR is perceived supports and reinforces this market logic and the business case for CSR dominates; the potential effect of this is that it reduces social and environmental elements to *supporting* financial performance, ensures that stakeholders are treated as a means to an end and fails to ensure that businesses are more accountable and responsible to society.[39]

Methods

This research sought to explore and better understand the social partnerships within the football industry by using the theoretical framework set out by Selsky and Parker[40] and with a particular focus on the perspective of CSTs. The main tool of data collection used in this research was the semi-structured interview. The first set of interviews was undertaken in 2006 (see Table 2). At this point in time, there were approximately 40 CSTs associated with professional football clubs. Although the charitable trust model had been in place since 1997, the majority of these CSTs had converted from FITC schemes between 2003 and 2006. So, whilst the model was not widespread, in 2006 it was becoming more prominent. Six interviews were conducted with individuals working in the sector. A further six interviews were undertaken in 2011. The fact that there was a significant time difference between the

Table 2. List of interviews.

Interviewee	Date	Position and organization
A	27 April 2006	Chief Community Officer, Football in the Community
B	14 September 2006	Chief Executive, Premier League football club
C	19 September 2006	Community Scheme Manager, Community Sports Trust (associated with a Premier League football club)
D	29 November 2006	Chief Executive, Community Sports Trust (associated with a League One football club)
E	4 December 2006	Vice-Chairman, League One football club
F	12 December 2006	Chief Executive, Community Sports Trust (associated with a Premier league football club)
G	21 June 2011	Project Co-ordinator, Community Sports Trust (associated with a Premier League football club)
H	29 June 2011	Director, Community Sports Trust (associated with a League One football club)
J	9 July 2011	Head of Community Sports Trust, (associated with a Premier League football club)
K	13 July 2011	Director, Social Enterprise that monitors and evaluates programmes run by community sports trusts
L	28 July 2011	Community Scheme Manager (directly employed by a Premier League football club)
M	30 August 2011	Chief Executive, Community Sports Trust (associated with a League One football club)

first and second set of interviews allowed for an understanding of the changes that had taken place over the five year period within the sector. This helped to provide further understanding of why the partnership model had become widespread as by 2011 the football club-CST partnership was dominant within the sector. Two key limitations with this approach were firstly, that the interviews were mainly drawn from individuals involved in CSTs and to a lesser extent, football clubs. While these interviews were appropriate in that all interviewees had knowledge of the partnerships between CSTs, football clubs and other organizations by virtue of their senior position within each of the organizations, it would also have been interesting to speak to a wider range of partners. However, it can be argued that the CSTs as the delivery agency are the key organization in these social partnerships. The second limitation is that the interviews are not a representative sample. Nevertheless, the aim of this research is to try to understand the partnerships in more detail and not to make any generalized conclusions. For example, one of the findings of this research demonstrated the diversity surrounding social partnerships in this particular sector.

Each interview lasted between 50 and 90 minutes and was carried out on the basis that all responses would be reported anonymously. The interviews relied on an interview guide that helped to structure the direction of questioning. As this article is part of a larger research project focused on organizational structures and governance within the CST sector in the professional football industry, there were a variety of themes that were used to structure the interviews. In regards to the specific focus of this article, the questions centred on the nature of the partnership, the relations between partners, resource-related issues and the motivations underpinning the different partner organizations. The interviews were recorded and transcribed by the authors. Transcripts of the interviews were sent to all of the interviewees to check for any errors or omissions. This process was helpful for fact-checking and also elicited further information in a number of instances. The interview transcriptions were read in full which enabled a general understanding of the responses.[41] Thereafter, the interviews were analysed using the five dimensions set out in Figure 1 from Selsky and Parker[42] as the broad coding scheme with the characteristics of each of the three theoretical platforms providing further themes to frame the analysis of the interviews. The five dimensions are used to structure the findings.

Findings and discussion

This article focuses on the social partnership between CSTs, football clubs and other organizations. Although a partnership approach is clearly in evidence, the importance of this particular approach to working was strongly emphasized in the interviews. For example, taking a historical perspective, partnerships were important in relation to the FiTC model, even when the community departments were integral to the club. The conversion to the CST model, and the increasing self-reliance of the schemes, further emphasized the fundamental role that partnerships played. As one interviewee stated:

> Our whole strap line is participation through partnership, I will give you a card and it is on there, but really our strategy has been to work in partnership with people. We couldn't have achieved what we've achieved without doing that, and we haven't gone into partnerships or relationships without really thinking about why we wanted to do in the first place and that is probably what has made them strong and sustainable. That is at the whole heart of our strategy. (Interviewee D)

Primary interest

Selsky and Parker[43] set out the differences between the three partnership platforms in relation to the primary interest for collaborating. It was clear from the interviews that there were differences in particular between the football clubs and the CSTs. For example, the CSTs clearly emphasized that they perceived the partnership as a way to address a social need, with social issues underpinning and framing their work. As two interviewees pointed out:

> All our projects are very much needs-led. From there we put in a claim, well a bid, to the Football Foundation of the Premier League. From there we got match-funding from the council, because we were already working with them. (Interviewee G)

> It started a few years ago where we jointly employed a community liaison officer who would do all that other stuff so that we could concentrate on our more youth work, tackling some real social issues in the community, which is what our raison d'être is really and what we enjoy doing. (Interviewee M)

There was an emphasis by some CST interviewees as perceiving the partnership as 'strategic'. However, the strategic element was not one that translates into organizational self-interest, rather it was focused on how the social partnership is a tool for the CST to address a social issue in such a way that the ultimate beneficiaries are the recipients of the initiatives. As one interviewee stated:

> If, by using (the football club), we can help pupils improve their maths; if by using the attraction of (the football club) we can have youngsters on an estate and join us for football sessions and be safe and have a good time together; if by the attraction of (the football club) we can help youngsters with any other school subjects we would be foolish not to. (Interviewee L, football club anonymised)

This was different from the way that the football clubs perceived the partnership. The interviews revealed that there is both self-interest and social interest associated with the social partnerships. For example, one of the club respondents clearly emphasized the business case but also the fact that 'it crosses both'; a direct reference to self-interest and a social interest:

> However, where it links is my point that the more communities you touch and the more people that see the (football club) brand name, because the trust activity is all carried out under the (football club) brand name, the more they become the future supporters of the club so that's the business case, that's why it crosses both. (Interviewee B, football club anonymised)

However, it was also found that self-interest, with a secondary interest in the social issue, underpins some social partnerships. This related to the formation of the CST (from the previous internal FiTC model) where the interviews revealed that in some cases the decision to convert to the charitable model was driven by the needs of the football club, for example, as a way to reduce costs in an area that was not considered fundamental to the business model of the clubs:

> So ours [the trust] came out of a very unique position here with the owner of the club at that point not wanting to fund any work and so we took the decision to do it ourselves. And some other club's community schemes did that at the same time. (Interviewee M)

Another key example that was discussed in the interviews where football clubs view the partnerships in a self-interested way related to the idea that they are able to build relationships with key stakeholders. One type of relationship is that between a football club and a local authority, particularly around the issue of planning applications relating to stadiums.

> ... and that's half the reason why clubs have these community schemes, because they want to show their CSR side of things... Because it gives them advantages over other planning consents. The reason why they do it is because they want to diminish the Section 106 commitments. (Interviewee M)

> Most would say that one of the major reasons why they got planning permission was the community work that the club do. I don't think that anyone would doubt that. It's agreed really. One of the overriding factors as to why we got planning permission was the community work. (Interviewee H)

These quotes from interviews in 2011 align with previous research that supported the idea that football clubs are aware of the 'degree of leverage' that the role of a CST can provide when it comes to planning consent.[44] More recently, we have seen this with the reduced section 106 commitment required by Haringey Council connected to Tottenham Hotspur's new stadium development. Arguably, the community programmes run by the Tottenham Hotspur Foundation played an important role in this, demonstrating the strategic CSR role that community programmes play in obtaining planning permission. One of the interviews also showed that the relationship with the local authority extended beyond planning permission and actually resulted in financial support for a football club:

> There is no way the Council would have given us that money unless they thought that we were good partners delivering good community programmes, so the partnership actually translated there into some hard cash which helped the football club to survive. (Interviewee E)

For the football club therefore the self-interest motive underpins involvement in a social partnership. Research on CSR in sport has demonstrated similar conclusions: for example, Hamil and Morrow[45] found instrumental reasons underpinning the CSR activities of Scottish Premier League clubs where the community work was part of the business model of the football club. Nonetheless, each partnership is different, and therefore, understanding the primary interest for partnering will differ across partners.

Contextual factors

Contextual factors set out the underlying pressures on organizations to engage in a social partnership. There are clear links with the societal sector platform and the pressure for adaptation to complexity and turbulence in regards to the formation of a CST. During the 1990s the internal FiTC departments at professional football clubs were primarily responsible for delivering coaching activities in the geographical communities around football clubs. However by the 2000s there was increasing calls for a new approach, emphasized by the report by Brown et al.[46] in which it was argued that the notion of 'the community' was complicated; that there was confusion surrounding club-community responsibilities; that football clubs did not really understand what is meant by the concept of community; and that a cohesive central government strategy was lacking. It was during this period that there was a shift in the institutional logic within the field. No longer were FiTC schemes predominantly seen as mechanisms to deliver coaching programmes but they were identified by the Department for Culture, Media and Sport as a way to target key policy objectives:

initiatives launched and funded by the government alongside other partners included *Positive Futures* and *Playing for Success* that were designed to tackle social inclusion, youth crime and raise educational standards. At the same time, the point mentioned above about football clubs becoming less willing to fund FiTC schemes led to an increasingly turbulent and complex environment. Many working within the FiTC departments recognized this, and as a result the move to the CST model and the development of social partnerships was seen as a way for the FiTC departments to become more self-reliant:

> That's why the community programmes in the late 80s and 90s have built up their own networks, their own connections, their own links and they had their relationships, their own funding partners and in some cases the funding partners were more important than the club in some instances, because that was the nature of it to keep it all going. (Interviewee M)

For a football club however it was clear that a social partnership can be understood as a result of increasing pressure on football clubs to address CSR (the social issues platform). This has also been seen in the broader sporting context. For example Babiak and Wolfe[47] demonstrated external pressures on sport organizations to engage in CSR from a range of stakeholders, including supporters, employees, and corporate partners. The growing commercialization within the professional football industry has led to pressures for football clubs to be seen as good neighbours and to be 'doing the right thing' (see Brown et al.[48]). In particular, football clubs were seen by the former Labour government as a means to deliver the 'third way' agenda and to demonstrate a commitment to socially responsible activities.[49] The social partnership with the CST is one way of doing this. However, when one considers the context underpinning the social partnership it was clear that the resource dependence platform and the pressure for 'mission-related performance' was highly relevant for a football club.[50] For example, the football club interviewees perceived that the social partnership with the CST had the potential to benefit a football club financially through commercial sponsorship deals in which the work of the CST is a key element in attracting commercial sponsors to a football club. Similarly, an additional financial benefit as a result of the social partnership was the potential to increase the supporter base. This was recognized by both the clubs and the CSTs that were interviewed, for example:

> We want people to feel that it's not that they just come here on a Saturday but that they actually are imputing into something, but there is a business case and this is where is often gets lost. If I have got 250 coaches out there working with 350 thousand people a year and they are giving out literature about matches and making them all membership ... things like that, a proportion of those will then become fans of the club. (Interviewee B, football club reference is kept anonymous)

This was mentioned previously in the section on primary interest, demonstrating that there is a strong sense of synergy between context and primary interest. This is understandable: contextual factors are likely to influence the primary interest for engaging in a social partnership.

An additional aspect that was mentioned that relates to the mission of the football club was that the social partnership has the potential to identify players for the football club. At two of the CST schemes interviewed the football coaching courses linked to the academies that the football clubs ran. There were a number of children within these academies that had been identified through the community programmes with a very small number even making it to the first team squad at one of the football clubs. Although this was not stated explicitly by the football club, one of the interviewees at a CST mentioned this:

> It's taken a while for us to demonstrate how much an asset the community scheme can be on all strands. It was important to show that quality players were coming through and we were giving the club very good players they are seeing those stats. (Interviewee C)

These are clear examples where mission related performance (the resource dependence platform) is an influential contextual factor underpinning the way that the football club and the CSTs frame their understanding of the social partnership. However, it was suggested that clubs were not solely pressured to engage in the social partnership for this reason. As two interviewees stated, there is the expectation that football clubs must also give back to society; in other words the clubs believe that community programmes offer a win-win situation:

> You either get your source of [financial] support from a sugar-daddy or you get it from the broader community, and if you want to get it from the broader community you have got to offer the community something back, which is where the social enterprise fits. So you have got to offer the social bottom line as well as the financial bottom line. (Interviewee E)

> Football clubs who are locally engaged and delivering real local benefit, whether it is their motivation or not and whether they are fan owned or not, find that they have better relations with a range of local stakeholders. (Interviewee K)

In this sense you can argue that there is overlap between the social issues platform and the resource dependency platform; this is what Porter and Kramer[51] contend as the interdependency between business and society. Whilst the need to be a 'good neighbour' was stressed by virtually all of the interviewees, it was clear that football clubs also felt pressure to ensure that the social partnership is tied to the mission of the club, in this case generating revenues to be able to improve on-pitch performance. The context in which an individual perceives the social partnership between a football club and a CST therefore determines the way the partnership is perceived.

Source of problem definition

The source of problem definition relates to who defines the issues that a social partnership is engaged in. One of the earlier interviews suggested that it is the CSTs that are the source of problem definition in that they respond to the needs of their local communities:

> I think what you'll find is that every scheme needs to look at what their opportunities are and what communities initially surround them and how they relate to those as well. (Interviewee D)

This aligns with the social issues perspective in the sense that it is local communities that are the source of the problem definition. This also concurs with the view stressed earlier that the programmes were 'needs-led' and supports the idea that it is the CSTs that are able to determine what programmes to develop based on a bottom-up approach in response to needs within the local communities. Whilst there was an acknowledgement of the need to align with government strategy in the early interviews it was evident that over time the issues that the social partnerships address appear to be driven more by external agents than by the CST. For example, there was overwhelming acceptance that community sport trusts, during the period in which the Labour government was in power, have benefitted from the receipt of government funding, both centrally administered and from local government. It is clear that the community sport trusts interviewed had aligned themselves with government, as mention was made about how this had been an explicit strategy of the community sport trust:

> We've started to more strategically align ourselves with the priorities of the council, things like that. We are starting to pay a bit more attention to that, rightly so. When we do that, we always find that what we are doing does fit in. (Interviewee G)

Where this is the case, it can be argued that government agendas act as a subtle coercive pressure that ultimately influences the type of activity that community sport trust deliver. This concurs with previous research that has identified that CSTs, as charitable organizations, are dependent upon sources of funding,[52] as the following demonstrates:

> We would shape where we're going according to where the funding is and sometimes you have to change that: if there's no more funding in that particular area then you have to stop. But by that time you'd have moved on to do other things. Sustainability is the key really. (Interviewee H)

The last point on sustainability is important. It is clear that underpinning the alignment with government agendas is that it can provide a certain level of financial sustainability. This demonstrates that government funding acts as an influence or a source of problem definition that can influence the activities of the social partnership. It was also found that the Football League Trust and the Premier League were also able to influence the types of community initiative. For example, the Premier League has the 'Creating Chances' brand that oversees community initiatives in five broad areas: community cohesion; education; health; sports participation; and international. The Football League Trust also has four similar overarching themes: education; health; sport; and inclusion. Both the Premier League and Football League provide funding for projects in these areas (although significantly more in the case of the Premier League), demonstrating that they set the community agenda centrally and community sport trusts deliver the programmes, for example:

> The Premier League provides 50% of our funding, so recently there is a big project, I am very proud of our new mental health project. We are one of the clubs working on that. So the Premier League knows what's needed. (Interviewee G)

> So they [the Football League Trust] try and be our watchdog, they try to be our governance scrutinisers, that's one role. It's a bit like the BBC Trust, it's a bit complicated, because they are our advocates, but they are also our police at the same time. So they police us in terms that we're all doing what we say we're doing. (Interviewee M)

This demonstrates that the source of the problem definition is often based on emerging public issues that are constructed over time, for example government agendas that demonstrate the relevance of the societal sector platform. However, it is also clear that the source of problem definition is externally defined by existing interest groups and public issues, for example by the Premier league and Football League, or by football clubs (social issues platform).

Dependencies

The resource dependence platform is underpinned by the idea that the organizations involved in a social partnership want to ensure the boundaries between the organizations are clear and that in doing so they are able to retain their autonomy. From a social issues platform, there is a focus on managing and segmenting interdependencies, whilst the societal sector platform focuses on integrating interdependencies. It was these latter two perspectives that came out in the interviews. For a CST, there was a clear perception that the charitable model allows a certain level of autonomy, for example, in relation to applying for grants and taking certain strategic decisions. This sense of autonomy between partners is reflected formally through the Football League criteria for receiving centralized funding:

> They've [the Football League] had this bronze, silver, gold accreditation and they've just revised bronze again and bronze is all about governance, forecasting, management, delivery, development, all the elements that make up a functional, independent business is what they are looking at. They want to see finances separate to the club. They want to see audited accounts. They want to see independent boards of trustees. (Interviewee M)

Whilst this would suggest that there is a clear sense of the need to retain autonomy within the context of the social partnerships, at the same time the fact that the CSTs enter into a contractual service-level agreement with the clubs indicates a certain level of interdependence. For example, when asked about the relationship between the club and the CST, two interviewees responded as follows:

> We have to be in agreement with the club in terms of the way we use the club's logo, etc. And why would we want to do anything they didn't want us to do. But the other thing is that you have to maintain your own independence in some areas. (Interviewee H)

> There's a very close working relationship with senior people at the club here to understand what the strategy is and how the club and the scheme can work together. More recently we have worked together on things like the (football club) deal where the scheme played a prominent role in that agreement. (Interviewee C, sponsorship deal anonymised)

This balance suggests that managing and segmenting social partnerships are important therefore aligning with the social issues platform. However, there was also evidence to suggest integration, particularly in the context of local authorities. With many local authorities providing funding for CSTs to deliver initiatives it was clear that a strong sense of integration was needed in order to obtain funding. This also relates to the previous section on the source of the problem definition. For example, if a CST is dependent upon a particular partner for funding, then it is likely that this partner will also be able to influence the nature of the programmes or initiatives (i.e. the source of the problem definition) that are delivered.

Time-frame

The time-frame dimension reflects the longevity of the social partnership. From a social issues platform, a partnership can be seen as finite of infinite depending on the social need or issue. The key factor underpinning the time-frame element of the social partnerships in this research was funding and from the perspective of the CSTs interviewed, this was dependent upon other partners:

> As much as we can be involved in social inclusion, and probably 60 per cent of our work at least is that, we still need to balance up everything because all you need is a change in government policy or a change in government possibly and half the rug could be pulled from you and you could then suddenly find that you completely shrink down again and you have got a problem. (Interviewee D)

> My particular project, you cannot get refunded. The Premier League does not refund projects. Obviously, with the current climate the council has less money now. So in its current form it will not go forward. (Interviewee G)

Whilst the social partnerships demonstrate a sense of longevity and in most cases are infinite in the sense that there have only been a very small number of social partnerships that have ceased to exist (due to the CST having been financially unable to continue), the nature of the work and the initiatives that are delivered therefore are determined by the social issues and the aspects that the partner organizations are prepared to fund. In this sense there is a strong level of stability in the social partnership. Where there is less stability is in regard to particular social issues. When one becomes less important or government prioritise other issues then it can lead to a particular initiative ceasing to receive any funding. This has led to CSTs effectively becoming more professional (due to the need to demonstrate they are a suitable organization to fund) but at the same time they have increasingly taken on the role of a service deliverer in the social partnership and therefore are less able to determine the types of projects that it gets involved in as these are driven by funding bodies. This is potentially problematic where a community sport trust is heavily reliant on funding from local or central government given the public sector budget cuts in the UK, or where it leads CSTs to deliver projects that they feel no longer demonstrate a commitment to address social issues:

> I mean the other thing is about taking risks, because in the old days we would do projects that interested us and we would take a financial hit on it and a risk because we thought it would lead to something else. In the current climate there's not so much of that, because the flip-side of all this is that you are creating a monster that you have to keep feeding. It gets bigger and bigger. On one side the XXXX scenario with what he said about staff, but also you become funding led and you're just a service deliverer based on contracts. The local authority in particular. You just spend your time doing stuff for them and you don't do any stuff that actually interests you. But you're doing it because you need to survive. This isn't all roses at all. (Interviewee M, reference to another individual anonymised)

Conclusion

This article has drawn on three theoretical platforms and five dimensions set out by Selsky and Parker[53] in order to better understand the social partnerships between CSTs, football clubs and other organizations. There are three key conclusions. First, this research has shown that organizations get involved in social partnerships for different reasons and perceive the partnerships in different ways. In the case of the social partnership between a CST, a professional football club, and other agencies such as local authorities, there are differing perspectives on the social partnership. This is particularly the case in regard to a football club as they align more with a resource dependence platform and view the social partnership firstly in regard to self-interest and secondly as a way to address a social concern. This is understandable given that the chief responsibility of a football club and for those running the club is to drive commercial revenues to be able to compete on the field of play. In contrast, a CST (the delivery agent of the social partnership) conceives of the partnership as a way for them to address social issues first and foremost. This is not a novel finding in and of itself: others have shown this to be the case in regards to business organizations (self-interested goals) and non-profit organizations (social goals) that engage in a social partnership.[54] However in the context of the sport industry there is little research that has shown the underpinning motivations for social partnerships although Sheth and Babiak[55] indicated that whilst sport executives focussed on philanthropic activities and ethical behaviours, they also viewed CSR as a strategic tool for their business.

The question that raises is whether this is a problem if two of the key partners involved in the social partnership have differing perceptions of the partnership? Previous research has shown the 'dysfunctional affiliation'[56] between football clubs and CST managers: if this dysfunction expands more broadly across the partners within a social partnership then this may be problematic as it may lead to a disconnect between a football club and CST. From the interviews that were conducted it was clear that there was a strong relationship between those involved in the social partnerships (despite differing perceptions of the partnerships) while the reflective position of the interviewees' demonstrated the complex, but sometimes close relationships, between football clubs and the CSTs. The interviews also provided evidence of how those working in CSTs come to understand the more strategic motivations of the football clubs. However, it was suggested that across the sector a strong relationship between a football club and CST is not always in evidence although this is not necessarily problematic if the two organizations can continue to work together in a social partnership and achieve their objectives.

A second, related point focuses on the theories, or platforms underpinning social partnerships. It has been shown that there are strong synergies between the five dimensions. So, for example, contextual factors clearly have an influence on the primary interest of a partner, whilst in the context of a social partnership, dependencies, the source of the problem definition, and time-frame elements are also closely related. However, whilst Selsky and Parker[57] contend that the three theoretical platforms exist on their own and set out clear characteristics (or dimensions) that underpin the platforms, this research has shown that it is difficult to perceive a social partnership from the perspective of one partner entirely in the context of one of the platforms. So, as mentioned above, it is clear that different organizations involved in a social partnership may get involved for different reasons. It was also argued that the platform that best describes the way that a professional football club perceives the partnership is the resource dependence platform in contrast to the social issues platform that underpins a CST. However, what this research has also shown is that the involvement in a social partnership may be underpinned by different theoretical platforms in relation to the five dimensions in this research. This was the case in relation to the primary interest of a football club to engage in a social partnership. This was more aligned with the resource dependence perspective yet at the same time when it comes to the source of the problem definition the social issues or societal sector platform is a better framework for understanding the partnership. What this demonstrates is that it is difficult to perceive a social partnership entirely in the context of one of the platforms.

The third conclusion from this research is that despite there appearing to have been a strong degree of homogenization within the organizational field over the past decade whereby internal FiTC schemes at professional football clubs have converted to the CST form of organization, this research has found that there are differences amongst social partnerships. For example, one of the themes that came out of the interviews was that social partnerships vary; some work well and address a range of social issues while others simply deliver football and coaching courses with little engagement in the social partnership. Therefore, to attempt to generalize across the sector would not necessarily portray an accurate picture of what is happening. Nevertheless, how can we explain the rapid adoption of the charitable structure over the past decade? One possible reason is that it provides a sense of legitimacy amongst the key actors involved in the social partnership. For a CST, it provides a sense of separation from a football club, thereby giving more confidence and ability to apply for grants. For a football club, the separation allows them to focus on their primary area of interest and leave the community side to the CST yet at the same time they draw on the social partnership as a source of legitimacy and create a socially constructed story about the community activities that the football club is involved in that can be used to create a social definition of the organization.[58] Scott[59] discussed institutionalization as a 'process of creating reality' and in part this can be seen in the way that football clubs draw on the work of the social partnerships to generate positive publicity, to help build a community brand, and to position themselves as a key organization within a community. However, there is a danger that in seeking legitimacy through the same organizational form, such arrangements will not be right for every social partnership. Perhaps now, with almost all professional football clubs having an association with a community sport trust, we may start to see critical reflection on whether this model is the most appropriate form for the future and whether alternative models will develop. Further research is therefore needed to be able to take into account a wider range of perspectives on social partnerships in the professional football industry, but also to focus specifically on the differences between social partnerships to better understand whether the charitable model is appropriate for all schemes and why some are able to grow and develop better than others.

Notes

1. Bondy, Moon, and Matten, 'An Institution of Corporate Social Responsibility'.
2. Brammer, Jackson, and Matten, 'Corporate Social Responsibility and Institutional Theory'.
3. Selsky and Parker, 'Cross-sector Partnerships to Address Social Issues'; Seitanidi and Crane, *Social Partnerships and Responsible Business*.
4. Waddock, 'Building Successful Partnerships'; Warhurst, 'Corporate Citizenship and Corporate Social Investment'; Selsky and Parker, 'Cross-sector Partnerships to Address Social Issues'; Seitanidi and Crane, *Social Partnerships and Responsible Business*.
5. Selsky and Parker, 'Cross-sector Partnerships to Address Social Issues'.
6. Selsky and Parker, 'Cross-sector Partnerships to Address Social Issues'; Seitanidi and Lindgreen, 'Editorial: Cross-sector Social Interactions'.
7. Husted, 'Governance Choices for Corporate Social Responsibility'; Albareda et al., 'The Changing Role of Governments in Corporate Social Responsibility'.
8. Watson, 'Football in the Community'; Walters and Chadwick, 'Corporate Citizenship in Football'.

9. Anagnostopoulos and Shilbury, 'Implementing Corporate Social Responsibility in English Football'.
10. Seitanidi, *The Politics of Partnerships*, six strands of partnership literature are outlined in regards to business-non-profit partnerships – the nature of the partnership; the managerial aspects; strategic use; legal and ethical considerations; partnership measurements; and societal implications.
11. Googins and Rochlin, 'Creating the Partnership Society'; Bryson, Crosby, and Middleton Stone, 'The Design and Implementation of Cross-sector Collaborations'.
12. Waddock, 'Building Successful Partnerships'.
13. Bingham and Walters, 'Financial Sustainability within UK Charities'; Anagnostopoulos and Shilbury, 'Implementing Corporate Social Responsibility in English football'.
14. Bingham and Walters, 'Financial Sustainability Within UK Charities'.
15. Anagnostopoulos and Shilbury, 'Implementing Corporate Social Responsibility in English Football', 278.
16. Selsky and Parker, 'Platforms for Cross-sector Social Partnerships'.
17. Waddock and Smith, 'Relationships'; Berger, Cunningham, and Drumwright, 'Social Alliances'; Seitanidi and Crane, 'Implementing CSR Through Partnerships'.
18. Seitanidi and Ryan, 'A Critical Review of Forms of Corporate Community Involvement', 413.
19. Selsky and Parker, 'Cross-sector Partnerships to Address Social Issues'; 'Platforms for Cross-sector Social Partnerships'.
20. Selsky and Parker, 'Cross-sector Partnerships to Address Social Issues', 21.
21. This table is taken from Selsky and Parker, 'Platforms for Cross-sector Social Partnerships', 30.
22. Selsky and Parker, 'Cross-sector Partnerships to Address Social Issues'.
23. Porter and Kramer, 'Strategy and Society'.
24. Graafland and van de Ven, 'Strategic and Moral Motivation for Corporate Social Responsibility'.
25. Donaldson and Preston, 'The Stakeholder Theory of the Corporation'.
26. Selsky and Parker, 'Platforms for Cross-sector Social Partnerships'.
27. Selsky and Parker, 'Cross-sector Partnerships to Address Social Issues'.
28. Bennett, 'Marketing of Voluntary Organizations as Contract Providers of National and Local Government Welfare Services in the UK'.
29. Kendall, *The Voluntary Sector*; Lusted and O'Gorman, 'The Impact of New Labour's Modernization Agenda on the English Grass-roots Football Workforce'.
30. Selsky and Parker, 'Platforms for Cross-sector Social Partnerships'.
31. Selsky and Parker, 'Cross-sector Partnerships to Address Social Issues', 852.
32. Fombrun, Gardberg, and Barnett 'Opportunity Platforms and Safety Nets'; Sagawa and Segal, *Common Interest, Common Good*; Porter and Kramer, 'Strategy and Society'; Jamali and Keshishian, 'Uneasy Alliances'.
33. Mahon and Wartick, 'Dealing with Stakeholders', 19.
34. Graafland and van de Ven, 'Strategic and Moral Motivation for Corporate Social Responsibility'.
35. Scherer and Palazzo, 'Toward a Political Conception of Corporate Responsibility'.
36. Lindgreen and Swaen, 'Corporate Social Responsibility'; Kotler and Lee, *Corporate Social Responsibility*.
37. Bondy, Moon, and Matten, 'An Institution of Corporate Social Responsibility'; Brammer, Jackson, and Matten, 'Corporate Social Responsibility and Institutional Theory'.
38. Brammer, Jackson, and Matten, 'Corporate Social Responsibility and Institutional Theory'.
39. Bondy, Moon, and Matten, 'An Institution of Corporate Social Responsibility'.
40. Selsky and Parker, 'Cross-sector Partnerships to Address Social Issues'; 'Platforms for Cross-sector Social Partnerships'.
41. Patton, *Qualitative Research and Evaluation Methods*.
42. Selsky and Parker, 'Cross-sector Partnerships to Address Social Issues'; 'Platforms for Cross-Sector Social Partnerships'.
43. Selsky and Parker, 'Platforms for Cross-Sector Social Partnerships'.

44. Walters and Chadwick, 'Corporate Citizenship in Football', 60.
45. Hamil and Morrow, 'Corporate Social Responsibility in the Scottish Premier League'.
46. Brown et al., *Football and its Communities*.
47. Babiak and Wolfe, 'Determinants of Corporate Social Responsibility in Professional Sport'.
48. Brown et al., *Football and its Communities*.
49. Mellor, 'The "Janus-faced Sport"'.
50. Selsky and Parker, 'Platforms for Cross-sector Social Partnerships'.
51. Porter and Kramer, 'Strategy and Society'.
52. Bingham and Walters; 'Financial Sustainability within UK Charities'.
53. Selsky and Parker, 'Cross-sector Partnerships to Address Social Issues'; 'Platforms for Cross-sector Social Partnerships'.
54. Selsky and Parker, 'Cross-sector Partnerships to Address Social Issues'.
55. Sheth and Babiak, 'Beyond the Game'.
56. Anagnostopoulos and Shilbury, 'Implementing Corporate Social Responsibility in English Football', 278.
57. Selsky and Parker, 'Platforms for Cross-sector Social Partnerships'.
58. Mizruchi and Fein, 'The Social Construction of Organizational Knowledge'.
59. Scott, 'The Adolescence of Institutional Theory', 495.

References

Albareda, L., J. Lozano, A. Tencati, A. Midttun, and F. Perrini. 'The Changing Role of Governments in Corporate Social Responsibility: Drivers and Responses'. *Business Ethics: A European Review* 17, no. 4 (2008): 347–63.

Anagnostopoulos, C., and D. Shilbury. 'Implementing Corporate Social Responsibility in English Football: Towards Multi-theoretical Integration'. *Sport, Business and Management: An International Journal* 3, no. 4 (2013): 268–84.

Babiak, K., and R. Wolfe. 'Determinants of Corporate Social Responsibility in Professional Sport: Internal and External Factors'. *Journal of Sport Management* 23 (2009): 717–42.

Bennett, R. 'Marketing of Voluntary Organizations as Contract Providers of National and Local Government Welfare Services in the UK'. *Voluntas: International Journal of Voluntary and Nonprofit Organizations* 19, no. 3 (2008): 268–95.

Berger, I., P. Cunningham, and M. Drumwright. 'Social Alliances: Company/Nonprofit Collaboration'. *California Management Review* 47, no. 1 (2004): 58–90.

Bingham, T., and G. Walters. 'Financial Sustainability within UK Charities: Community Sport Trusts and Corporate Social Responsibility Partnerships'. *Voluntas: International Journal of Voluntary and Nonprofit Organizations* 24, no. 3 (2013): 606–29.

Bondy, K., J. Moon, and D. Matten. 'An Institution of Corporate Social Responsibility (CSR) in Multi-National Corporations (MNCs): Form and Implications'. *Journal of Business Ethics* 111, no. 2 (2012): 281–99.

Brammer, S., G. Jackson, and D. Matten. 'Corporate Social Responsibility and Institutional Theory: New Perspectives on Private Governance'. *Socio-Economic Review* 10, no. 1 (2012): 3–28.

Brown, A., T. Crabbe, G. Mellor, T. Blackshaw, and C. Stone. *Football and Its Communities: Final Report*. London: The Football Foundation, 2006.

Bryson, J., B. Crosby, and M. Middleton Stone. 'The Design and Implementation of Cross-sector Collaborations: Propositions from the Literature'. *Public Administration Review*, no. 52 (2006): 44–55.

Donaldson, T., and L.E. Preston. 'The Stakeholder Theory of the Corporation: Concepts, Evidence and Implications'. *Academy of Management Review* 20, no. 1 (1995): 63–91.

Googins, B.K., and S.A. Rochlin. 'Creating the Partnership Society: Understanding the Rhetoric and Reality of Cross Sector Partnerships'. *Business and Society Review* 105, no. 1 (2000): 127–44.

Graafland, J., and B. van de Ven. 'Strategic and Moral Motivation for Corporate Social Responsibility'. *Journal of Corporate Citizenship* 22 (2006): 111–23.

Hamil, S., and S. Morrow. 'Corporate Social Responsibility in the Scottish Premier League: Context and Motivation'. *European Sport Management Quarterly* 11, no. 2 (2011): 143–70.

Husted, B. 'Governance Choices for Corporate Social Responsibility: To Contribute, Collaborate or Internalize'. *Long Range Planning* 36, no. 5 (2003): 481–98.

Jamali, D., and T. Keshishian. 'Uneasy Alliances: Lessons Learned from Partnerships Between Businesses and NGOs in the Context of CSR'. *Journal of Business Ethics* 84, no. 2 (2009): 277–95.

Kendall, J. *The Voluntary Sector*, London: Routledge, 2003.

Kotler, P., and N. Lee. *Corporate Social Responsibility: Doing the Most Good for Your Company and Your Cause*. Hoboken, NJ: Wiley, 2005.

Lindgreen, A., and V. Swaen. 'Corporate Social Responsibility'. *International Journal of Management Reviews* 12, no. 1 (2010): 1–7.

Lusted, J., and J. O'Gorman. 'The Impact of New Labour's Modernisation Agenda on the English Grass-roots Football Workforce'. *Managing Leisure* 15, no. 1–2 (2010): 140–54.

Mahon, J.F., and S.L. Wartick. 'Dealing with Stakeholders: How Reputation, Credibility and Framing Influence the Game'. *Corporate Reputation Review* 6, no. 1 (2003): 19–35.

Mellor, G. 'The "Janus-faced Sport": English Football, Community and the Legacy of the "Third Way"'. *Soccer & Society* 9, no. 3 (2008): 313–24.

Mizruchi, M.S., and L.C. Fein. 'The Social Construction of Organizational Knowledge: A Study of the Uses of Coercive, Mimetic, and Normative Isomorphism'. *Administrative Science Quarterly* 44, no. 4 (1999): 653–83.

Patton, M. *Qualitative Research and Evaluation Methods*. Thousand Oaks, CA: Sage, 2002.

Porter, M., and M. Kramer. 'Strategy and Society: The Link Between Competitive Advantage and Corporate Social Responsibility'. *Harvard Business Review* 84 (2006): 78–92.

Sagawa, S., and E. Segal. *Common Interest, Common Good: Creating Value through Business and Social Sector Partnerships*. Boston: Harvard Business School Press, 2000.

Scherer, A.G., and G. Palazzo. 'Toward a Political Conception of Corporate Responsibility: Business and Society Seen from a Habermasian Perspective'. *The Academy of Management Review* 32, no. 4 (2007): 1096–120.

Scott, W.R. 'The Adolescence of Institutional Theory'. *Administrative Science Quarterly* 32 (1987): 493–511.

Seitanidi, M.M. *The Politics of Partnerships: A Critical Examination of Non-profit-business Partnerships*. London: Springer, 2010.

Seitanidi, M., and A. Crane. 'Implementing CSR through Partnerships: Understanding the Selection, Design and Institutionalisation of Nonprofit-business Partnerships'. *Journal of Business Ethics* 8, no. 2 (2009): 413–29.

Seitanidi, M.M., and A. Crane, eds. *Social Partnerships and Responsible Business: A Research Handbook*. London: Routledge, 2014.

Seitanidi, M.M., and A. Lindgreen. 'Editorial: Cross-sector Social Interactions'. *Journal of Business Ethics* 94 (2010): 1–7.

Seitanidi, M., and A. Ryan. 'A Critical Review of Forms of Corporate Community Involvement: From Philanthropy to Partnerships'. *International Journal of Nonprofit and Voluntary Sector Marketing* 12 (2007): 247–66.

Selsky, J.W., and B. Parker. 'Cross-sector Partnerships to Address Social Issues: Challenges to Theory and Practice'. *Journal of Management* 31, no. 6 (2005): 1–25.

Selsky, J.W., and B. Parker. 'Platforms for Cross-sector Social Partnerships: Prospective Sensemaking Devices for Social Benefit'. *Journal of Business Ethics* 94, no. S1 (2010): 21–37.

Sheth, H., and K. Babiak. 'Beyond the Game: Perceptions and Practices of Corporate Social Responsibility in the Professional Sport Industry'. *Journal of Business Ethics* 91, no. 3 (2010): 433–50.

Waddock, S. 'Building Successful Partnerships'. *Sloan Management Review* 29, no. 4 (1988): 17–23.

Waddock, S.A., and N. Smith. 'Relationships: The Real Challenge of Corporate Global Citizenship'. *Business and Society Review* 105, no. 1 (2000): 47–62.

Walters, G., and S. Chadwick. 'Corporate Citizenship in Football: Delivering Strategic Benefits through Stakeholder Engagement'. *Management Decision* 47, no. 1 (2009): 51–66.

Warhurst, A. 'Corporate Citizenship and Corporate Social Investment: Drivers of Tri-sector Partnerships'. *Journal of Corporate Citizenship*, no. 1 (2001): 57–73.

Watson, N. 'Football in the Community: 'What's the Score?'' In *The Future of Football: Challenges for the Twenty-first Century*, ed. J. Garland, D. Malcolm, and M. Rowe, 114–29. London: Frank Cass, 2000.

Little United and the Big Society: negotiating the gaps between football, community and the politics of inclusion

Annabel Kiernan and Chris Porter

Centre for the Study of Football and its Communities (CSFC), Manchester Metropolitan University, Manchester, UK

The UK government's Big Society vision is a source of fierce debate and controversy, particularly when set alongside severe austerity measures. This has revealed a glaring disconnect between rhetoric of empowered, inclusive communities and the burgeoning reality of cuts to publicly funded community provision. This puts pressure on organizations that rely on or promote volunteering as a means of participatory community inclusion, not just financially through loss of funding, but also potentially on ideological grounds. To explore this, research was conducted within the community projects of FC United of Manchester, a not-for-profit, cooperative, fan-owned, non-league English football club. Findings reveal extremely positive perceptions of its community and inclusivity work, with volunteering and the club's ownership structure being seen as major factors in that success. Despite clear opposition to the coalition government's policies, from a community inclusion perspective and on wider ideological grounds, the club aims to increase its capacity as a community provider, acknowledging the potential contradictions and conflicts this may bring.

Introduction

The old way of doing things: the high spending, all-controlling, heavy-handed state, those ideas were defeated ... It's not government abdicating its role, it is government changing its role ... It's about government helping to build a nation of doers and go-getters, where people step forward not sit back, where people come together to make life better.[1]

This article is concerned with the ways in which English football clubs may be enabled, by the current UK public reform agenda, to insert themselves more deeply into the communities of which they claim to be an active part. Football clubs attach importance to community engagement, with charitable work, soccer schools and other outreach and inclusion programmes constituting a typical part of the offering of football clubs at all levels of the pyramid.[2] It has been argued, however, that existing models of community engagement, particularly by English Premier League clubs, can be less about improving access and inclusion and more about talent spotting and marketing. Indeed, evident contradictions between (many) clubs' community inclusion claims and their aggressive market-driven, corporate direction have led elite-level English football in the Premier League era to be characterized as 'the

---

Little United is a term occasionally used to describe FC United of Manchester; it is a reference to the club and fans being a breakaway from Manchester United (Big United).

Janus-faced sport'.[3] At the opposite end of the pyramid, in non-league football, the nature of the clubs and the composition of the team (often part-time, local men balancing paid employment with playing in the first team) more often means that the clubs rely on volunteers from the community and have a broader form of engagement, precisely as a function of the more limited resources they have at their disposal.

FC United of Manchester (FCUM) is one such non-league football club, established in 2005 and currently playing in the Evo-Stik Premier division (three steps below the Football League). FCUM has consciously sought to be an engaged community football club from its inception and may even be best described as 'activist' in terms of the ways in which it has both embedded itself in the local community for support as well as, in turn, supporting on-the-ground community development and outreach work. In that sense, FCUM is a model community football club: it relies on a phalanx of volunteers and seeks out positive means of promoting inclusion and access, not just to football but in the wider sense of social inclusion using the vehicle of football, via its community development work. It is, therefore, particularly well placed to take advantage of new legislation which empowers local and third sector providers to enter in to the market of local service provision, as is envisioned in the Localism Act, 2011.[4] An additional feature of the organization of FCUM is that it positions itself politically as a left-leaning football club. This has informed the structure and governance of the club as well as its outward profile and strategy for engagement. This potentially poses an interesting conundrum for the forward strategy of the club; does it actively exploit the new legislative framework to enhance its community position or does it step back from an agenda which facilitates the replacement of local service provision with a volunteer labour force?

This article considers the role and strategy of FCUM in light of the current public sector reform proposals. Using insights from volunteers and community groups who have engaged with the club, as well as the vision of the General Manager of FCUM, we consider the impact of the new legislation on the role of football clubs and ask whether this is a significant opportunity for football to add value and build capacity for meaningful social change within the lives of its communities.

Legislative context 2010–2013

The extent of the financial meltdown of 2008 which has produced a long-term recession has brought forward an economic and therefore political crisis. In the UK, the political debate about the appropriate response to the economic crisis – mostly in terms of a traditional Keynesian-Monetarist strategic split – saw a marginal victory for the programme of the Conservative party in the 2010 General Election. In Coalition with the Liberal Democrats, their formula for economic recovery rested on a traditional neo-liberal strategy of cutting debt through directly challenging what they saw as costly state provision of public services. In its early development, the economic rebalancing act of shifting responsibility for service provision from the state to local communities was characterized as falling within the rubric of 'the Big Society', which in turn was twinned with the Conservatives' other electoral slogan of 'we're all in it together'. Calling to mind the Kitchener instruction 'Your Country Needs You', the Big Society was a conjuring up of a core Conservative principle of self-help; state services were identified as costly, not representing good value in the market and contributing to economic sclerosis. Instead, the legislative proposals called for a more agile and innovative public service sector with more cost-effective business models and a diversity of providers in the supply chain. At the core of this new blueprint for service delivery was the withdrawal of local authority provision in favour of both existing market actors and new market entrants drawn from the voluntary and community sector (VCS).

There is no agreed definition of 'the Big Society', and its lack of traction with the public has seen the term now more or less disappear from public discourse; indeed, Jeffares's analysis points to just 1000 days of the Big Society.[5] Most discussion of the meaning of the 'Big Society' point to the contribution by Conservative MP, Jesse Norman, who first articulated the new 'compassionate Conservative' vision of a smaller and more agile state, complimented by voluntary cooperation and a stronger society.[6] Norman developed a vision for the UK, which fed into the Conservatives' electoral machine and served as the party's big idea for the 2010 election, serving a dual purpose as one of the mechanisms for detoxifying the Tory brand. In addition, there are the practical implementation challenges raised by Philip Blond (of right-leaning think tank ResPublica), who developed an argument which transcends the traditional state vs. market convention, by overlaying it with the need for the social glue of families and individuals, who are identified as an untapped resource in the core economy.[7] Blond's contribution was significant for the development of the policy tools brought forward by the government, but Blond subsequently became disenchanted by the government's apparent lack of investment in the necessary infrastructure to bring about a real Big Society and with it an enduring shift in social values and behaviour in relation to community self-reliance, volunteering and co-production of services.

Despite the lack of an agreed definition of 'Big Society', or a consensus on the ways in which it is used and understood by different stakeholders, the core of the government's proposals and enacted legislation under the Big Society umbrella have resulted in an opening up of public service contracts to a wider range of providers, specifically enabling the VCS and social enterprises to tender for local contracts; organizations who are seen by government as offering more cost efficient and innovative business models. Having volunteer labour at the heart of the new architecture is also fundamental to the Big Society agenda. Volunteering speaks to the self-help and self-reliance narratives, as well as offering a clear economic make-weight in the rebalancing of an economy deep in recession.

Despite the evident shelving of 'Big Society' terminology as a result of its lack of traction with the public,[8] the framework for delivering the conceptual heart of the Big Society has been delivered in both the Localism Act 2011 and the Open Public Services Act 2012. In that sense, we may be able to agree on the outcomes of what is in reality an ideological project to reduce the size and reach of the state and therefore the public sector.

Public service reform: opportunities for football

There may be opportunities for football clubs, at all levels of the game, to take advantage of the new legislation relating to localism and community empowerment. Arguably football clubs are particularly well placed to make positive use of the further opening up of the market in public service provision, given their community location, their extensive use of volunteer labour and their capacity for carrying cultural capital. In this way, the Big Society agenda may find in football clubs ready opportunities to become a functioning reality in terms of public service provision. Indeed, there have been several studies developed on the specific role which sport might play in the Big Society initiatives, precisely because sports clubs tend to be embedded in local communities and rely on volunteers to remain a going concern; local sports clubs and teams also add to community bonds, thus holding the potential to create social capital and to increase community resilience.[9]

The most recent available figures show that only 44% of people feel that local public services act on the concerns of local residents and only 33% feel that their council provides value for money in the provision of services.[10] Consequently, football clubs have the potential to be at the forefront of some service delivery and community asset development as a local provider; a role which may offer advantages in terms of identity (esteem) and community value for service users,[11] a factor certainly supported in the findings of this research. The government uses the term 'differently or better'[12] to describe the kinds of approaches and business models they expect to gain and encourage from moves towards decentralizing service provision: this can be interpreted positively in terms of innovation, social and/or community value and local needs' responsiveness. In this way, clubs or trusts which 'do things differently' and can demonstrate impact should be well positioned.

Echoing Thatcher-era terminology that trumpeted the freedom (right) of individuals to buy council houses, and thus remove them from public ownership, the Localism Act introduces provision for communities' *Right to Bid*, *Right to Challenge*, *Right to Reclaim* and *Right to Build*. These openings suggest significant possibilities for football clubs, particularly those which can leverage a meaningful community presence.

The *Right to Bid* enables community groups and organizations to bid for community facilities which have fallen into disuse and the *Right to Challenge* enables community groups and organizations to bid to run a local service if they can demonstrate that they would do it 'differently or better'. There are potentially significant mutually beneficial opportunities here for football clubs and their local community support structures in terms of additional mechanisms for engagement. In turn, there are longer term benefits for football clubs in terms of financial self-sufficiency and the potential to expand. This may further enable the development of increased social capital in local communities, which can have knock-on benefits for both supporter groups and the local community more broadly defined.[13] The legislation has, for instance, already been used by football supporter campaign groups to protect their clubs' stadium from potentially being sold by club owners: both Manchester United's and Liverpool's home grounds have in this way been designated as 'assets of community value', despite legal challenges from the clubs' owners.

As already noted, the Department for Communities and Local Government (DCLG) is especially keen on the implementation of innovative business models which it sees as a core means of revitalizing an area. The DCLG's Localism Act cites community shares and a volunteer workforce as positive examples[14]; both areas in which community football clubs and supporters trusts are already engaged and thus again could be seen to represent a model of 'Big Society' type working, thereby finding favour under this legislation should football clubs seek to insert themselves so directly in local service provision.

This particular model of localism offers a good fit for Greater Manchester in terms of the possibility for further leveraging the economic growth and community capacity-building potential of the football industry. Given the current dominant position of Manchester's two main clubs, as well as the arrival of the National Football Museum in Manchester city centre, this may be seen as a particularly advantageous moment to harness football as a driver of economic recovery. As the leader of Manchester City Council has claimed, growth in this current period of recession is driven by cities, with the Manchester city region capable of achieving above average growth with global potential. Manchester is described as having adapted Local Enterprise Partnership[15] architecture, thus allowing an organic development of what was already there, enabling economic development on a whole conurbation basis, embracing a bottom-up model of growth.[16]

The broader economic and legislative landscape of the UK in the period since 2010 has produced a significant political response in terms of the reorganization and re-framing of public services and their delivery. In effect, the legislation accelerates a shift from public sector provision to more private and voluntary provision of local services which has been packaged as 'community empowerment', but which critics see as an ideological challenge to public services and the provision of publicly funded social programmes. In either scenario, the opportunities for football clubs, particularly community and supporter-led football clubs, to enter into the redrawn market of community capacity-building and service delivery has been significantly enhanced. The example of FCUM is particularly interesting in this regard given its constitutional commitment to community working and its need therefore to deliver good community projects in order to pursue the interests of its other core community, its fans and members.

FC United: a football club and its communities

Football Club United of Manchester was formed by supporters in 2005 in protest at Malcolm Glazer's takeover of Manchester United. The new club was intended to provide a means for boycotting fans, as well as those otherwise excluded, to have the kind of match-day experience, as well as close, active participatory relationship with their club that they felt was no longer possible with Manchester United. Many of the boycotting fans who were most active in setting up FC United had been prominent within independent supporter campaign groups over the previous two decades.[17]

Indeed, boycotting fans have been keen to stress that rather than representing a reaction merely to the Glazer takeover, their actions were, and still are, based on concerns over longer term processes of commercialization and commodification at Manchester United in particular, and top level English football in general.[18] The notion of community had risen to prominence not only in critiques of the more commodified relationships elite football clubs were pursuing with their main constituents, the supporters, but also more generally around understandings of social exclusion. This tended to rest on the increasingly widely held perception that football clubs could, and should, perform more pivotal and pro-active roles as community institutions.[19]

In protesting against the dominant market-led approach of elite levels of club football in England, FC United therefore have attempted to become a more active, engaged and therefore 'genuine' community institution. The heterogeneity of that 'community' is a crucial factor to acknowledge, as a number of different 'types' of community can be identified as having a stake in the progress and direction of the club.

Amongst FC United supporters, the distinction between the politically motivated boycotting fans and those who could not afford to attend Manchester United games is significant as it reveals a fundamental problem in any attempt to imagine a homogeneous supporter community at FC United. Further to this, when the definition of 'community' is extended to also include various 'communities of disadvantage' or 'neighbourhood communities',[20] the need to acknowledge the differences, and potential conflicts, within and between FC United's various communities is greater still.

As well as providing a 'sanctuary' for disenfranchised and disenchanted Manchester United supporters therefore, FC United has also actively positioned itself as a community institution which aims, according to its manifesto, 'to be seen as a good example of how a club can be run in the interests of its members and be of benefit to its local communities'.[21] In its efforts to secure a home ground in Manchester, FC United launched a successful 'community share' scheme which enabled the club to raise funds without challenging its 'one-member, one-vote' co-operative structure. This entailed a rule change in the form of an 'asset lock', thereby legally binding FC United to ensure that club assets (including any future stadium) are accessible to and of benefit to the community. This asset lock was voted in to FC United's rules by the club's member owners.

In attempting to assess FCUM's engagement with, and impact upon, the various communities it works with in Greater Manchester, it is important to consider not only the particular structural and organizational characteristics of FC United, but also the relationships football clubs more generally have had with what they and others have regarded as their communities, both historically and in the contemporary context. FC United were constituted and are structured with particular ideas of community engagement in mind,[22] in many ways seeking to enable and facilitate the kind and level of community impact that its founders believed was lacking in English football.[23]

As touched upon above, possibly the most important distinction to bear in mind when considering FCUM's sense of community, and indeed one that has often been less than clearly articulated within general understandings of football clubs and community, is that which exists between supporters and what we might loosely term the 'local community'. Of course, there can often be overlap between supporters and locally based residents, even when considering the largest and most globally oriented of football clubs, but the distinction is nevertheless an important one to recognize.

This was a central feature identified in a report commissioned by the Football Foundation into 'Football and its Communities',[24] which recommends a more nuanced approach to conceptualizing 'community' in the context of football clubs. As well as supporters and 'neighbourhood' or 'geographical' communities, the authors also highlight the emphasis that has in recent years been placed on so-called 'social problem communities',[25] with football clubs seen – particularly under the policy context of the 'New' Labour government from 1997 – as ideally placed to deliver community 'solutions'. The scope of football clubs' presumed influence under this 'cultural inclusion' approach was by then seen to include 'health, education, community cohesion, regeneration and crime reduction'.[26]

It was broadly from within this context that the founders of FC United sought to build a football club that would 'genuinely' embrace its roles and responsibilities as a community-based football club. The democratic, cooperative structure of the club, in providing members with a say in how the club is run and therefore making the club more accountable to stakeholders not motivated by financial profit, was seen as the best way to ensure that the club would live up to its promises. However, with the above qualifications in mind regarding the plurality of football clubs' community stakeholdings, it is important to emphasize that the interests of the supporters – who make up the vast majority of the club's membership – are not necessarily the same interests as those of either local residents or of so-called 'communities of disadvantage'.

Methods

This paper focuses on research findings drawn from individual interviews with FC United staff and representatives of partner organizations, as well as a number of focus group interviews with community project participants and volunteers. After establishing contact with FC United's Community and Education Officer, six focus group discussions were planned, though due to logistical difficulties in coordinating activities for two of these groups during the time data were being collected, just four focus groups went ahead.

Focus groups:

- **Future Jobs Fund (FJF) employees**: *March 2011, FC United office, Ancoats, Manchester*
    - 7 participants, employed temporarily[27] in various aspects of the club's work – coaching, administration, community projects
- **FC United Youth Forum**: *March 2011, Gigg Lane, Bury*
    - 11 participants, including 7 volunteers from various club community projects
- **Refugee and Asylum Seekers**: *March 2011, Gigg Lane, Bury*
    - 9 participants, including 6 volunteer coaches
- **Apprentices/NVQ trainees**: *March 2011, Levenshulme Youth Centre, Manchester*
    - 12 participants, all members of FC United's apprentice coaching scheme

Individual interviews;

- **Andy Walsh, FCUM General Manager**: *September 2011, FC United office, Ancoats, Manchester*
- **Jenny Loudon, Inter Mancunia**[28]: *September, 2011, Manchester*
- **Eric Allison, West Gorton FC**[29]: *October 2011, Manchester*

It must be noted that there is some fluidity in the labels of 'participant' and 'volunteer', in that volunteering is regarded and utilized by the club and partner organizations as a way of engaging more deeply with project participants. Becoming a volunteer rather than 'mere' participant is therefore seen to be a valuable step in building esteem as well as active, sustaining relationships. It was such engaged participant–volunteers that were, understandably, most accessible as research participants, rather than less engaged, or what might be termed 'end user', participants.

A consciously unobtrusive approach was taken in communications, as concerns had been expressed of over-burdening some of the participants and partner organizations, due in part to other recent research and evaluation exercises. We were also mindful of adding to the workload of volunteers and casual workers at both FC United and its partner organizations. Contact with participants was then largely limited to projects who it was felt could accommodate us without too much disruption, and to those times already scheduled for FC United community work. These difficulties and limitations immediately draw attention to the voluntary nature of much of the work carried out by these organizations, which goes to the heart of the conceptual focus of the research. Indeed, experiences reported by participants in various community projects reflect the limitations, along with the benefits, of volunteer-led community work.

The rationale for data collection therefore was to gather the views of those with practical experience of the community work carried out by FC United. Of key concern was an attempt to establish whether the organizational structure and approach of FC United, as a largely volunteer-led, social enterprise cooperative and of course as a football club, was felt to be a pivotal factor in facilitating whatever kinds of experience participants and partner organizations reported of their contact with FC United.

Focus groups were considered the most appropriate method of data collection when interviewing the community project participants, due in part to the relative informality and reduced sense of individual scrutiny of a group setting.[30] As in each instance, participants were already well acquainted with each other, the benefit of social interaction accrued through a focus group was also a key consideration.[31]

For both focus groups and individual interviews, semi-structured interview questions and key themes were initially drawn up to guide discussion. This approach shares Kvale's observation that the interview is above all 'a construction site of knowledge',[32] and in this spirit focus groups were held prior to individual interviews, thus allowing emerging themes from the former to inform and prompt more engaged discussion in the latter. All sessions were digitally audio-recorded and later transcribed. Transcriptions were then analysed by noting emerging themes and topics and their relation to the key conceptual focus of the project.

Findings

The rhetorical and ideological conflict over the meaning, intended or supposed, of the term Big Society is now quite familiar. Equally, clear is a widespread mistrust of the underlying motives of such populist terminology, led by fears of back-door privatization of currently publicly funded services. How then might FC United be positioned within such an environment? The anti-corporate, left-leaning *raison d'être* of the club perhaps places it more precariously than organizations without such overtly ideological principles, and the findings here do highlight a very reflexive awareness of such pitfalls. FC United are attempting to balance long-term aspirations as an inclusive community provider, with the danger of becoming, or representing, an unwitting justification for cuts to local services.

FC United's General Manager Andy Walsh (AW) tackles the thorny issue of the Big Society head on:

> If you're asking 'is what FC United are doing important for community cohesion, for developing capacity within communities, for giving people opportunities for activity, education and physical engagement with sport and other people in their communities?', then yes that's what we do. Do we want to badge it as Big Society? No.

It isn't just a matter of labelling however for AW, who goes on to explain that they certainly don't see themselves as sole providers of what they do, while recognizing that they are relative newcomers to the scene, with plenty of wrong turns and mistakes surely still ahead.

The need to be fully aware of the tricky terrain they have set themselves up to exist within is readily acknowledged, with the danger of being cast as a vanguard of the Big Society agenda paramount in such concerns. AW explains further:

> we've got to guard against being used in that way. I think the experience we've now got within the staff and within the board, will allow us to guard against that, but it means that we face some very difficult questions that are not easy to provide a straight answer to.

So FC United, as with many other community stakeholders, are at risk of finding themselves, however genuine their motives, unwittingly aligned with what many feel to be a disingenuous co-option of community-friendly rhetoric.

'Our approach has always been about partnerships and working with other organizations' says AW, as he defends FC United against suggestions that they may in future prove to be rivals to current community providers. This cooperative approach is reflected particularly well in the way the club decided from the outset not to establish its own junior teams, and instead to work alongside the many pre-existing junior football clubs in Greater Manchester. So, rather than taking the most promising players from perhaps less glamorous junior sides, FC United provides coaching support, and through its youth and first team can act as a safety net to provide a good level of competitive football to those players not signed up, or perhaps later dropped, by professional clubs.

Being a football club also carries weight for other kinds of community engagement FC United are involved in. Even the club's relatively lowly status compared to the big professional clubs in the city isn't a hindrance to engaging with hard-to-reach groups. As well as youths, AW explains that older men have been shown to respond positively to an approach by a football club, rather than for instance social services or a charity. Football then acts as an 'in' according to AW, so that as part of the club's well-being project, for instance, older people have enjoyed days out at FC United matches in the company of young volunteers (one of which had been employed through the FJF scheme).

The volunteers are crucial to FC United's success in engaging with target groups, mainly because as a football club, the kind of volunteers attracted are often quite different from those who volunteer with more traditional community-oriented agencies. AW suggests that it helps in this regard that many of FC United's volunteers, particularly those working on community-based coaching projects 'are drawn from estates and environments, social groups that are very similar to the people that we're working with'.

A resource at a time when resources are few

'FC is giving something really special' according to Ahmed, a football coach on FC United's projects that work with migrant, refugee- and asylum-seeking communities across the city. Representatives of Manchester's Sudanese community, Bolton Immigration Integration Group and Spotlight of Cheetham Hill together explained that FC United provide practical support in putting together football teams for young people, entering tournaments and help with funding applications. A key strength of FC United's approach, related by the project leaders, was a willingness to go out to actively engage with local communities, rather than merely put on events and expect people to come to them, as had been their experience of other football clubs in the city. A general lack of resources amongst those groups most in need was cited as a key factor, with volunteers having to find creative solutions in order to bring together young people who may benefit most from such activities.

Consequently, despite being a smaller organization than other local football teams, FC United is still a relatively important resource in a market where resources are increasingly squeezed. Given both the economic climate and the public sector reforms implemented as a response, the VCS is chasing a smaller financial pot from both local authorities and funding agencies. The arrival of a football club which brings its own resources, tapped from a fan community which is additional to that of the local communities it engages with, offers new opportunities to grassroots community organizations for partnership working and resource transfer. The peculiarity of FC United's fan base is significant here as, for a membership of 3–4000, a relatively high proportion of volunteers can provide organizational, bidding and community engagement experience. Resource exchange and transfer is key, with FC United able to offer expertise and a successful track record of gaining funding for its activities as well as experienced football training and coaching provision, including from first team players and staff.

A core advantage of football clubs as service providers then is that they bring with them an additional community in the form of the supporters, who are a resource both financially and in terms of knowledge and skills' exchange.

Esteem factors and cultural 'capital'

There are some indicators that football can deliver personal esteem rather than the stigma that can be associated with engaging with a state service, providing further reason for their engagement with the new legislative reform initiatives.

A focus group of 12 young men, aged between 17 and 21, engaged as FC United Apprentices and training for their NVQ Level 2 football coaching qualification, revealed that before joining the scheme, despite trying a wide range of trades, nothing had resulted in sustainable employment. While previous knowledge of FC United amongst the group was limited (they described themselves as Manchester United, Manchester City or Liverpool supporters), they all appreciated the added-value of their NVQ training sessions being run by a football club, even a smaller, community-based club. FCUM's involvement was seen to provide a more professional approach, partly through the involvement of first-team manager Karl Marginson and also through the chance to attend first team matches at Gigg Lane. A clear advantage of accessing training through a football club was identified early on, as the group was clear that wearing FC United's training kit rather than their own training clothes was important. Wearing the club's official training kit delivered a sense of professionalism and belonging, and was seen as a source of pride and status amongst friends and family: 'you know when you're walking down the street? People see you're doing something with your life'.

A similar perception of esteem emerged from the focus group with young people working with FC United under the previous government's *FJF* initiative.[33] Young people in this group explained that wearing the club badge while carrying out their roles again helped them to feel more professional, and was also seen as helping to convince partners that FC United is a serious, established organization. The FJF group also expressed pride outside of their work in seeing others wearing the club's colours, knowing that they work for FC United. In particular, for those working in coaching roles and other project-based volunteers, the importance of feeling that they were representing the club was seen to be crucial for sustaining their engagement.

In the same vein, a focus group held with FC United's Youth Forum[34] expressed the importance of identifying with the club and being socially identified as belonging to the club. During the period of research (2011), FC United had a high profile FA Cup run, playing established teams further up the football pyramid, notably Rochdale and Brighton & Hove Albion; seeing FC United on television and in the newspapers was a source of pride for these volunteers, especially when considering the attitudes of friends and family to their involvement. Again, the volunteer coaches stressed the importance of wearing the club badge and training kit, not just during their coaching sessions but in other social circles too.

What seems clear then is, for marginalised youth, the ability to identify with an organization was important for a sense of belonging and professionalism and, more so, the identification with a football 'brand' (wearing the training kit, club badge) provided esteem factors for the young people in their family and social circles. One young man in the Apprentices' focus group was keen to have a copy of the group photo taken for the research with a request to add the club badge to the picture so that he could post it on his Facebook page. In that sense, football clubs, and particularly those which are truly embedded in communities, have an advantage in becoming service providers as they can deliver important social and cultural capital to individuals and groups which may be absent from other, particularly state-led, services which seek to engage young people or hard to reach groups. The apparent stigma associated with state support still resonates with young people, with a clear need to be distant from the notion of 'dependency'. In that way, football clubs are well positioned to move into community service provision with good potential for more sustainable engagement by client groups.

Structures of real engagement

FC United's particular ethos plays just as vital a role according to AW, who feels that fans are more likely to become volunteers if they have a closer, more participatory relationship with their football club:

> our governance structure, the way we've set ourselves up, the language we use, the way we communicate with our members and talk about what we're trying to do, means that it's an accepted part of working for FC, you're not just coming to do a job, you're coming to deliver a message, and you're coming to deliver a change, and make a difference in your local area – community is not a bolt-on for FC United, it's central to everything we do.

Such sentiment may appear clichéd to those familiar with the public relations outputs of football clubs, but AW is quick to point out that these are more than just words in FC United's case:

> we deliberately set ourselves up as an IPS, a community benefit society – community benefit is enshrined within our constitution, and the board are charged with delivering

community benefit, even before we put a team out on the pitch, if we do not deliver community benefit, then the board are not acting within the legal requirements, so that's a deliberate move by us.

Since their formation in 2008, Inter Mancunia have worked with FC United intermittently on various joint community projects with a focus on providing football-playing opportunities to migrants, refugees and asylum seekers, such as tournaments and open training sessions held in the city. Accessibility to these sessions is seen as vital for many within Manchester's migrant communities, mainly down to cost. Jenny Loudon, who was instrumental in setting up Inter Mancunia, feels that accessibility is reflected in the structure and ethos of FC United:

it's grassroots led, from the bottom up, and ... everybody has a voice and an opinion that's valued, and it kind of governs the direction of the club ... and what I've found with FC is that unlike every other big club in Manchester that are like fortresses if you want to get any support from them, they are much more accessible than Man City, than Oldham Athletic, than United, and it's not a case of 'we'll help you if you're involved in our projects' (rather) 'we'll help you if we can, and if we can't we'll say so'.

The nature of the club's structures and governance is also well known to core volunteers. In the FJF focus group, there was broad awareness of FC United's democratic structure, as well as the Community Share Scheme.[35] These elements of the club's constitution were described as very positive, factors which, according to one FJF participant, 'keep fans happy by giving them a say in how the club is run'. While there was acknowledgement that many of the young people the club works with through its community initiatives will not understand or appreciate this aspect of the club, it was felt that the work carried out by the club benefits from its more open, accessible nature compared to the bigger, less democratically structured clubs, who also deliver community engagement work.

Employment enhancement

The wide range of roles and areas of responsibility available for volunteers at FC United also means that personal development and individual employability is a positive outcome of this way of working, and is a clear articulation of the public service reform agenda's aspiration for people to move closer to the labour market through volunteering.

The Apprentices, on completion of their training, could progress to the NVQ Level 3 qualification, which would open up more employment possibilities such as working in schools, for example as PE instructors. The Apprentices described how, since starting the scheme, they have had a clearer focus on their career aspirations, and had already discussed setting up their own 'soccer school'. However, their employment horizons had also been expanded; aside from directly football-related skills, some spoke of transferable skills such as teaching, management and communication which they felt would be beneficial for other career paths.

Similarly, the seven young people employed by the club FJF scheme, working in administration, coaching and other community outreach projects, worked a 35-hour week with the club giving them direct employment experience. The FJF focus group agreed that volunteering was generally a positive thing and that 'things would be better' if more people volunteered in their local communities, with the FJF workers' own experiences highlighting the benefits for those involved. They also emphasized that it was important that people have a passion for the thing they volunteer for, as was felt to be the case with FC United volunteers. They felt projects would be less effective if volunteers did not have passion and enthusiasm, especially if they were forced or coerced in to giving up their time (perhaps a note for George Osborne's most recent JSA-linked community work proposals). The Youth Forum volunteers also discussed that they had all learned new skills during their time with FC United, and claimed to have grown in confidence through their roles. The group felt that participating in these projects provides valuable experience that reflects positively when they apply for jobs, college or university places. Again, this seems to point to the rationale for the Big Society agenda of improving the employability of target groups of unemployed, young people, hard to reach groups and the long-term unemployed. Further, the added advantage of passion and enthusiasm which can come from engagement with a football club rather than a local authority provider also points to a positive model of more sustainable volunteering.

Have 'politics', can mobilize

An area which has been highlighted by critics of the government's reform agenda is that one unintended consequence of the local empowerment strategy by government is to create activist organizations on the ground that can organize against the government's agenda. In particular, as stated at the outset, FC United in its constitutional structure and forms of governance is open and democratic; in its politics, it is left of centre; in its community role, it is active if not overtly activist. Jenny Loudon from Inter Mancunia recognized that the campaigning background of FC United, and of many of the people involved with the club, makes a big difference to some of the issues facing the communities she works with. This had been shown when FC United helped mobilize support for Mehdi Mirzae, a volunteer community coach involved with both organizations who was threatened with deportation to Afghanistan. As Jenny explained 'I was fairly overwhelmed by FC's response … that they wanted to get involved … we wouldn't have had a campaign without FC'.

It is possible, therefore, that by exploiting the leverage they have to take advantage of the government's reform and local empowerment agenda, organizations can become empowered not only for on the ground community development work but also for engaging with the agenda in order to challenge it. In one sense, for an organization like FCUM, this would be a straightforward form of social democratic entryism; that is, take what's there to provide the best services and opportunities for people in need of those forms of support but also empower people to social action and political engagement. Indeed, as well as seemingly ideal vehicles for community engagement, football clubs have been identified as potential 'hooks' to political activism, where more direct 'politics' is often seen to fail.[36]

The hope, for FC United, is that it will develop more capacity, and despite reservations, AW cannot rule out potential future bids for local service provision contracts, arguing that such a move could be justified 'if it meant us doing it or it not happening'. Setting out how the club could best prepare for such scenarios, AW continued:

> we as a club … need to establish our moral and political purpose … we need to have a clearly defined and easily understandable strategic position on that … and so long as it's done clearly, which again is a problem, then at least people know where you're

starting from, and it allows the board some comfort in what decisions they're actually taking.

The main challenge therefore will of course be to articulate an agreed 'moral and political purpose' that represents the different values and meanings that the club's various communities have invested the club with:

> but we've set ourselves that problem, because of where we've come from ... if we defined ourselves as a political organisation, then we'd turn as many people off as not, but we do have a socio-political role ... and for me, it's about tackling youth issues, and trying to create opportunities for youth.

Conclusion

FC United initially came into existence because there was a space for them, and they now appear to be thriving as an engaged community partner because there is still a need for what they provide. As General Manager Andy Walsh stated, 'we do fill gaps, we fill gaps where there's a lack of provision'. Public service shortfalls are likely to grow in the coming years of funding cuts, providing – from a pragmatic perspective – further opportunities for the club in developing deeper and wider community provision. That this may also place a club set up with self-evidently left-leaning principles in a difficult position, will clearly not prevent it from carrying out the functions it was set up for, and is legally constituted, to provide.

An important role for FC United, however, identified during the research process, is one which is about more than filling the gaps. The identification of esteem factors by NEET young men (i.e. Not in Education, Employment or Training) and the sense of belonging identified in the youth forums illustrate that football clubs can make an important contribution to social capital and community resilience. The club is creating bonds of trust within and across communities, which are significant at times when the responsibilities and pressures on communities are much more significant, as a result of the economic environment and the political shift to community delivery of services.

Secondly, the employment opportunities created by the club via the FJF, as well as the apparent impact on widening the youth coaches' horizons and expectations is also significant. In other words, the economic and employment purchase the club has could be an important driver of local regeneration. Further, improved local economic prospects also contribute to community cohesion and the ability to develop community assets. In addition to this of course is the skills and training 'resource transfer' taking place through the significant numbers of volunteers who work with and for the club. The research highlighted the heady mix of academic, public sector and small business skills available, as well as marketing and campaigning capacity that individuals bring to FC United, and which have been a major part of the club's success. Set against shrinking local budgets this is a very attractive and very important local resource, which in fact creates ripples across a broad geographical area in Greater Manchester.

Finally, of great value to a squeezed public service front line is a consistency of approach. The club's constitutional commitment to community capacity building, as well as the longevity of a relatively high profile but community-focused football club, signifies the development of a sustainable resource. In combination with the asset lock on the new stadium currently being built in Moston, an area of relative deprivation in North Manchester, the club can be regarded as a model of Big Society working, in a way as envisioned by Jesse Norman and Philip Blond. FC United are part of the glue that binds communities together and it is a very successful example of community self-organization. From that point of view, the politicized nature of the backbone of the club has been actualized through this process of community building and asset development. The notion that the club could simply be cast as a Trojan horse for a Coalition project, which challenges public service provision as universal and government-based, is of course a result of the neoliberal co-opting of terminology seemingly free of politicized intent, such as inclusion, volunteering and community. Two things are important here. Firstly, the co-option of terminology by the government cannot impact the intent or the outcomes of this type of community working. Secondly, an overt articulation, by the club, of their recognition of the political problematic and their use of the legislative framework for their own ends would likely represent a challenge to some of the club's fans. For some, watching football is not and should not be a political act. For others, immediate challenges of economic recession and a lack of opportunities may well express themselves in a different political hue than that which predominantly characterizes FC United. The extent to which different people and different communities may acknowledge the 'politics' in the issues the club is faced with, or rather chooses to be faced with, is pivotal here. Can FC United negotiate a role as a meaningful community provider within an environment of public service cuts and austerity measures, while avoiding becoming an agent of the 'Big Society' agenda?

The great challenge therefore for FC United is to set out its stall unambiguously, through the democratic processes that are required by its members, to say clearly what it stands for and what its role is to be within that. The club acknowledges that this will be an extremely difficult task, and may require them to state political positions more overtly than many of its members, and potentially partners, end-users and funders, would be comfortable with. This difficult process though is looking increasingly necessary, so that the club's board, staff and volunteers are able to steer the club confidently towards being the club its member-owners, and its various communities, want it to be.

Notes

1. PM David Cameron, speech to Conservative Party conference, October 6, 2010.
2. Breitbarth and Harris, 'The Role of Corporate Social Responsibility in the Football Business'; Brown et al., *Football and its Communities: Final Report*; Football Association, *The Football Development Strategy 2001–2006*; Parnell et al., 'Football in the Community Schemes'.
3. Mellor, 'The Janus-faced sport'.
4. Department for Communities and Local Government, *Localism Act* (HMSO, 2011).
5. Jeffares, 'The Big Society Lasted 1000 Days. Will We Ever See Ideas of its Like Again?'
6. Norman, *The Big Society*.
7. Blond, *How Left and Right Have Broken Britain and How We Can Fix It*.
8. Figures from Ipsos/Mori polls 2010: 42% had heard of the Big Society the day after the election.
9. See Misener and Doherty, 'Connecting the community through sport club partnerships'.
10. *Place Survey: England – Headline Results and Place Survey: England – Further results* (DCLG, 2008).
11. Brown et al., *Football and its Communities: Final Report*.

12. Department for Communities and Local Government, *Localism Act* (HMSO).
13. http://www.supporters-direct.org/wp-content/uploads/2013/02/Locality-Paper_pdf.pdf.
14. Department for Communities and Local Government, *Localism Act* (HMSO).
15. Local Enterprise Partnerships replaced the Regional Development Agencies in 2010 as a more localized unit of strategic economic development.
16. Sir Richard Leese, leader of Manchester City Council, speech to Local Government Association Summit, Whitehall 2012.
17. Brown, '"Not For Sale?" The Destruction and Reformation of Football Communities in the Glazer Takeover of Manchester United'.
18. Porter, 'Manchester United, Global Capitalism and Local Resistance'.
19. Blackshaw et al., 'English Football and Re-definitions of Community'; Brown et al., *Football and its Communities: Final Report*; Mellor, 'The Janus-faced Sport'.
20. Brown et al., *Football and its Communities: Final Report*, 5.
21. http://www.fc-utd.co.uk/m_manifesto.php.
22. Fans had developed a critical perspective in recent years over what they viewed as a disembedding of top-level football clubs from their traditional, local communities (see Brown, '"Not For Sale?" The Destruction and Reformation of Football Communities in the Glazer Takeover of Manchester United'; Porter, 'Manchester United, Global Capitalism and Local Resistance'; Porter, 'Cultures of Resistance and Compliance'.
23. In some ways, therefore, fans shared the 'social inclusion' view of sport that Tony Blair's New Labour government espoused, that sports clubs had a duty of care to their local communities, albeit in Blair's case within a market-friendly, laissez-faire regulatory environment (see Mellor, 'The Janus-faced Sport').
24. Brown et al., *Football and its Communities: Final Report*.
25. Blackshaw et al., 'English Football and Re-definitions of Community'.
26. Mellor, 'The Janus-faced sport', 319.
27. This interview with FJF employees came within weeks of the announcement by the Conservative-led coalition UK government to scrap the scheme (an initiative of the previous Labour government).
28. Inter Mancunia is a volunteer-run football club primarily focused on the participation of locally based migrants, refugees and asylum seekers. They have worked alongside FC United on a number of community projects.
29. This local youth football club worked with FC United to establish the apprentice scheme and NVQ Level II football coaching course.
30. Kitzinger, 'Qualitative Research: Introducing Focus Groups'.
31. Merton, Fiske, and Kendall, *The Focused Interview: A Manual of Problems and Procedures*.
32. Kvale, *Interviews: An Introduction to Qualitative Research Interviewing*, 42.
33. In 2010, FC United took part in the FJF, a young people's employment scheme initiated by the then Labour government. Entitlement to the FJF was dependent on the young people having been out of work and seeking employment for at least six months.
34. FC United's Youth Forum is a representative group of young people who participate in the club's various community programmes, meeting regularly to discuss and reflect on identified strengths and weaknesses.
35. FC United's pioneering 'Community Share' scheme allows people to invest money in the club without disrupting its one-member, one-vote democratic structure.
36. Evanson, 'Understanding the People: Futebol, Film, Theatre and Politics in Present-day Brazil'; Giulianotti, *Football: A Sociology of the Global Game*; Porter, 'Cultures of Resistance and Compliance: Football fandom and political engagement in Manchester'.

References

Blackshaw, T., T. Crabbe, C. Stone, A. Brown, and G. Mellor. 'English Football and Re-definitions of Community'. Paper given at North American Society for the Sociology of Sport (NASSS) Conference, Montreal, Canada, October 2003.

Blond, P. *Red Tory. How Left and Right Have Broken Britain and How We Can Fix It*. London: Faber & Faber, 2010.

Breitbarth, T., and P. Harris. 'The Role of Corporate Social Responsibility in the Football Business: Towards the Development of a Conceptual Model'. *European Sports Management Quarterly* 8, no. 2 (2008): 179–206.

Brown, A. '"Not For Sale?" The Destruction and Reformation of Football Communities in the Glazer Takeover of Manchester United'. *Soccer & Society* 8, no. 4 (2007): 614–35.

Brown, A., G. Mellor, T. Blackshaw, T. Crabbe, and C. Stone. *Football and its Communities: Final Report*. Manchester: The Football Foundation & Manchester Metropolitan University, 2006.

Department for Communities and Local Government. *Place Survey: England – Headline Results 2008 and Place Survey: England – Further results*. London: HMSO, 2008.

Department for Communities and Local Government. *Localism Act*. London: HMSO, 2011.

Evanson, P. 'Understanding the People: Futebol, Film, Theatre and Politics in Present-day Brazil'. *South Atlantic Quarterly* 81, no. 4 (1982): 399–412.

Football Association. *The Football Development Strategy 2001–2006*. London: The Football Association, 2001.

Giulianotti, R. *Football: A Sociology of the Global Game*. Cambridge: Polity Press, 1999.

Jeffares, S. http://inlogov.wordpress.com/2014/02/05/big-society/February2014

Kitzinger, J. 'Qualitative Research: Introducing Focus Groups'. *British Medical Journal* 311 (1995): 299–302.

Kvale, S. *Interviews: An Introduction to Qualitative Research Interviewing*. London: Sage, 1996.

Mellor, G. 'The Janus-faced Sport: English Football, Community and the Legacy of the Third Way'. *Soccer & Society* 9, no. 3 (2008): 313–24.

Merton, R., M. Fiske, and P. Kendall. *The Focused Interview: A manual of problems and procedures*. New York: Free Press, 1990.

Misener, Katie E., and A. Doherty. 'Connecting the Community through Sport Club Partnerships'. *International Journal of Sport Policy and Politics* 4, no. 2 (2012): 243–55.

Norman, J. *The Big Society*. Buckingham: University of Buckingham Press, 2010.

Parnell, D., G. Stratton, B. Drust, and D. Richardson. 'Football in the Community Schemes: Exploring the Effectiveness of an Intervention in Promoting Healthful Behaviour Change'. *Soccer & Society* 14, no. 1 (2013): 35–51.

Porter, C. 'Manchester United, Global Capitalism and Local Resistance'. *Belgeo* 2008, no. 2 (2008): 181–92.

Porter, C. 'Cultures of Resistance and Compliance: Football Fandom and Political Engagement in Manchester'. PhD thesis, Manchester Metropolitan University, 2012.

Growing the football game: the increasing economic and social relevance of older fans and those with disabilities in the European football industry

Juan Luis Paramio Salcines[a], John Grady[b] and Phil Downs[c]

[a]*Departamento de Educación Física, Deportes y Motricidad Humana, Universidad Autónoma de Madrid, Madrid, Spain;* [b]*Department of Sport and Entertainment Management, University of South Carolina, Columbia, SC, USA;* [c]*Disability Liaison Officer and Secretary of Manchester United Disabled Supporter Association, Manchester United FC, Manchester, UK*

> In trying to grow the customer base of the football game, recent studies have argued that relevant key actors in the European football industry such as football governing bodies and professional clubs must attend to the needs of all their supporters as well as consider the economic and social relevance of older supporters and those with disabilities, described as the 'new' generation of sport customers. Through analysis of major trends in legislation, demography, consumer expenditures and sport and leisure interests over time, coupled with a series of interviews with representatives of three of the main football leagues in Europe, this article contends that these two growing segments of sport consumers should be valued as important stakeholders, with enhanced access to all types of services, goods and experiences, not only considered a legal and moral imperative but one which also makes good business sense. To attend to the needs of these two groups of supporters will not only create managerial challenges but also significant opportunities for sustainable business growth that the football industry cannot underestimate as they seek to activate this latent consumer demand. Improving access to stadia is also a timely issue that football clubs should integrate into their organization's culture and operations in order to provide an inclusive environment at club level.

Introduction

The success of global sport organizations relies upon identifying the profile of existing and prospective customers and effectively meeting their needs and expectations. As the current chairman of UEFA (the governing body of European football), Michel Platini, clearly stated, fans are considered major stakeholders in football. 'Supporters are the lifeblood at the very heart of professional football. Without its supporters, professional football would not be very different from an amateur sport or pastime'.[1] Similar sentiments can be found in the mission statements of many European football leagues[2] and professional football clubs. In the same way, UEFA has made explicit reference to the importance of increasing the fan base of the football game by treating fans with disabilities as valuable customers based on their large economic impact. According to UEFA 'disabled people should therefore be seen as valued customers, with good access not only as a moral issue but also as good business sense'.[3]

Ageing coupled with disability has become a major demographic trend worldwide. The latest statistics have revealed that large sections of the population within the European Union's 28 countries[4] have a variety of disabilities[5] and also the population is getting older[6] (see Table 1). This suggests that such large numbers of potential football consumers could have a multiplier effect as older people and those with disabilities are able to influence their relatives, friends and caregivers who often accompany them to leisure and sporting events. As the European Commission and the recent Census from the UK, Germany and Spain data supports, the share of people with disabilities and the older population is not only increasing quickly, but most importantly it will continue to rise in the next five decades.[7] This data provides anecdotal evidence that this market segment is worthy of attention by the football industry and other related industry sectors.[8] As the general population ages, people develop age-related disabilities. Obviously, this demographic growth has created challenges as well as significant opportunities for sustainable business growth that the European football industry can no longer underestimate as they seek to activate this latent demand in the upcoming decades. As in other related industry sectors, this article contends that Corporate Social Responsibility (CSR)[9] demands that relevant stakeholders in the European football industry, such as national governing bodies as well as professional clubs, should respond to the needs and expectations of all their customers, including people with disabilities and older people.

Understanding football stadia and inclusivity

Over the past decade, research into understanding the sport and leisure habits, needs and consumer expenditures of individuals and groups represents an important area of study within the sport management field worldwide.[10] Similarly, past studies in the area of football and inclusivity, as this special issue seeks to address, have not devoted sufficient attention to understanding the main characteristics and demands from individuals with disabilities and older people as consumers and spectators. Both groups are increasingly deemed important subsets of football consumers; that is, while attending football matches is recognized as one of the most popular forms of leisure activities worldwide,[11] analysis of the economic and social relevance of these two 'new' market segments as well as analysing the connection (and similarities) between these two groups of sport consumers is still an under-researched area, both for the football industry and the sport management sector.

Much of the academic literature on the European football industry has focused on diverse economic, sociological and managerial themes, such as the development of clubs and their stadia,[12] the relationships and level of representation of football fans within their clubs as part of the governance of European clubs,[13] the level of attendance of football fans to their stadia[14] or the social profile of fans who attend live matches at large venues. Other areas of interest have included the commercial opportunities found in postmodern stadia, given that these facilities rely on extending their operations throughout the whole year and not just during the traditional football calendar.[15] Therefore, contemporary stadia are now expected to draw large audiences, including older fans and those with disabilities, by offering all types of services, goods and experiences on match and non-match days. As a consequence, managers are developing new strategies to make stadia appeal to wider audiences, such as offering VIP experiences and including more entertainment features in their stadia as part of the sport experience. However, few studies in sport management

Table 1. Population at the European Union's 28 state members (including the UK, Germany and Spain) at 1 January 2012 including older people and those with disabilities by size and % of total population.

	Total population (million)	Aged 50–64 (% of total population)	Aged 65 and over (% of total population)	People with disabilities	Overall figures of older people and those with disabilities
EU-28	506.8 million	19.1% 95 million	17.8% 90.2 million	15% 80 million	51.5% 258.4 million
UK	62 million	18.1% 11.2 million	16.4% 10.1 million	19.3% 12 million (2013)	53.8% 33.3 million
Germany	81.8 million	19.3% 15.8 million	20.7% 16.9 million	8.9% 7.3 million	48.9% 40 million
Spain	46.8 million (2011)	17.4% 8.14 million	17.3% 8.04 million	9% 3.8 million (2008)	43.3% 20 million

Source: Adapted from Eurostat, *Basic Figures on the EU*. Office for Disability Issues, *National Population Projections*; Office for National Statistics, *National Population Projections*; Department for Work and Pensions, *Fulfilling Potential*, for the UK; Federal Statistical Office, *Germany's Population by 2060*, for Germany; Spanish Statistical Institute, *Spain in Figures 2013* for Spain.

have explored the implementation of stadium policies in order to provide a high quality experience for customers with disabilities attending events at European stadia.[16] Moreover, improving access for fans with disabilities and older fans in European football stadia still remains a managerial challenge for most European clubs. As Phil Downs, one of the pioneers in this area and former chairman and co-founder of the National Association of Disabled Supporters (NADS) (renamed Level Playing Field since 2011) and currently in charge of the operations for all Manchester United events and services for disabled fans at Old Trafford Stadium said, 'improving the accessibility to stadia in most European football clubs should be one of the main concern of the next decade'.[17] More recent scholarship has analysed access for all types of users, including the needs and demands of individuals with disabilities, when they plan to attend a sporting event in European stadia[18] and in US stadia,[19] and has examined the level of accommodations for spectators with disabilities in European stadia.

In general, many practitioners and academics still view the provision of universal accessibility at large sports venues as an imperative based on non-economic motivations, most notably ethical, legal and social justifications, rather than based mainly on economic reasons.[20] To extend this argument, there is also a paucity of studies in this area of sport management scholarship that present sufficient evidence of a strong business case of this growing segment market at football leagues and clubs in Europe.[21] As part of this claim, studies conducted in Europe and in the United States have argued that the sport industry must address the needs and requirements of this important subset of sport consumers.

In this paper, we contend that improving access in stadia in most European football clubs for spectators with disabilities and older people should become a strategic priority for governing bodies and individual football clubs. Downs appeals to the Corporate Social Responsibility (CSR) efforts of football clubs. Commenting on the successful experience of Manchester United, he remarked:

> ... we need to generate awareness within football not only in England but also in European clubs to improve their stadium facilities considering the social aspects that accessibility produce.[22]

Football clubs can provide total inclusion within their stadium operations and CSR actions at the club level through common-sense solutions, such as the provision of an 'Ability Suite' which provides a comfortable (and fully accessible) place for disabled supporters and older supporters and their companions to gather at Old Trafford Stadium on match and non-match days.

Increasingly, as accessibility has become a major political issue for UEFA, some European Leagues such as the Premier League and Bundesliga and some individual clubs, notably Manchester United, Arsenal, Manchester City and Bayern Munich, have approached the promotion and implementation of accessibility and disability as part of their organization's culture and everyday business operations.[23] However, there are still a number of physical barriers to stadium accessibility but also a notable resistance by senior and middle managers to the implementation of actions and policies that facilitate individuals with disabilities attending matches regularly at stadia and enjoying the same experience as the rest of able-bodied spectators.[24] One of the reasons that might explain this resistance from upper level managers to the implementation of an inclusive business environment, as Scott-Parker and Zadek clearly contend in the United Kingdom, is that:

> ... most managers, including many in public sector and non-profit organizations, remain unconvinced that people with disabilities can enhance their overall business performance.[25]

As a result, there is a concomitant underestimation of the significance of disabled people as an emerging and recognizable customer group and a lack of attention to the older market, described as the 'new old market of the early twenty first century', as Luker and Stone claim based on the US sport industry. In particular, Luker reinforced this lack of attention by calling for action to attend to the needs of older fans considering that most of the US sport industry focuses on fans between the ages of 18 and 34, while a large number of loyal and avid fans are those aged over 35.[26] There is a need to identify and understand the characteristics of those sport customer groups that bring the greatest economic and social value to the sport industry. In this article, the following recommendation by Scott-Parker and Zadek is adapted:

> ... it is critically important to understand why organisations remain unconvinced [of a sound business case for older fans and fans with disabilities].[27] Once these reasons are understood, they can be addressed by people with disabilities and their advocates.

As one of the aims of the study, researchers seek to provide sufficient indicators that might contribute to convince relevant key actors of the European football industry, such as CEOs, club managers and officials, that meeting effectively the demands of these growing generations of consumers in the football industry as one that makes good business sense. This will contribute to overcome some of the misconceptions that prevent managers to promote inclusive environments as football stadia:

> The challenge is therefore to present arguments that go beyond short-term cost-benefit analyses and to describe a long-term strategic case integrated into the broader diversity perspective: it is essential to simultaneously address the ignorance and fear that currently prevent potential business benefits from being realized.[28]

Building the business case for inclusivity

This paper builds the 'business case for inclusivity' by combining economic, social and sporting indicators that include: (a) current and upcoming demographic trends of people with disabilities and older adults within all EU member states; (b) sport and leisure interests for older adults and those with disabilities; (c) social composition and levels of attendance to football matches in stadia of the three football leagues considered in our analysis (English Premier League, Bundesliga and Spanish Primera Liga); (d) the spending power of those groups and (e) the relationships and level of representation of those fans with their clubs and football governing bodies.

Method

This exploratory study draws on both primary and secondary sources. Primary data was collected by means of in-depth semi-structured interviews with six key stakeholders in three of the most prestigious football professional leagues in Europe. These leagues were selected based on sporting performance, financial performance, level of attendance and level of provision for fans with disabilities to their clubs' stadia over recent years. Four relevant Disability Liaison Officers of Premier League and Bundesliga clubs were also interviewed and were followed up by ongoing personal communications via email or Skype from early 2008 to January 2014. The analysis also included personal observations at the stadia as well as the long-time experience and knowledge of Phil Downs, based on over 20 years of experience at one of the world's largest football clubs and responsible for the accessibility operation of Manchester United's Old Trafford Stadium.

These two data collection processes enhanced the level of analysis and helped to bridge the gap between theory and practice. Parallel to this original data collection, documentary analysis was conducted using documents produced from the European Commission and European countries, European and national Census, different European (UEFA) and national football governing bodies (Premier League, Bundesliga and Spanish Professional League), advocacy organizations of fans with disabilities (Centre for Access to Football in Europe (CAFÉ), Level Playing Field and BBAG (Bundesbehindertenfanarbeitsgemeinschaft), National (English) Fans Surveys (Premier League) and football clubs from our three target leagues. Analysis of these documents offers comprehensive and reliable statistics about the profile and characteristics of older people and those with disabilities as spectators and consumers. Furthermore, additional evidence from newspapers, official and unofficial reports and club websites have been relevant to building and documenting the argument that the two market segments make a good business case to the European football industry.

Findings

Demographic trends of people with disabilities and older people in Europe

Demographic trends such as ageing and people with disabilities have a substantial economic impact on the sport and leisure industry in general and on the football industry in particular. The latest statistics show that ageing within the European Union's 28 state members is a reality. Overall, the number of older people has increased exponentially over the last decades in Europe. Generally, the EU's population was estimated at 506.8 million people as of 1 January 2012. Of these people, there were about 185 million aged 50 years and over which represent about 36.9% of the total population[29] (see Table 1). Apart from this, Eurostat population projections 'foresee that the number of people over 60 years will increase by about two million persons per year in the coming decades'.[30] These figures will substantially increase when people with disabilities are also included. The European Commission itself estimates there are more than 80 million people with disabilities in Europe, representing about 15% of the population.[31] Together both segments represent more than 50% of the population.

This study focused on three countries: the United Kingdom, Germany and Spain. In the UK, the Department of Work and Pensions recently calculated that there are almost 12 million people with disabilities, which include those with a limiting long-term illness, impairment and disability.[32] In addition, two UK governing bodies, the Office for Disability Issues and the Office for National Statistics, concur in estimating that there are currently 19 million people aged 60 or over, a figure which is projected to rise to 22.5 million by 2020.[33] Unlike the United Kingdom, the German Federal Statistics Office (*Statistisches Bundesamt*) only recognizes people with severe disabilities, excluding a wide variety of types of disabilities. Bearing this criteria in mind, the overall number of people with severe disabilities has increased from 7101,682 in 2009 to 7289,173 in 2011 (Statistisches Bundesamt officer, personal communication, 4 November 2012) which represents an increase of 2.6%. However, the number of people with different types of disabilities in Germany would be larger. Focusing on those people aged 50 and over in Germany, the figure accounts for 30% of the overall population. In Spain, despite difficulties to obtain reliable and current data on the number and type of people with disabilities, the Spanish Statistics Institute (*Instituto Nacional de Estadística*) showed that there were almost four million disabled people in 2008, representing around 9% of Spain's overall population.[34] The 2011 Census estimated the Spanish population is growing increasingly older considering that life expectancy exceeded 82 years old, with the population aged over 64 accounting for 17.3% of the Spanish population.

The share of individuals with disabilities and older people significantly will continue to rise over the next five decades.[35] As Ahtonen and Pardo stressed,[36] Eurostat predicts that by 2060 the number of people aged 65 and over in the European Union will have increased to around 30%. Already, over 32% of those aged between 55 and 65 years report a disability and this figure increases to over 40, 60 and 70%, respectively, for each additional decade.[37]

While there are obvious limitations within these figures in that there are differences in the criteria used to estimate the number of people with disabilities and older people within the European Union, there is still a strong sense when considering that one in four Europeans has a family member with a disability and six out of ten Europeans have a disabled person within their circle of friends, colleagues and relatives.

Sport and leisure interests for older people and those with disabilities

A second common indicator of the economic and social relevance of older fans and those with disabilities focuses on analysis of the level of participation of our target groups in sport and leisure activities, such as attending matches at stadia. One of the challenges that different studies and advocacy organizations concur in identifying is how to quantify the number of European individuals with disabilities as well as older people attending those matches. In this aspect, the level of accessibility at stadia in Europe can be a major facilitator or barrier to increasing the number of people from both market segments that attend matches at those venues. As noted by Grady and Paramio Salcines,[38] a recent study commissioned by UEFA found that 33% of people with disabilities do not attend the matches because the facilities are not accessible to them. Somewhat surprisingly, the Pan European advocacy organization CAFÉ[39] estimated that:

> ... around 50 percent of people with disabilities have never attended a sporting or public event and at least one third of disabled Europeans have never travelled abroad or even participated in day excursions because of inaccessible venues and services.

Although there is no similar data about participation of older people at football matches, the *Taking Part survey* evidence for England shows, as Taylor[40] remarked, some aspects that might be relevant for different stakeholders, in that 'attending historic sites, arts events, museums and galleries, and for gambling, participation rates increase until middle age, then fall with older age'. What is more relevant to this study is that age is one of the main influences on sport and leisure participation and is a major challenge to sport and leisure managers. But as this study concurs with the evidence from the adult leisure time in Spain in 2010,[41] older people are one of the groups with more disposable time (and income) for leisure activities such as attending matches at stadia.

Levels of attendance and social composition in football matches in England, Germany and Spain

Despite the fact that not all individuals with disabilities and older populations in Europe are football fans,[42] an initial conservative estimation by the advocacy organization CAFE considers that there are approximately 500,000 people with disabilities who are deemed to be football fans with a growing number of them who regularly attend, either alone or accompanied, matches at European stadia as one of their preferred leisure activities.

After examining the level of attendance of football matches in our target football leagues clubs' stadia (summarized in Table 2), it is worth noticing that attendances to German Bundesliga 1 clubs' stadia totalled the remarkable figure of 13.8 million spectators in the 2011–12 season,[43] which represented a 5.2% increase compared to the 2010–11 season (with an overall attendance of 12.8 million). Premier League clubs' stadia also attracted similar overall figures to the Bundesliga. According to Richard Scudamore, Chief Executive of the Premier League, 'our clubs deserve great credit for a range of supporters' initiatives that brought 13.6 million supporters through the turnstiles last season (2011/2012) producing a record stadium capacity of 95.3%'.[44] However, as one representative of the Spanish Liga de Fútbol Profesional noted, the Primera Division's attendance in the 2012–13 season decreased

Table 2. General trends of people with disabilities and older people attending football matches at clubs' stadia of the three main leagues in the season 2011–12.

Main football leagues in Europe	Average stadium capacity (2009/2010)	Average attendance per match (2011/2012)	Capacity utilization (2011/2012)	Total number of attendance (2011/2012)	Number of seats for disabled fans at clubs' stadia
UK Premier League	37,121	34,601	95.3%	13.6 million	2900
Germany Bundesliga 1	48,295	44,293	91%	13.6 million	2985 2541 (wheelchairs) 410 (blind people) 61 (for other types of disabilities)
Spanish Primera Division	38,748 (2009/10)	28,268	73% (2009/10)	9.9 million (2011/2012) 9.6 million (2012/2013)	

Source: Sartori, *European Stadium Insight 2011*; Bundesliga, *Bundesliga Report 2013*; Premier League, *2012/13 Premier League Season Review*; LFP, *Memoria 2011–2012 Liga de Fútbol Profesional* and Paramio, Campos and Buraimo, 'Promoting Accessibility for Fans with Disabilities to. European Stadiums and Arenas: A Holistic Journey Sequence Approach'.

slightly to 9.6 million spectators, compared to the 9.9 million spectators in the 2011–12 season (LFP officer, personal communication, January 2014).

When trying to understand the type and demographic profile of fans that attend football matches at those Leagues' stadia and how professional leagues value individuals with disabilities[45] and older people as spectators, we found that the Premier League[46] clearly focused on attracting youngsters, families and ethnic minorities to the football game saying that '19% of those who attended the 2011/2012 season were fans aged 18–24 years (12% of the population is in this age range), 13% of season tickets holders are children, 23% of match fans are women and 12% are ethnic minorities, while 41 is the average age of an adult fan going to matches'. In addition, the Premier League targeted families when half of fans (51%) attend matches with friends, 20% with their spouses and 34% with other family members; 29% attended with children.

In the case of the Deutsche Football League (DFL) in 2009 it was estimated that *'out of 800,000 wheelchair users living in Germany, 30,400 are interested in football'* (M. Rühmann, personal communication, 18 December 2009). Nevertheless, the Bundesliga itself as a governing body does not have accurate figures on the number of fans with disabilities and older fans that regularly attend matches at Bundesligastadia. As one of the DFL officers confirms to us:

> … the Deutsche Football League (DFL) does not collect this data, only the clubs themselves might be able to evaluate the access of their fans. Most of them do have an electronic access control, but no club has and even with the access control you can normally evaluate the different categories but not the whole personal data …. For home games the advance ticket offices as well as the box-offices usually sell the tickets without recording personal data (personal communication, December 10 2013).

At the time of writing, the English advocacy group Level Playing Field (LPF)[47] estimated that there are more than 30,000 people with disabilities actively attending matches regularly in England and Wales. At club level, Manchester United has implemented a wide range of accessibility services and programmes for individuals with disabilities at Old Trafford Stadium. This long-term commitment has been a central part of their Corporate Social Responsibility (CSR) policy. As a result, the club estimates that over 2200 people with disabilities, which also include some companions, are able to access football matches and enjoy similar services, activities and experiences as the rest of their large fan base.[48]

In contrast to their English and German counterparts, these numbers are reduced considerably when considering the level of provision and operation of Spanish stadia.[49] In a 2008 study, which analysed the existing facilities and services available for fans with disabilities and their companions on match days by six Spanish Primera Division clubs' stadia, it was found that, in general, except in two stadia like La Santiago Bernabeu, Real Madrid, there were an inadequate number of seats for fans with disabilities in stadia. Most of the accessible features and services were for wheelchair users, but there was a complete lack of provision for the visually impaired, people with ambulatory disabilities or other types of disabilities as happens at Bundesliga and Premier League stadia. Despite these poor conditions, it was estimated that more than 30 disabled fans plus their companions still regularly attend each match.[50] Yet, it is still unknown how many more follow the league's matches on television or via print or electronic media. The representative of the Spanish Liga Profesional clearly stated that 'the LFP does not have any data on fans with disabilities and older fans attending to clubs' stadia' (LFP officer, personal communication, 20 January 2014). In 2013, FC Barcelona attempted to quantify the number of fans with different disabilities within their fan base. In their study, the club estimated that there are 4051 members with a broad range of disabilities, where over 2000 fans (2.170) are wheelchair users, followed by sensory (hearing and vision) (1.850) and learning (difficulties) (31) disabilities.[51] Despite these numbers, the level of provision of seats for fans with disabilities at the FC Barcelona Stadium, Camp Nou, is at the time of writing extremely poor (only 40 seats for wheelchair fans) considering the overall capacity estimated at 98,784 compared to other clubs in Spain and even worse compared with European football stadia generally.[52]

The empirical data presented shows that there is no consistently available data which has considered both market segments over time. In the same way, older fans and fans with disabilities as spectators in Europe have been ignored by those Leagues and their clubs, with some relevant exceptions, in favour of other groups such as youngsters, families and other minorities.

Spending power of people with disabilities and older people

Another critical indicator of sport and leisure's importance in society is spending by consumers.[53] Focusing on this economic indicator, in the last two decades, average spending per household in the UK on leisure services has doubled in real terms[54] and leisure spending is typically around 27% of total consumer spending in the UK. Similarly, and drawing on general official statistics, the Office for Disability Issues[55] concurs with the Level Playing Field (LPF)[56] to state that disabled people in the UK nowadays have over £80 bn. a year available to spend on goods and services. In addition, this organization offers other appealing figures saying that disabled customers may account for up to 20% of the customer base for an average UK business. Beyond Europe, the Americans with Disabilities 2010 and the US Department of Justice offer also much more compelling figures than the UK's case on the economic impact of people with disabilities and older people. For the first group, it is estimated that this group make up a significant market of consumers, representing more than $200 bn. a year available to spend on goods and services,[57] while the economic impact of older people is also quite significant after the US Department of Justice clearly stated that 'more than 50% of the total US discretionary income is controlled by those 50 years and older. This is not a market that businesses should turn away from their doors'.[58]

When analysing the spending power of either fans with disabilities or older fans, Level Playing Field only focused on people with disabilities; they do not analyse the economic spending of older fans. Meanwhile, the other two leagues have not attempted to estimate the economic power of people with disabilities in general or fans with disabilities in particular. As the DFL's representative confirmed to us the lack of data on the spending power of football fans with disabilities and older fans in Germany by saying:

> We do not have data on this issue. Maybe some of the clubs (who are working with registered cashless card systems) have some data. But I am not sure if any club has evaluated the spending power of those two groups yet (personal communication, December 10 2013).

Football governing bodies and professional football club policies for older fans and those with disabilities

As previously published,[59] within the football industry, the Premier League and the Bundesliga were the first to establish guidelines and policies to try to address the needs of people with disabilities. Meanwhile, the Spanish Professional Football League has not issued any specific guidelines or policies to address the needs and expectations of fans with disabilities. Additionally, the best documents to guide anyone with the design, planning and operation come from the US (Accessible Guidelines for Stadia and Arenas 2004 and Tickets Sales 2011) and also from Europe (Accessible Stadia Guide 2004 and the UEFA and CAFE 'Good Practice Guide to Creating an Accessible Stadium and Match day Experience').

Concluding remarks and managerial implications for clubs and football governing bodies in Europe

As in other industry sectors like retail, hospitality and tourism and leisure and culture that have gradually started treating people with disabilities like valued customers, the current investigation represents an initial exploration of the analysis of the economic and social importance of older people and those with disabilities as spectators of stadia within three of the main football leagues in Europe.

When evaluating the potential of the two market segments for the football industry, the current and future demographic projections make this an attractive market for sustainable growth. This market has now expanded to over 258 million people (including people with disabilities and older people) in Europe. This data as well as the additional indicators discussed above demonstrate that these market segments are clearly deserving of management's attention which should include the prospect of additional resources being directed to providing a superior sport experience or at least a base level experience equivalent to that which other fans receive.

Another factor that supports the relevance of these combined market segments as customers is the fact that they have well-defined sport and leisure interests forming part of their everyday consumer spending. It is the confluence of the demographic shift, the sport and leisure interests, their leisure time available and the consumer spending that now make these even more attractive market segments for European football clubs.

Clearly our target populations are not necessarily all football fans, although there is a growing number of fans with disabilities and older fans regularly attending stadia in Europe, whether alone or accompanied by friends or family. Data from the main football leagues in Europe show that this number is steadily increasing, except for a slight decline in attendance at Spanish Professional League stadia. This increase in consumer demand naturally extends to these two market segments.

In light of these factors, the relevant stakeholders of European leagues and clubs like the CEO's, club managers and officials are forced into thinking how to demonstrate organizational commitment, overcoming the traditional and long-term resistance, to the implementation of specific policy actions capable of meeting the needs of all supporters which justifiably now include the combined market segments of disabled and older people. Universal accessibility become the key to implementation of such policies and will ultimately enhance the customer experience of these fans.

The challenge for managers and marketers has always been a combination of meeting effectively the needs and expectations of this growing demographic as well as attempting to broaden the appeal of the venues' physical characteristics in order to retain this segment of customer base and create opportunities for an extended period of increase by this market segment in the football industry. We are still at this early stage of understanding and appreciating the emergence of this growing demographic of disabled and older people visiting stadia, which has been characterized by a process of 'ad hoc' development in producing a coping strategy to meet current needs. As we look forward toward the middle stage of development, the challenge will become considering and developing a much more structured approach that is capable of addressing the needs of this market segment in respect of the existing customer base as well as the projected expansion of the future customer base.

Ideas to overcome resistance, as Scott-Parker and Zadek have previously argued, include upper and middle managers implementing inclusive environments at clubs stadia and organizations. It is now essential that upper and middle managers and senior stakeholders begin the process of understanding the characteristics of this market segment. They need to connect with these groups and integrate their feedback and experiences which will then assist in defining the new criteria needed to produce desired future enhancements. This could prove to show that further consideration needs to be given to potential changes to physical characteristics which impact the level of accessibility of the stadium. Many ideas can be brought in to the sphere of consideration when thinking of how we move forward with our attempts to enhance our services for fans. Changes to the physical characteristics of some parts of the stadium and possibly extending our thinking to re-imagine the immediate areas around the stadium and considering better options in respect to parking areas, transport links and connection between the two now become top priorities.

There is no doubt that disability increases with age, making it true to say that there is a definite 'squeeze' on the stadium event staff involved in an stadium operation context when dealing with this demographic. This situation has led Phil Downs to describe the successful approach Manchester United has used to appeal to this new generation of sport customers:

> ... Many years ago, we accepted that the average age of our fans was going to steadily increase as the official statistics show. We also acknowledge that a football stadium environment is not normally one of the easiest to negotiate if you have any kind of mobility difficulty. Hence, we have already taken steps to increase the overall numbers of accessible parking bays. At one time, the number of people with walking difficulties trying to get to a standard seat was so small that they could walk up to the stadium and ask to use the lift without any problem. That is not the case now. We have a tried and trusted structure for accommodating supporters such that those who need this consideration no longer have to worry about whether or not their particular need will be provided for them.[60]

Mounting evidence shows that we are moving into an epoch where companies must concentrate more of their efforts on expanding their customer base to include an increasing number of people with disabilities (including those with severe difficulties) and older people. Finally, European governing bodies and football clubs need to commit additional resources to better understand the number of fans with disabilities and older fans that attend matches regularly at European clubs' stadia as well as the customer preferences of those groups. In addition, these governing bodies and clubs should start considering the needs of these two growing segments of sport consumers, as other related industry sectors, in order to increase their fan base, to promote inclusivity at the football sector as well as to provide a high-quality customer to all fans, including our two growing segments of fans.

Acknowledgements

This study is part of the research project entitled 'Estudio Comparativo de las Funciones y Competencias del Experto en Accesibilidad Universal en Instalaciones y Eventos Deportivos: Perspectiva Norteamericana y Europea' (*Comparative Study of the Role and Competencies of the Disability Liaison Office on Sport Facilities and Events: North American and European Perspective*) led by Dr Juan L. Paramio Salcines, Universidad Autonoma de Madrid with Dr John Grady, University of South Carolina and funded by the Spanish Bank, Banco de Santander (2ª Convocatoria de Proyectos de Cooperación Interuniversitaria UAM-Banco de Santander con EEUU, 2013–2014).

Notes

1. UEFA, *Supporter Liaison Officer Handbook*, 3.
2. See this statement in different football leagues such as Premier League, *Premier League Guidance for Clubs on Disabled Fans and Customers 2010; 2012/13 Premier League Season Review; Premier League Research and Insight Season 2011/12*; Liga de Fútbol Profesional, *Memoria 2011–2012 Liga de Fútbol Profesional*; The Football League, *Supporters Survey 2010*; Bundesliga, *Bundesliga Report 2013*. See also Deloitte, *Fan Power Football Money League*.
3. UEFA, *Access for All. UEFA and CAFÉ Good Practice Guide to Creating an Accessible Stadium and Match day Experience*, 11. See a more detailed discussion on Paramio Salcines and Kitchin, 'Institutional Perspectives on the Implementation of Disability Legislation and Services for Spectators with Disabilities in European Professional Football' and Grady and James, 'Understanding the Needs of Spectators with Disabilities attending Sporting Events'.
4. At the time of writing, there are 28 countries within the European Union after the adhesion of Croatia on July 1, 2013.
5. To clarify the term disability will be important to locate this concept as part of the ongoing debate about the main perspectives concerning disability; the medical and social models. Based on both approaches, the term disability has different and distinctive meanings. On the light of this comment, disability can mean something entirely different in relation to football fans with disabilities, based on the medical and social models of disability. From the football industry, and as an advocacy group as the English Playing Field states, each club has a different approach to definition and qualification of disability and even between individuals within a club. For the purposes of this study, we follow what this advocacy group defines as a disabled supporter: 'any person who, because of their disability or impairment, is unable to use ordinary stand seating without contravening Health and Safety Regulations, Guidelines or Policy OR where the club has provided a "reasonable adjustment or "auxiliary service" to enable that supporter to attend the venue". Any such person will be considered for use of the "designated areas" of the stadium in line with the procedures set out in this policy' (Level Playing Field, 2013). See more details in Paramio Salcines and Kitchin, 'Institutional Perspectives on the Implementation of Disability Legislation and Services for Spectators with Disabilities in European Professional Football'.
6. For the purpose of this paper and considering that there is neither recognised statistical definition of 'old' or 'older' people (Eurostat 2010, 2012, 2013), though in their statistics, Eurostat starts measuring the number of older people as those people aged 50 and over, nor general consensus on who should be classed as old people we have defined in our study as those people over 50 years old as 'older people', considering that, at this age, the incidence of disability begins to increase significantly with this age. Different academics, practitioners and advocacy organisations have started to contend that the segment market

of older people, known as the 'grey market' or 'baby boomers', and those with disabilities should be valued as two 'new' customer segments by the sport industry in general (see Stone, 'The "New" Older Market'; Luker, 'Why Sport Industry must Recognize Importance of Older Fans'; Dolliver, 'The Stats on Older Fans'; Wolfe, 'Older Markets and the New Marketing Paradigm' for a more detailed analysis of the US Sport Industry on the relevance of older people segment) and the football industry in Europe in particular (CAFÉ, *Annual Report 2011–2012*; Grady and Paramio Salcines, 'Global Approaches to Managing the Fan Experience for Patrons with Disabilities'; Downs and Paramio Salcines, 'Incorporating Accessibility and Disability in the Manchester United Culture and Organization as part of their CSR policies'; Paramio Salcines and Kitchin, 'Institutional Perspectives on the Implementation of Disability Legislation in Professional Football'; Waterman and Bell, *Disabled Access to Facilities*; and Grady and James, 'Understanding the Needs of Spectators with Disabilities attending Sporting Events'.

7. See more details of this demographic trend in European countries, in Eurostat, *Demography Report 2010; Active Ageing and Solidarity between Generations*; *Basic Figures on the EU*; Office for National Statistics, *National Population Projections* for the UK; Federal Statistics Office, *Germany's Population by 2060* for Germany or Spanish Statistics Institute, *Spain in Figures 2013* for Spain. Beyond Europe, see Erickson, Lee and von Schrader, *2011 Disability Status Report. United States*; Brault, *American with Disabilities: 2010*; and Werner, *The Older Population: 2010* to analyse this demographic trend and the large economic impact and social importance of our two segments of population in the United States.

8. Similar concerns for the travel industry are found in Hudson, 'Wooing Zoomers: Marketing to the Mature Traveler', hospitality (Grady and Ohlin) or sport (Grady and Paramio Salcines; Grady and James).

9. Breitbarth and Harris, 'The Role of Corporate Social Responsibility in the Football Business. Towards the Development of a Conceptual Model'; Downs and Paramio Salcines, 'Incorporating Accessibility and Disability in the Manchester United Culture and Organization as part of their CSR policies'; Walters and Tacon, '*Corporate Social Responsibility in European Football*'; and Walter and Kent, 'Do Fans Care? Assessing the Influence of Corporate Social Responsibility on Consumer Attitudes in the Sport Industry'.

10. To analyse the sport and leisure habits, needs and consumer expenditures of individuals and groups in European countries, see Taylor, *Torkildsen's Sport and Leisure Management* for the UK; Lera-López and Rapún-Gárate, 'Sports Participation versus Consumer Expenditure on Sport'; Ministerio de Educación, Cultura y Deporte, 'Anuario de Estadísticas Deportivas 2013'; Spanish Statistics Institute, *Spain in Figures 2013* for Spain; and Pawlowski and Breuer, 'The Demand for Sport and Recreational Services' for Germany.

11. In the twentieth century, football became the national sport in many countries worldwide, with an estimated fan base over 3 bn. people. See Sartori, *European Stadium Insight 2011*, 6. However, these figures do not estimate the number of fans with disabilities and older fans.

12. To analyse the relevance of the commercial development of the latest generation of stadia in Europe see Sartori, *European Stadium Insight* 2011; Paramio, Buraimo, and Campos, 'From Modern to Postmodern'; and Kitchin, 'Planning and Managing the Stadium Experience'.

13. See more details at Hassan and Hamil, 'Introduction: Models of Governance and Management in International Sport'; Giulianotti, 'Supporters, Followers, Fans and Flaneurs'; Cleland 'From Passive to Active: The Changing Relationship between Supporters and Football Clubs'; and Llopis-Goig, 'Propiedad y Gestión de los Clubes de Fútbol. La Perspectiva de los Aficionados'.

14. Premier League, *2012/13 Premier League Season Review*; *Premier League Research and Insight Season 2011/12*; The Football League, *Supporters Survey 2010*; and Bundesliga, *Bundesliga Report 2013*.

15. See Sartori, *European Stadium Insight* 2011; and Paramio, Buraimo, and Campos, 'From Modern to Postmodern' and see more details of the case of Arsenal and the Emirates Stadium in Kitchin, 'Planning and Managing the Stadium Experience'.

16. Paramio Salcines and Kitchin, 'Institutional Perspectives on the Implementation of Disability Legislation and Services for Spectators with Disabilities in European Professional Football'; Grady and Paramio Salcines, 'Global Approaches to Managing the Fan Experience for Patrons with Disabilities'; Grady and Paramio Salcines, 'Global Disability Laws and their Impact on the Stadium Experience'; Kitchin, 'Managing the Stadium Experience'; and Grady and James, 'Understanding the Needs of Spectators with Disabilities attending Sporting Events'.
17. See Paramio, Buraimo, and Campos, 'From Modern to Postmodern', 530.
18. Paramio, Campos, and Buraimo, 'Promoting Accessibility for Fans with Disabilities to European Stadiums and Arenas'; and Paramio Salcines and Kitchin, 'Institutional Perspectives on the Implementation of Disability Legislation and Services for Spectators with Disabilities in European Professional Football'.
19. In the United States, see Grady and James, 'Understanding the Needs of Spectators with Disabilities attending Sporting Events'.
20. As was reflected in Paramio, Campos, and Buraimo (2011: 385), 'Both individual clubs and governing bodies (in Europe) should become more proactive in the promotion of accessible stadia in decades to come. Those clubs that are still reactive and do not explore the benefits of dealing with providing good standards of accessibility within their stadia will be considered, as Downs states, as part of the problem rather than the solution, especially when some top clubs in Europe are moving forward on this issue'.
21. Grady and Paramio Salcines, 'Global Approaches to Managing the Fan Experience for Patrons with Disabilities'; Paramio, Campos, and Buraimo, 'Promoting Accessibility for Fans with Disabilities to European Stadiums and Arenas'; Paramio Salcines and Kitchin, 'Institutional Perspectives on the Implementation of Disability Legislation and Services for Spectators with Disabilities in European Professional Football'; and Downs and Paramio Salcines, 'Incorporating Accessibility and Disability in the Manchester United Culture and Organization as part of their CSR policies'.
22. See more details on Downs and Paramio Salcines, 'Incorporating Accessibility and Disability in the Manchester United Culture and Organization as part of their CSR policies', 144.
23. Downs and Paramio Salcines, 'Incorporating Accessibility and Disability in the Manchester United Culture and Organization as part of their CSR policies'.
24. This issue has been analysed on Grady and Paramio Salcines, 'Global Approaches to Managing the Fan Experience for Patrons with Disabilities'; Paramio, Campos, and Buraimo, 'Promoting Accessibility for Fans with Disabilities to European Stadiums and Arenas'; Paramio Salcines and Kitchin, 'Institutional Perspectives on the Implementation of Disability Legislation and Services for Spectators with Disabilities in European Professional Football'; and Grady and James, 'Understanding the Needs of Spectators with Disabilities attending Sporting Events'.
25. Scott-Parker and Zadek, 'Managing Diversity', 120. See also Zadek and Scott-Parker, 'Unlocking Potential'.
26. Luker, 'Why Sport Industry must Recognize Importance of Older Fans'.
27. Ibid., 120.
28. Ibid., 120.
29. Eurostat, *Demography Report 2010; Active Ageing and Solidarity between Generations; Basic Figures on the EU*.
30. Eurostat, *Active Ageing and Solidarity between Generations*, 15. Similar demographic projections are provided by the Office for National (UK) Statistics where it is stated that the UK population will increase from 62.3 million in 2010 to reach 70 million by mid-2027 with the average (median) age rising from 39.7 years in 2010 to 39.9 years in 2020 to 42.2 by 2035 (See more at the Office for National Statistics, *National Population Projections*). Beyond Europe, the U.S. Census Bureau states that the 65 years and over population grew at a faster rate than the total population. Trend that it will continue to rise in the next decades (See more at Werner, *The Older Population: 2010).*
31. Ahtonen and Pardo, 'The Accessibility Act'.
32. *Department for Work & Pensions, Fulfilling Potential, VI.*
33. Office for Disability Issues, *Growing your Customer Base to Include Disabled People*, 5.
34. Spanish Statistics Institute, *Spain in Figures 2013*.

35. Eurostat, *Demography Report 2010; Active Ageing and Solidarity between Generations*; *Basic Figures on the EU*.
36. Ahtonen and Pardo, 'The Accessibility Act'.
37. Waterman and Bell, *Disabled Access to Facilities*.
38. Grady and Paramio Salcines, 'Global Approaches to Managing the Fan Experience for Patrons with Disabilities'; and Grady and Paramio Salcines, 'Global Disability Laws and their Impact on the Stadium Experience'.
39. CAFÉ, *Annual Report 2011–2012*. Similar argument can be found in UEFA, *Access for All. UEFA and CAFÉ Good Practice Guide to Creating an Accessible Stadium and Match day Experience*, 10.
40. Taylor, *Torkildsen´s Sport and Leisure Management*, 42.
41. García Ferrando and Llopis Goig, *Ideal democrático y bienestar personal: Encuesta sobre hábitos deportivos en España 2010*.
42. CAFÉ, *Annual Report 2011–2012*.
43. See Reiche, 'Drivers behind Corporate Social Responsibility in the Professional Football Sector: A case study of the German Bundesliga'.
44. Premier League, *2012/13 Premier League Season Review*, 7.
45. See more details in Paramio, Campos, and Buraimo, 'Promoting Accessibility for Fans with Disabilities to European Stadiums and Arenas'; Paramio Salcines and Kitchin, 'Institutional Perspectives on the Implementation of Disability Legislation and Services for Spectators with Disabilities in European Professional Football'.
46. Premier League, *2012/13 Premier League Season Review*, 29.
47. Level Playing Field, *Annual Report 2012/2013*.
48. As the Manchester United Foundation impact report 2012/2013 stressed, the club, through Manchester United Disabled Supporters Association (MUDSA), provided nearly 10,000 (9831) tickets for disabled supporters and their caregivers for the season 2012/2013. Additionally, an increasing number of children and adults with disabilities engaged in different disability programs as Ability Counts in the club since 2000. In particular, 156 players were registered on the Ability Counts program. See more details at Downs and Paramio Salcines, 'Incorporating Accessibility and Disability in the Manchester United Culture and Organization as part of their CSR policies' and Manchester United Foundation. *A Season Review. Taking Manchester United to the Heart of the Community. Impact Report 2012/13*.
49. Paramio Salcines et al., 'Disability Provision in European stadia within a CSR framework'; and Paramio, Campos, and Buraimo, 'Promoting Accessibility for Fans with Disabilities to European Stadiums and Arenas'.
50. Ibid.
51. See FC Barcelona, Presentació Web Accessible.
52. See more details of the provision for fans with disabilities at top main stadia of the Spanish Primera Division, Bundesliga and Premier League´s clubs as well as the new Wembley Stadium at Paramio, Campos, and Buraimo, 'Promoting Accessibility for Fans with Disabilities to European Stadiums and Arenas: A Holistic Journey Sequence Approach', 380–83.
53. Taylor, *Torkildsen´s Sport and Leisure Management*.
54. Ibid., 63.
55. Office for Disability Issues, 'Growing your Customer Base to Include Disabled People', 5; Waterman and Bell, *Disabled Access to Facilities*; Scott-Parker and Zadek, 'Managing Diversity'; and Zadek and Scott-Parker, 'Unlocking Potential'.
56. Level Playing Field, *Annual Report 2012/2013*.
57. Brault, *American with Disabilities: 2010*.
58. U.S. Department of Justice, *Accessibility Benefits Older Adult Customers*.
59. Paramio Salcines and Kitchin, 'Institutional Perspectives on the Implementation of Disability Legislation and Services for Spectators with Disabilities in European Professional Football'.
60. Personal communication, 30 September 2013.

References

Ahtonen, A., and R. Pardo. *The Accessibility Act – Using the Single Market to Promote Fundamental Rights*. Brussels: European Policy Centre, 2013.

Baker, S., J. Holland, and C. Kaufman-Scarborough. 'How Consumers with Disabilities perceive "Welcome" in Retail Servicescapes: A Critical Incident Study'. *Journal of Services Marketing* 21, no. 3 (2007): 160–73.

Baker, S., J. Holland, and C. Kaufman-Scarborough. 'How Can Retailers Enhance Accessibility: Giving Consumers with Visual Impairments a Voice in the Marketplace'. *Journal of Retailing and Consumer Services* 9 (2002): 227–39.

Brault, M.W. *American with Disabilities: 2010. Current Population Reports*. Washington, DC: United States Census Bureau, http://www.census.gov/prod/2012pubs/p70–131.pdf. 2012. Accessed December 1 2013.

Breitbarth, T., and P. Harris. 'The Role of Corporate Social Responsibility in the Football Business. Towards the Development of a Conceptual Model'. *European Sport Management Quarterly* 8, no. 2 (2008): 179–206.

Bundesliga. *Bundesliga Report. 2013. The Economic State of German Professional Football*. Frankfurt/Main: DFL Deutsche FuBballLigaGmbh, 2013.

CAFÉ (Centre for Access to Football in Europe). *Annual Report 2011–2012*. London, 2012.

Cleland, J.A. 'From Passive to Active: The Changing Relationship between Supporters and Football Clubs'. *Soccer and Society* 11, no. 5 (2010): 537–52.

Deloitte. *Fan Power Football Money League*. Manchester, NH: Deloitte, 2012.

Department for Work and Pensions. *Fulfilling Potential. Making it Happen*. London: Office for Disability Issues, Department for Work and Pensions, 2013.

Dolliver, M. 'The Stats on Older Fans'. *Brandweek*, October 12, 2009, p. 19.

Downs, P., and J.L. Paramio Salcines. 'Incorporating Accessibility and Disability in the Manchester United Culture and Organization as Part of Their CSR Policies'. In *Routledge Handbook of Sport and Corporate Social Responsibility*, ed. Juan Luis Paramio Salcines, Kathy Babiak, and Geoff Walters, 135–46. London: Routledge, 2013.

Erickson, W., C. Lee, and S. von Schrader. *2011 Disability Status Report. United States*. Ithaca, NY: Cornell University Employment and Disability Institute. 2012. http://www.disabilitystatistics.org/reports/2011/English/HTML/report2011.cfm?html_year=2011&fips=2000000&subButton=Get+HTML (accessed January 16, 2014).

Eurostat. *Demography Report 2010. Older, More Numerous and Diverse Europeans*. Luxembourg: Eurostat, 2010.

Eurostat. *Active Ageing and Solidarity between Generations. A Statistical Portrait of the European Union 2012*. Luxembourg: Eurostat, 2012.

Eurostat. *Basic Figures on the EU*. Luxembourg: Eurostat, 2013.

FC Barcelona. *Presentació Web Accessible* [FC Barcelona Officially Launched its Accessible Website]. Barcelona: FC Barcelona, L'OficinaAtencióEspecialitzada, 2013.

Federal Statistics Office. *Germany's Population by 2060*. Wiesbaden: Federal Statistical Office, 2009.

García Ferrando, M., and R. Llopis Goig. *Ideal democrático y bienestar personal: Encuesta sobre hábitos deportivos en España 2010* [Democratic Ideal and Personal Well-being: Survey of Sports Habits in Spain 2010]. Madrid: CIS and CSD, 2011.

Grady, J. 'Accessibility doesn't Happen by Itself: An Interview with Betty Siegel, J.D., Director of The Kennedy Center Accessibility Program'. *Journal of Venue and Event Management* 2 (2010): 69–73. http://www.hrsm.sc.edu/JVEM/vol2issue2.shtml.

Grady, J., and J.D. James. 'Understanding the Needs of Spectators with Disabilities attending Sporting Events'. *Journal of Venue and Entertainment Management* 4, no. 2 (2014): 46–61.

Grady, J., and J.B. Ohlin. 'Equal Access to Hospitality Services for Guests with Mobility Impairments under the Americans with Disabilities Act: Implications for the Hospitality Industry'. *International Journal of Hospitality Management* 28 (2009): 161–9.

Grady, J., and J.L. Paramio Salcines. 'Global Approaches to Managing the Fan Experience for Patrons with Disabilities'. Paper presented at the 10th Annual Conference of the Sport Marketing Association, Orlando, North America, October 24, 2012.

Grady, J., and J.L. Paramio Salcines. 'Global Disability Laws and their Impact on the Stadium Experience'. Paper presented at the Sport Entertainment & Venues Tomorrow (SEVT) Conference, Columbia, South Carolina, North America, November 21, 2013.

Guilianotti, R. 'Supporters, Followers, Fans and Flaneurs: A Taxonomy of Spectators Identities in Football'. In *The New Sport Management Reader*, ed. John Nauright and Steven Pope, 209–31. West Virginia: FIT, 2009.

Hassan, D., and S. Hamil. 'Introduction: Models of Governance and Management in International Sport'. *Soccer and Society* 11, no. 4 (2010): 343–53.

Heo, J., I.H. Lee, J. Kim, and R. Stebbins. 'Understanding the Relationships among Central Characteristics of Serious Leisure: An Empirical Study of Older Adults in Competitive Sports'. *Journal of Leisure Research* 44, no. 4 (2012): 450–62.

Hudson, S. 'Wooing Zoomers: Marketing to the Mature Traveller'. *Marketing Intelligence & Planning* 28, no. 4 (2010): 444–61.

Kitchin, P. 'Planning and Managing the Stadium Experience'. In *Managing Sport Business: An Introduction*, ed. Linda Trentberth and David Hassan, 350–66. London: Routledge, 2011.

Lera-López, F., and M. Rapún-Gárate. 'Sports Participation versus Consumer Expenditure on Sport: Different Determinants and Strategies in Sport Management'. *European Sport Management Quarterly* 5, no. 2 (2005): 167–86.

Level Playing Field (LPF). *Annual Report 2012/2013. Promoting Good Access for All Fans*. Chester: LPF, 2013.

Liga de Fútbol Profesional (LFP). *Memoria 2011–2012 Liga de Fútbol Profesional* [Annual Report 2011–2012 Spanish Professional Football League]. Madrid: LFP, 2012.

Llopis-Goig, R. 'Propiedad y Gestión de los Clubes de Fútbol. La Perspectiva de los Aficionados' [Football Clubs Ownership and Management. The Fans Perspective]. *Revista Internacional de Ciencias del Deporte* 35 (2014): 16–33.

Luker, R. 'Why Sport Industry must Recognize Importance of Older Fans'. *Street & Smith's Sport Business Journal*, June 25, 2012. http://www.sportsbusinessdaily.com/Journal/Issues/2012/06/25/Research-and-Ratings/Up-Next.aspx (accessed September 10, 2013).

Manchester United Foundation. *A Season Review. Taking Manchester United to the Heart of the Community. Impact Report 2012/13*. Manchester, NH: Manchester United Foundation, 2013.

Ministerio de Educación, Cultura y Deporte (Spanish Ministry of Education, Culture and Sport). *Anuario de Estadísticas Deportivas 2013*. Madrid: Ministerio de Educación, Cultura y Deporte, 2013. https://sede.educacion.gob.es/publiventa/detalle.action?cod=15922 (accessed September 3, 2013).

Office for Disability Issues. *Growing your Customer Base to Include Disabled People. A Guide for Business*. 2012, http://www.odi.gov.uk/involving-disabled-people (accessed September 28, 2012).

Office for National Statistics. *National Population Projections, 2010-based Statistical Bulletin*. 2011, http://www.ons.gov.uk/ons/dcp171778_235886.pdf (accessed September 30, 2013). 1–22.

Paramio, J.L., B. Buraimo, and C. Campos. 'From Modern to Postmodern: The Development of Football Stadia in Europe'. *Sport in Society* 11, no. 5 (2008): 517–34.

Paramio, J.L., C. Campos, and B. Buraimo. 'Promoting Accessibility for Fans with Disabilities to European Stadiums and Arenas: A Holistic Journey Sequence Approach'. In *Managing Sport Business: An Introduction*, ed. L. Trenberth and D. Hassan, 267–88. London: Routledge, 2011.

Paramio, J.L., C. Campos, P. Downs, E. Beotas, and G. Muñoz. 'Disability Provision in European stadia within a CSR framework: The case of Primera División-Spanish Football League'. Paper presented at the 17th European Sport Management Congress 'Best Practices in Sport Facility and Event Management, Amsterdam, 2009.

Paramio Salcines, J.L., K. Babiak, and G. Walters, eds. *Routledge Handbook of Sport and Corporate Social Responsibility*. London: Routledge, 2013.

Paramio Salcines, J. L., and P. Kitchin 'Institutional Perspectives on the Implementation of Disability Legislation and Services for Spectators with Disabilities in European Professional Football'. *Sport Management Review* 16, no. 3 (2013): 337–48.

Pawlowski, T., and C. Breuer. 'The Demand for Sport and Recreational Services: Empirical Evidence from Germany'. *European Sport Management Quarterly* 11, no. 1 (2011): 5–34.

Premier League. *Premier League Guidance for Clubs on Disabled Fans and Customers 2010.* London: Premier League, 2010. http://www.nads.org.uk/ddaguidance_downloads/4.html (accessed August 10, 2011).

Premier League. *Premier League Research and Insight Season 2011/12.* London: Premier League. http://fansurvey.premierleague.com/ (accessed September 10, 2013).

Reiche, D. 'Drivers behind Corporate Social Responsibility in the Professional Football Sector: A case study of the German Bundesliga'. *Soccer and Society* 15 no. 4 (2014): 472–503.

Sartori, A. *European Stadium Insight 2011.* KPMG: Prospects for football stadium development and commercialization across Europe, 2011.

Scott-Parker, S., and S. Zadek. 'Managing Diversity: A Key Factor in Improving Efficiency, Productivity, and Overall Business Success'. *Journal of Vocational Rehabilitation* 16 (2001): 119–23.

Siegenthaler, K.L., and I. O'Dell. 'Older Golfers. Serious Leisure and Successful Aging'. *World Leisure Journal* 45, no. 1 (2003): 47–54.

Spanish Statistics Institute (Instituto Nacional de Estadística) (INE). *Spain in Figures 2013.* http://www.ine.es/inebmenu/mnu_cifraspob.htm (accessed September 30, 2013).

Stone, M. 'The 'New' Older Market'. *Racquet Sport Industry Magazine* (2011), http://www.racquetsportsindustry.com/articles/2011/08/19_the_new_older_market.html (accessed September 10, 2013).

Taylor, P., ed. *Torkildsen's Sport and Leisure Management.* London: Routledge, 2011.

UEFA. *Access for All. UEFA and CAFÉ Good Practice Guide to Creating an Accessible Stadium and Matchday Experience.* Nyon: UEFA, 2011.

UEFA. *Supporter Liaison Officer Handbook.* Nyon: UEFA, 2011.

U.S. Department of Justice. *Accessibility Benefits Older Adult Customers.* Washington, DC: U.S. Department of Justice, 2006. http://www.ada.gov/olderaccess.pdf (accessed February 1, 2014).

Walter, M., and A. Kent. 'Do Fans Care? Assessing the Influence of Corporate Social Responsibility on Consumer Attitudes in the Sport Industry'. *Journal of Sport Management* 23 (2009): 743–69.

Walters, G., and R. Tacon. '*Corporate Social Responsibility in European Football*'. Report funded by the UEFA Research Grant Program, Birbeck University of London, 2011.

Waterman, I., and J.A. Bell. *Disabled Access to Facilities.* London: Routledge, 2013.

Werner, C.A. *The Older Population: 2010. 2010 Census Briefs.* Washington, DC: United States Census Bureau, 2012. http://www.census.gov/prod/cen2010/briefs/c2010br-09.pdf (accessed December 1, 2013).

Wolfe, D. 'Older Markets and the New Marketing Paradigm'. *Journal of Consumer Marketing* 14, no. 4 (1997): 294–303.

Zadek, S., and S. Scott-Parker. *Unlocking Potential: The New Disability Business Case.* London: Employers Forum on Disability, 2003.

Fit Fans: perspectives of a practitioner and understanding participant health needs within a health promotion programme for older men delivered within an English Premier League Football Club

Daniel David Bingham[a,b], Daniel Parnell[c], Kathryn Curran[d], Roger Jones[e] and Dave Richardson[f]

[a]*School of Sport, Exercise and Health Sciences, Loughborough University, Leicestershire, UK;* [b]*Bradford Institute for Health Research, Bradford, UK;* [c]*Centre for Active Lifestyles, Carnegie Faculty, Leeds Metropolitan University, Leeds, UK;* [d]*Academic group of Engineering, Sports and Sciences, University of Bolton, Bolton, UK;* [e]*Older Men's Health and Well Being, National Older Men's Network, Liverpool, UK;* [f]*The Football Exchange, Research Institute for Sport and Exercise Sciences, Liverpool John Moores University, Liverpool, UK*

> Fit Fans was a men's health promotion intervention delivered within an English Premier League Football Club (2010–2011), which aimed to support the local community dwelling older men in lifestyle promotion (physical activity [PA], diet and well-being). The purpose of this study was to provide a reflexive account of a practitioner and the needs of participants. Seven men (mean age 58 years) attended weekly PA and lifestyle sessions over an eight-month period. Baseline physiological measurements included body mass index, resting blood pressure and abdominal girth. Principles of ethnography and observational research (i.e. field notes, reflective diary) were adopted by the practitioner. Unexpectedly, the cohort exhibited a range of serious diagnosed illnesses that challenged the practitioner's skill base and experience in the delivery of the intervention. Reflections of the practitioner and the stories of the progression that participants made add insight to future football in the community programmes.

Introduction

Older men (50 years and over) in the UK are living longer compared to half a century ago.[1] However, this increase in life expectancy has occurred alongside the increase in the prevalence of lifestyle-related illness and/or disorders such as non-insulin-dependent diabetes and obesity.[2] The UK Government highlighted that these poor public health occurrences are underpinned by decreasing levels of physical activity (PA) and the greater consumption and availability of processed foods.[3] These public health issues have led the UK government to support and finance health promotion schemes.[4]

Sport and specifically (the brand of) football (or soccer) has been championed by the UK Government as a vehicle to address health issues such as PA and exercise participation as well as wider social issues such as social inclusion and regeneration in order to spread health messages.[5] In 1986, the national Football in the Community (FitC) programme was launched in order to address an array of social issues and help build a greater connection between football clubs and their community.[6] Whilst football interventions have proved to be both popular and enjoyable, they have tended to lack sufficient empirical evidence to confirm their status as a significant facilitator of positive behaviour change.[7] Historically there has been a lack of research to suggest that sport-based policy interventions can have a positive impact upon health behaviour(s).[8] However, recent published studies strongly suggest this to be untrue.[9] Research within older (50+) and at risk populations is still scarce, however, preliminary findings from an older men's health intervention based in Scottish football clubs, have shown promising findings in terms of feasibility and outcomes.[10] Such a position has been echoed by studies which have called for a more rigorous evaluation of FitC schemes.[11] Health behaviours including PA are complex behaviours and are influenced by a number of different determinants that include social, political, economic and environmental factors.[12] Health promotion schemes such as exercise referral programmes and FitC schemes are typically multi-disciplinary. In the context of FitC schemes, past studies have been unable to capture the true nature, complexity and subsequent outcomes of the (apparently) numerous interventions.[13] For these reasons it has been suggested that evidence from health interventions are required from a range of disciplines including psycho-social and sociocultural sciences in order to fully understand the complex nature of health promotion, and especially, in populations such as older men.[14]

Qualitative-based research methodologies have been suggested to be more suitable in order to fully understand the person (in this case older men) and the nature of their existence, (i.e. thoughts, feelings, historical and situational context) and also better understand the difficulties and challenges that occur within interventions from a practitioner's perspective.[15]

The Fit Fans intervention (referred to as Fit Fans throughout this article) was a novel older men's health promotion project targeted at men over the age of 55 years with a view to elevating the importance of engaging in health behaviours. Fit Fans was delivered within an English Premier League Football Club within the City of Liverpool. Fit Fans is part of Age UK's nationwide Fit as a Fiddle (FaaF) programme which aims to support people over the age of 50 years with services to promote PA, healthy eating and mental well-being. FaaF, hosts innovative projects promoting healthy ageing based around the needs of local people. Programmes are run in partnership with local, regional and national organizations with FaaF working alongside partner organizations for older men to access activities tailored to their needs. The projects are not just designed *for* older men but also designed *with* and *by* older men with additional support from the programme's practitioners.[16]

The aims of this study are twofold. Firstly, we aim to explore the participants' needs and how those needs developed throughout the intervention; and secondly we aim to provide a reflexive account of a practitioner leading the intervention. These two aims offer a critical insight and future guidance for practitioners, coaches and allied health professionals into the realities of delivering health promotion programmes for older men.

Methods

Participants and setting

The Fit Fans programme took place at Everton Football Club and was delivered within the Everton Active Family Centre (EAFC). EAFC was a community fitness centre located in the grounds of Goodison Park (English Premier League Football stadium). EAFC was part of a longitudinal collaborative research venture between the School of Sport and Exercise Sciences at the Liverpool John Moores University and the community arm of Everton Football Club, Everton in the Community (EitC – a registered charity), and Everton Football Club. More information on the different projects and history of the EAFC, along with the issues of brand power of a football club reaching out to the local community are explored elsewhere in this special edition journal.[17] Everton Football Club and the EAFC are situated in the North West of England. The surrounding catchment area is classified as an area of multiple high deprivations.[18]

Fit Fans took place one day a week and was one of a range of health interventions that were delivered within EAFC. A total of seven participants were recruited. All participants were men (mean age 58 years(y); $1n=63y$; $3n=62y$; $2n=58y$; $1n=47y$), white British and were all from the local surrounding community (low socioeconomic status). Three of the men were retired, one was unemployed and a further three were out of work due to health issues/disability. Three of the men lived at home with a partner and four of the men lived alone. All of the men volunteered to join the programme through the recommendation of different community health workers from different National Health Service services (nurse, general practitioners and community well-being advisors). The inclusion criteria originally stated that any male over the age of 55 years who showed an interest in the project and who had medical clearance could be included. All but one participant met these criteria, the individual (47 years) that did not, still took part. Ethical approval was obtained from the Liverpool John Moores University ethics committee.

The programme and measurements

Fit Fans took place every Tuesday for an eight-month period (October 2010 – May 2011). The programme was structured as six-week continuous cycles with participants taking part in a range of one-to-one activities devised in conjunction with the practitioner (1st author). A typical six week cycle is depicted in Figure 1.

Each of the men took part in at least one six-week cycle. The programme commenced with an introductory session and the completion of baseline physiological measurements including body mass index (BMI),[19] resting blood pressure (RBP)[20] and abdominal girth (AG).[21] Following the initial session, the practitioner designed a personalized behaviour change programme using different behaviour change techniques (e.g. information on consequences, intention formation, setting grading tasks, modelling of behaviours, self-monitoring of behaviour, instruction of time management and aspects of motivational interviewing) derived from the theory of planned behaviour, social cognitive theory and control theory.[22] During the following six weeks, the individual attended their allocated one h weekly time slot. Weekly sessions consisted of individualized lifestyle support (including nutritional advice, PA/exercise provision and health advice) alongside participant–practitioner goal setting and other behaviour change techniques previously stated. Weekly diaries were issued to participants to allow them to record PA levels and daily dietary intake. Diaries were not used within any data analyses but were used as a practical method of self-awareness and goal setting for the participants and practitioners alike.

Following the initial six week cycle, the practitioner repeated baseline measurements with each participant to highlight positive changes and areas for improvement

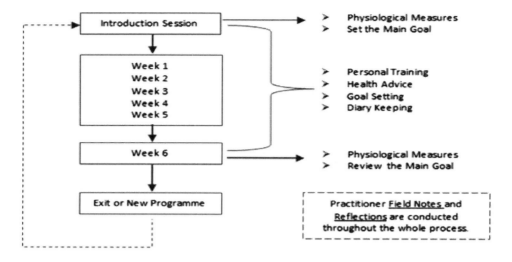

Figure 1. Outline of the 6 week cycles within Fit Fans.

with a view to guiding future programme development. The flexibility of the programme allowed the practitioner and the participants to consult and agree any extensions to the following six-week cycle.

Physiological measurements

In order to measure any physiological adaptations, a number of measurements were collated. Height and weight measures were recorded to calculate BMI (kg/m^2) (Overweight = BMI $\geq$ 25 kg/m^2) (Obese = BMI $\geq$ 30 kg/m^2).[23] BMI, RBP and AG measures are widely accepted as valid and reliable mechanisms for assessing levels of cardiac risk associated with older men.[24] It is critical that such measures were recorded due to the increased cardiac risk associated with men aged 50 years and over.[25] Moreover, such measures enabled a more bespoke, appropriate and safe exercise/health intervention to be designed.[26] BMI, RBP and AG were also recorded as measures of physiological progression.

Immersion and observation

The first author, here by referred to as the practitioner, utilized the principles of ethnography and observational research in adopting a practitioner-cum-researcher approach to data collection.[27] Principally, the practitioner became immersed in the weekly working environment of EAFC and Fit Fans.[28] The practitioner led all weekly sessions of the intervention over the eight-month period. During this prolonged period of engagement (developing rapport and acceptance with each of the participants), the practitioner adopted a range of informal and open approaches to data collection (e.g. informal practitioner–participant conversations). Such approaches enabled the practitioner to explore issues as they evolved between themselves and with the participants. Throughout data collection, the practitioner recognized the importance of not being perceived to be collecting data and that ultimately personal exchanges should be as near to 'normal' in order to achieve acceptance with all individual participants.[29] The practitioner's personal reflections and observations were recorded through informal field notes and a reflective diary.[30] The reflective diary and informal field notes were continually developed in an attempt to capture the context, culture and practice of the intervention and the viewed opinions and perceptions of all those involved.[31]

Data analysis and representation

The 1st author prepared his respective field notes and reflections, before engaging in a period of close reading in order to become immersed in the data.[32] Content analysis procedures were adopted to identify and code themes arising from the data.[33] Key themes emerging from the data are presented and discussed. Verbatim citations (identified in *italics*) are applied to illustrate the contextual features of the participants to illuminate the rich detail of the collected data. The practitioner's field note extracts, and personal reflections are evidenced as indentations, single-spaced lines and a smaller (font 10) within the text. A first-person writing style was adopted in elements of the results and discussion in order to help contextualize the data and the on-going story for the reader. Pseudonyms are used for all participants and select 'others' throughout. No statistical models or analyses were conducted within the objective data (i.e. physiological measurements). Physiological data were taken predominately to track the progress of each of the participants. The reporting of the participants' physical states within the data analysis alongside the qualitative data helps the reader understand the journey of each of the participants.

Results

Participant's needs: physiological results and health needs

The physiological results of all seven men can be found in Table 1. The results in Table 1 show that the physiological markers did not change in terms of reducing the risk of health consequences. For instance, all the participants that were classified as obese at the beginning of the programme were still obese at the end (see Table 1).

Table 2 outlines the health conditions of each of the participants when they first registered on the Fit Fans programme. Table 2 shows that some of the participants' health conditions were quite serious, and knowledge of these conditions helped to contextualize the journey that each of the participants went through and provides an insight into the personalized and relative goal setting outlined within Table 3.

Participant's needs: goals and perspective

Table 3 provides an insight to the breadth and range of strategies that the practitioner developed with each of the participants during their time with Fit Fans. Robert's first week goal to *'Aim for 30 min on the exercise bike (at home) per day',* was far too ambitious when considering his health status (see Table 2). Such over-ambitious goals are not uncommon and can be typically explained by the limited participant knowledge gleaned in the early stages of engagement alongside the practitioner's willingness not to damage the early stage eagerness of the men. During the following weeks it became clear that, as the practitioner and Robert became better

Table 1. Physiological measures (BMI, RBP, Resting Heart Rate & AG changes) across the duration of the intervention.

Name	Week 1 BMI	Week 1 RBP	Week 1 RHR	Week 1 AG	Week 6 BMI	Week 6 RBP	Week 6 RHR	Week 6 AG	Week 12 BMI	Week 12 RBP	Week 12 RHR	Week 12 AG	Week 18 BMI	Week 18 RBP	Week 18 RHR	Week 18 AG
Robert	38.1	150/88	70	143	39.1	152/89	69	150.11	39.1	152/89	68	151.89	38.4	117/73	75	142.75
Ant	39.9	137/75	70	141.73	40.6	139/78	68	145.54	39.6	136/85	70	141.73	37.4	137/79	67	126.63
Nigel	38.5	144/82	61	129.8	38.5	162/78	66	131.06	38.9	143/77	68	135.38	38.9	148/69	57	130.56
Mick	36.1	129/89	71	132.84	35	126/85	75	128.51	34.7	128/80	72	125.48	33.6	119/81	78	113.03
Lee	29.3	123/88	95	109.73					31.4	128/92	101	123.95	29.4	127/86	89	119.13
Ryan	24.8	132/85	75	98	24.5	129/83	72	94.49	21.4	131/81	76	91.69	21.7	132/81	74	93.73
Ben	32	168/95	73	107.7	31.3	165/90	76	121.16								

Table 2. Participant health demographics.

Name	Age	Health demographics
Robert	63	Physical Disability/chronic pain (spinal injury); Obesity; Hypertension (M); High Cholesterol (M); Osteoarthritis
Ant	62	Obesity; Gout; Hypertension (M); High Cholesterol (M); Osteoarthritis
Nigel	64	Diabetes Mellitus (Type II); Obesity; Hypertension (M); Osteoarthritis
Mick	56	Depression (M); Anxiety (M); Obesity
Lee	47	Depression (M); Anxiety (M); Addiction (Alcohol and Substance)
Ryan	62	Bowl Cancer (within 12 month remission)
Ben	59	Post-polio syndrome (M)

acquainted; they were able to modify the goal to something more suitable and palatable for Robert.

> Being new to working with older men, especially those with a range of serious illnesses I (the practitioner) had to forget some of the behaviour change skills and messages that I'd learnt at University and more importantly how to apply them in the 'real' world. I knew I had to forget a lot of the health messages (including government guidance) and begin to understand Robert's day-to-day existence, in order to help adjust his goal setting to reflect his expectations and ability on a week to week basis.

Table 3 provides an insight into the individual goal setting for each of the men. Robert's weekly goals were based mainly upon increasing PA. Other men had goals that were aimed more at becoming familiar with an alien (fitness) environment (see Mick's goals on weeks 5 and 6) or more habit changing (and forming), such as walking into town rather than taking the bus (Nigel, Week 2). Such low-level 'entry' points (to PA) are worthy of consideration especially when working with such populations. It is evident that more bespoke, subtle, meaningful and achievable goal setting was required in order to 'hook' the participants into (small) positive exercise and health behaviours before introducing them to potential longer term achievements.

Participant's needs: understanding perceived impact(s) of the intervention

A major observation of Fit Fans was that whilst some of the men did not always reach their original goal, which was primarily of a physical orientation, they reported to have achieved something 'much more', as they alluded to both social and psychological benefits of the programme:

> I haven't lost weight Dan (practitioner) but I tell you what, I feel on top of the world! After sweating it out on that treadmill. I mean ... I get down (sad) a fair bit especially living by myself, not working no more and our kid (brother) being ill and living in that care home. And just coming here talking to you about all this health and fitness stuff. You just feel fitter and better just talking about it. (Nigel)

> I have been out of work for a long time and felt rubbish about myself. I knew that my depression is not going to be helped by meself staying at home eating rubbish and doing nothing. It's a struggle sometimes you know, to leave the house. But coming here and talking to nice people (i.e. other men) who have similar issues and who care and understand. Well it's just good. My confidence is growing and I find it easier each week to leave the house, and hopefully I will get myself back into work soon (i.e. employment). (Mick)

Table 3. Participants' weekly goal setting.

1st 6W cycle

Goal setting	Main goal	W1	W2	W3	W4	W5	W6
Robert	'Increase exercise levels'	Aim for 30 min on the exercise bike (home) a day	Try again with the exercise bike but aim for 5 days a week	Try again with the exercise but aim for 3 days	Aim to just go on the exercise bike once a week any time	Aim for 1x 10 minutes of the exercise bike a day	Aim for 2x5 minutes of the exercise bike a day
Ant	'Weight loss and to get fitter and more active'	Walk more often	Walk three times a week, 40 minutes each time	Walk twice a week 30 minutes at a time	Drink less beer and record all.	Now walk three times a week 40 minutes at a time and drink 2 pints of beer less than usual	Same as last week
Nigel	'Lose weight get more active'	Go on the exercise bike at home for once a week	Aim to do 3 walks and record it, walk to town get bus home	30 min over the whole week on the exercise bike at home and continue walks	Same as last week	Go on the bike three times a week, drink 3 glasses of water	Illness
Mick	'Lose Weight and get fitter and I want to join a gym'	Walk more and attempt to attend a local gym	Same as the week before	Continue to increase walking, try and just go to the gym door.	Walk 2 days a week, take the dog and record	Have a cup of coffee at the gym's cafe and walk to town instead of bus/car	Inquire about the prices of the gym
Lee	'To gain structure, programme, lose weight'.	Get in the habit of recording everything that is done in a week (food and activity diary).	20 min of cardio each gym session	Cut the amount of coffee from around 10 cups to 5 cups	Cut the amount of coffee from around 10 cups to 7 cups, and also look into stopping smoking.	Increase the amount of water drank in a week, (buy 1 litre bottle and drink daily).	Arrange meeting with GP to start a quit smoking programme.
Ryan	'Become stronger and fitter'	Investigate how to use unused lower body equipment at the gym, and use them	Change to 'salt light' rather than cut all salt out.	Aim to 25 min of CV x 2 weekly (walking/ running)	Go for one 1 jog	Drink 1.5 litres of water a day and eat 3 pieces of fruit a day	Had some bad news, so week off.

	Goal setting	Main goal	W7	W8	W9	W10	W11	W12
Ben		'Get healthier, get back into healthier stuff again'	Record everything I do and look into local swimming	Joined swimming pool and gym	Absent	Go swimming twice a week and eat less packets of crisps and try and get out if bed and do something	Only eat fruit as snacks, and aim to go gym, not just swimming	Begin to eat regular breakfast.

2nd 6W cycle

	Goal setting	Main goal	W7	W8	W9	W10	W11	W12
Robert		'Be more active'	Use food and exercise diary, 2 × 5 min on exercise bike in week	3 × 5 min on exercise bike	Aim for 1 continuous bout of 10 minutes one day a week	Aim for 1 continuous about of 12minutes one day a week	Same again	Missed week
Ant		'Lose weight and improve general fitness.'	Do two walks (2–3miles)	Do three walks (2–3 miles)	Bring in complete food diary and drink more water (litre a day)	Drink 500 ml of water a day, 3 walks this week (2–3 miles)	To prepare and make a 'healthy' meal for family	Absent
Nigel		'Lose the weight I put on over Xmas'	Find a gym, aim for 6000 steps a day (pedometer)	Use the gym once a week, try new machines and aim for 8–10,000 steps a day	Try out new designed programme in gym, maintain walking steps	Reduce salt in diet, continue with gym and walking when possible	Absent	Aim to do 90 min this week at the gym
Mick		'Lose weight, have better eating habits and improve my lifestyle.'	Walk an hour a day with the dog and aim to drink 1litre of water a day.	Buy a 1litre bottle and drink that a day. Replace Breakfast 'Burger' for more healthier option	Join the local gym and have introduction and only 2 burgers this week	Consume only 1 burger in the week and attend one gym session a week (Sunday)	No burgers this week, have porridge for breakfast, keep to gym session	Go to the gym and use the hand out practitioner has designed. And enjoy holiday
Lee	Absent							
Ryan		'Stay as active as possible'	Continue to come to the centre (illness)	Continue to come to the centre (illness)	Continue to come to the centre (illness)	Continue to come to the centre (illness)	Continue to come to the centre (illness)	Continue to come to the centre (illness)

(*Continued*)

Table 3. (Continued).

3rd 6W Cycle

Goal Setting	Main Goal	W13	W14	W15	W16	W17	W18
Robert	'Lose weight and get healthier'	10 min on exercise bike 1 day a week and 5 min another day	12 min on exercise bike 1 day a week and 5 min another day	15 minutes on 2 days a weeks on exercise bike, drink more water (record)	Week off	Week off	Same as week 15 get back into things
Ant	'Lose more weight'	Eat a piece of fruit with every meal	Get back into the garden	Take the grandkids to the park and join in and encourage playing football	Go for one big of walk 5 miles	Absent	Try and choose more healthier options when on holiday
Nigel	'Lose weight'	When at gym aim for 30 minutes of continuous cadio exercise	Include resistance activities in the gym, get back into the garden.	Same as last week	Drink less alcohol when out, 9 pints instead of 10	Aim to go the gym twice a week	Continue with the gym twice a week
Mick	'Continue to lose weight, and exercises and try my best to swim'	Walk to the gym, attend the gym for 1 h and use pedometer	Aim to go to the gym twice a week. Aim for 12,000 (pedometer) for the whole week	Look to eat a healthy lunch with a healthy breakfast, keep up the gym (2x week)	Inquire about going to swimming and aim for 1300 steps a week	Go gym at leisure centre, have lunch and if comfortable go swimming at the leisure centre.	Go swimming again along with going the gym twice a week
Lee	'Loose body fat percentage, stop smoking and coffee'	Drink the same amount of water after every coffee, to reduce dehydration, continue with smoking programme.	Buy a 1litre water bottle	Absent	Getting very stressed so aim to start going yoga every Thursday	Absent	Carry on with Yoga and aim to go gym every Tuesday.
Ryan	'Stay as active as possible.'	Continue to come to the centre (illness)	Absent (Holiday)	Absent (holiday)	Get back into fitness routine	Gym 2 h a week and drink more water	Eat less when going on holiday

It was found that through applying health messages such as healthy eating ideas (see Table 3) and increasing PA participation in an informal non-intimidating manor (i.e. small, subtle and manageable changes set by a caring practitioner) the men appeared to engage and apply what they had been taught and the results appeared to lead to small changes within their everyday life.

> I did not know that salt could affect my blood pressure. I am on tablets to sort me out (high blood pressure) but never heard anything about salt. Makes sense really I have a good lot of salt on everything really, especially on boiled eggs which I have for breakfast every day, but I have changed that to some high fibre stuff and to be fair feel I feel a bit better and happier. (Ant)

> You always hear that runners get a high or something, but I just always felt knackered. But what I will say is, having a bit of banter with Dan (practitioner), and having him keep banging on about getting out there and doing a little bit extra ... well really he is right. I look back and I felt knackered walking around, but now no problem, easy! (Nigel)

> Coming here once a week and me starting to go the gym in my own time, has really improved my confidence, I was putting weight on, but the advice I've been given has really made me believe I can get rid of this weight and get back into work. (Mick)

> For me coming here (EAFC) one hour a week and then going to my community gym once a week, is enough for me. I feel better in myself and our kid (his brother) has noticed that I ain't down the dumps no-more. (Nigel)

Although positive physical changes (i.e. changes in BMI, weight and RBP) were not present across all the men, they agreed and believed that they felt they had improved their physical health and felt better about themselves after their last week in comparison to their first week. These small positive lifestyle changes may not create initial physiological changes. However, the immediate positive psychological changes help in their habit formation through commitment to the whole process of behaviour change (and long-term PA and exercise).

Practitioner's perspectives: reality check

The first author was responsible for the delivery of the Fit Fans intervention, whilst near the completion of his undergraduate degree within Sport and Exercise Science. During this time, he had accrued a number of practitioner-based qualifications, including his Fitness Instructor Level 3 award. However, he had little experience of working with older populations, nor any experience of the subsequent challenges that emerged. Table 3 complimented with the results within Table 1 and the men's views offer some empirical and contextual findings of the programme. However, at this juncture, it appears appropriate to explore the practitioner's personal insights concerning the challenges and successes that may be helpful for the future of similar interventions:

> One of the initial aims of the intervention was for the men to increase their physical activity levels. My (practitioner) initial perception was to get the men aiming towards and reaching the then UK health guidelines (i.e. 150 min split by 30 × 5 a week, 5 a day). As a health and exercise practitioner (with a degree in Sport and Exercise Science), I was aiming to get these fellas, off the couch and out there; walking more, going to the gym, cycling, swimming, all those types of activities. I believe that age is only a number and when you are retired you should have plenty of time to keep healthy and active. There is no reason why you can't reach 30 min of moderate

exercise per day, or even an hour! However, it soon became apparent that the men on the programme would not be able to reach, or in some cases even imagine reaching, some of current health guidelines, and/or my expectations of them. After I finished my first session, I realised that my blinded enthusiasm was very much ill informed. The majority of the men looked at me in shock when I suggested that they jogged on the treadmill, or even asked them to aim for walking 30 min every day *"... what walk 30minutes! It ain't happening lad, simple."* I asked Robert if he could try and do an extra two reps on the chest press (he had only done 4). He replied clearly without the slightest hesitation, *"I will do what I can do lad, have you forgot I am not 21 like yourself."* I replied, *"Well how about aiming higher. It's my job to try and increase your intensity so that you can achieve your health goals, and it's only two reps."* Robert replied, *"Well two reps fucking hurts lad!"*

It was clear that following set guidelines was not going to be realistic or positive. The practitioner re-engaged with the men, learnt from experiences, built up a rapport and then began to set more suitable goals (see Table 3).

I realised each individual participant had their own needs. These men all came from a poor (low socio-economic) background from the areas surrounding the football club. Some men had disorders and disabilities, some psychological and some physical. All the men knew they were overweight and most were told from their fabled General Practitioners (GP) (aka community medical practitioner/doctor) that they needed to lose weight and get more active. This information was evidently not enough for any of the guys to actually 'get out there' and change their behaviour, as they all lacked a basic understanding of what constituted a 'healthy' lifestyle.

When engaging the men in the goal setting aspect of the programme, it became clear that this meeting was all about 'compromise'. It would be very easy for me to set goals (and I did at first) the way my degree had prepared me – what everyone (with a few exceptions) tended to bang on about in the classroom and textbooks! But these were not fit for purpose, ideal or realistic to these men. Overtime I adopted the personal philosophy that 'doing anything was better than doing nothing'.

I realised that by week 3 and 4 I had begun to develop a rapport and level of trust (and understanding) with the men. This was critical in even creating modest changes. In all, there may have been no drastic weight loss; you know the classic picture with someone grinning like a Cheshire cat while wearing their old trousers, holding and lifting them out to show how much weight they'd lost. But in all I think, so what! These men were beginning to get control of their lives again, doing more activity and thinking more about what they eat, with some even contemplating getting back into employment. I mean thinking of the health conditions these men have, how dumb struck and amazed I was of how something like a mild form of gout could have a real and detrimental impact on someone's well-being. These men during their time started to take control, and a few did lose (some) weight. But in my opinion what is important is that by taking control and making these small changes these men were increasing their quality health and ultimately dignity; to them (and me) surely this makes Fit Fans a success!

The increase of rapport led to more suitable and palatable goals for the men, but the role of the practitioner working within community populations was at times much more than a professional exercise or lifestyle specialist, solely concentrating on the goals of each of the men. Trials and tribulations of the men's lives were brought to the attention of the practitioner:

Ryan was down today, I asked a few times whether he was ok. He said "yeah just tired lad." I knew something was wrong. Half way through the session I just decided to ask Ryan what was up. He looked to the floor and I knew that it was not going to be good news. "The cancer (bowl) is back and no cure. I might have chemo (therapy) to increase the time I have but I am unsure whether I want to feel that sick again and know I am not getting better." I was overwhelmingly shocked. No words could explain the sheer shock of hearing this. I had no idea, professionally, what should be done in this situation, but I just spoke to Ryan the way I would a friend and/family. What was clear though was that whether he decided to go for treatment or not the centre (EAFC) and I would be here for him, even if we just changed his goals to 'coming here for a cup of coffee for a few weeks'. (see Table 3-Ryan week 7)

It was two weeks after Ryan told me about the cancer coming back. I was so happy that he still made the time to come along to his session. I was even happier that he seemed himself, seemed in good spirits and had decided to undergo chemotherapy. I also knew and told Ryan that I knew colleagues and researchers at the University who were specialist in exercise and cancer. Although exercise is not a cure, it could be used a treatment against the side effects of chemotherapy and also positive self-determining nature that someone is being proactive. He was happy with this and so was I.

The empathy and respect the practitioner had for the participant and vice versa was clear to see, and the fact that the participant continued to attend sessions was a success and the support and resources the practitioner had availed allowed Ryan to continue to come along and most importantly be safe.

Discussion

The Fit Fans intervention was primarily designed for older men. However, the ages of the participants (47–63) would suggest that the term 'older men' was applied liberally. In essence, the average age of the men (i.e. 58 years), seven years under the UK legal retirement age of 65 years, suggest that these men were 'young-older men'. All of the men involved had pre-existing health conditions that are common within older men (e.g. diabetes, gout, hypertension, high cholesterol, cancer, depression and obesity). All of these conditions have been reported to have increased in prevalence over the last few decades within older men.[34] What is clear from the high level of health conditions along with the 'young-old age' is that the men were prime candidates for a lifestyle intervention, and if they had not taken part in the intervention, it could be assumed that the continuing of their hazardous lifestyles would have increased the risk of more sinister health conditions which would decrease quality or even longevity of life.

Participant needs

It was clear from the beginning of the intervention that the health conditions of the men were seen by the practitioner as factors affecting the men's ability to being active and meeting personal set goals. The practitioner in this study initially attempted to apply PA guidelines,[35] as a target and overall goal for each of the men to reach. Opinions and views expressed by the men made it clear and apparent that this method was not suitable for this group of men. Results, stemming from the practitioner's reflections, suggested that aiming for recommended guidelines had damaging effects upon the men's perspectives on what they were able to do. It appeared that current guidelines were inappropriate, unachievable and 'out of reach' for populations most 'at risk'. Learning this lesson and having a personalized approach, the practitioner allowed the participants to discuss, adapt and agree achievable goals that were individualized to each of the men which led to greater success in meeting the goals set. Current guidelines do not account for, nor reflect the landscape, nor connect with those that are most risky and most unlikely to get involved in such health interventions, particularly men and men from low socio-economic backgrounds.

The health conditions reported by the men in this study were not the only barriers perceived by the practitioner to impact engagement of positive health behaviours. It appeared that the construct of self-efficacy was also seen by the practitioner to be a barrier. Whilst self-efficacy was not measured, within this study, it has been previously shown to be a significant psychological correlate to older men's health behaviour.[36] Although not measured, self-efficacy appeared to be evident in the practitioner's reflections. The participants clearly struggled with the ability to succeed in certain tasks that they perceived to be well beyond their reach (i.e. a lack belief in one's own competence and/or ability to achieve 'what others would perceive to be 'ordinary and/or achievable' tasks). Future interventions involving similar participants should take these issues into consideration when designing interventions. It was evident from this intervention that greater consideration is needed to explore individual contexts to increase the likelihood of achieving successful behaviour change. Practitioners must develop activities that are appropriate to the individual and be mindful that whilst recommended guidelines (e.g. PA) are laudable, they are not achievable for many, especially at a low-level entry points. More bespoke, subtle, meaningful and achievable goal setting(s) are required in order to 'hook' the participants into (small) positive exercise and health behaviours before introducing them to potential long-term achievements.

The practitioners role

It was found that the positive and evolutionary relationship between the practitioner and participant was critical to facilitating 'any' behavioural change.[37] Building a rapport and adopting a familiar, caring and empathic approach as a practitioner appeared to facilitate the level of the men's engagement which has been shown to be an effective and recommended aspiration in both this study and the previous research.[38] However, much of the past research advocating such an evolutionary practitioner–participant (client or patient) relationship has been doctor–patient focused[39] with very little research within community health settings.

The Fit Fans intervention was delivered within the community arm of a football club; however, what made Fit Fans unique was that the FitC programme worked closely with a University-based School of Sport and Exercise Sciences. Having such a relationship allowed the programme to recruit a degree-educated practitioner (including expert supervisory support). Although he did not have the experience of the extreme health conditions found within the Fit Fans participants, the practitioner did have the knowledge of health promotion strategies and behaviour changing techniques. This type of relationship is not 'usual' within FitC programmes and others may not be able to recruit or have the training capabilities to employ practitioners or coaches that are capable of running and maintaining an intervention in such high needs of older men. Similar findings were found by Parnell and colleagues,[40] who although reporting on a FitC coach leading a children's session, the reported issues around the inability to be effective in promoting health are relevant to the current study. Fit Fans could not have been possible without the practitioner, but also vitally the support and sport and health expertize the practitioner received from the University.

The relationship between the University and this particular FitC programme allowed the Fit Fans programme to be led by a team of multi-skilled practitioners, whose skills were mainly within health promotion rather than a sports performance focus of which football community coaches/practitioners have been reported to be commonly trained to focus upon.[41] The serious nature of some of the situations the practitioner encountered shows the importance of FitC programmes having the capabilities to cater for the needs of high-risk individuals. The cost of such training could well be high, the practitioner was undergoing a £9000 a year degree, which is not a possibility for every individual. However, building links with universities with expertize and the students, who could well undertake teaching/coaching roles educating existing and future FitC coaches/practitioners in areas of health promotion, behaviour change techniques and understanding social needs and considerations of different populations (e.g. older men, children and disabilities), should be considered.

Whilst this study has reported a number of positive health behaviours resulting from the men's involvement within the Fit Fans project, we acknowledge some limitations to the study. Fit Fans was aiming to promote health (i.e. positive changes to diet, PA and well-being). The practitioner was predominantly qualified within sport and exercise science. Although each participant had individual tailored programmes, the practitioner could well have focused much of the intervention and attention upon PA where perhaps a greater focus could have been placed on the nutritional goals of the participants.[42] Although a qualitative-based study and PA were subjectively measured via informal conversations and during the process of goal setting, the inclusion of an objective measure of PA would be of added strength to the current study, and has been found to be feasible and be an effective instrument within recent research.[43] Finally, by not having a followup period (i.e. beyond the protracted nature of the study) any claims or suggestions of long-term (e.g. over a 12 month period) behaviour change have no merits of assumption.

Conclusions

Fit Fans (a community setting intervention) engaged (young) older men with multiple health complications that although not uncommon in this population, were found to be problematic. Future engagement with similar groups of participants in similar settings requires practitioners to understand the negative effect health complications can have. Practitioners must have the skills and ability to complement subtle progressive goal setting based around building a positive and evolutionary relationship of trust between themselves and participants. This study provides evidence that practitioners in health promotion interventions have just as an important role in the engagement of community populations, as coaches have with sports performers and health professionals with clinical populations. However, there is currently limited research within community-based health promotion interventions which requires addressing.

Acknowledgements

The authors would like to thank Age UK's Fit as a Fiddle Project funded by The BIG LOTTERY and supported by Age Concern Central Lancashire. Further thanks to the National Older Men's Network www.oldermenswellbeing.org. The authors would like to express their gratitude to all the "chaps" who were part of Fit Fans. A special acknowledgement goes to 'Ray' who sadly lost his battle with cancer, such a lovely and dignified man. The authors would also like to thank the staff of Everton Football Club and Everton in the Community for their support with this research and permission to identify the club explicitly in this publication. Matt Malone, Scott Robinson, Susan Jones and Daniel Webber for their time, effort, passion and help during their time volunteering within the EAFC and specifically within Fit Fans.

Notes

1. Leon, 'Trends in European Life Expectancy'.
2. World Health Organisation, *Global Recommendations on Physical Activity*.
3. Department of Health, *Healthy Weight, Healthy Lives*.
4. Idem.
5. Department for Culture, Media and Sport, *Social Exclusion Unit*.
6. Football Association, *Football Development Strategy* 2001–2006.
7. Idem.
8. Priest, 'Promoting Healthy Behaviour Change (Review)'; Priest, 'Interventions Implemented Through Sporting Organisations'.
9. White, 'Men's Under Use of Health'; Pringle, 'pre-adoption Demographic and Health Profiles'; Pringle, 'Effect of a National Programme of Men's Health'; White, *Premier League Health*.
10. Hunt, 'It's Given Me a Good Kick up the Backside … the First Thing I Do is Put My Pedometer On'; Gray, 'Football Fans in Training: The Development and Optimization of an Intervention Delivered Through Professional Sports Clubs to Help Men Lose Weight, Become More Active and Adopt Healthier Eating Habits'.
11. Parnell, 'Monitoring and Evaluation'.
12. Biddle, *Psychology of Physical Activity*.
13. Parnell, 'Monitoring and Evaluation'; Tacon, 'Football and social inclusion'; Schorr, *Strengthening Families and Neighbourhoods*.
14. Gidlow, 'Physical Activity Promotion'.
15. Parnell, 'Monitoring and Evaluation'.
16. Age UK, 'Fit as a fiddle'.
17. Curran, 'What works? Ethnographic Engagement'.
18. Liverpool City Council. 'The Indices of Multiple Deprivation 2007'.
19. Expert Panel, 'Executive Summary of the Clinical guidelines'.
20. National High Blood Pressure Education Programme, 'Prevention, Detection, Evaluation and Treatment'.
21. Agarwal, 'Waist Circumference Measurement'.
22. Abraham and Michie, 'A Taxonomy of Behaviour Change Techniques used in Interventions'.
23. American College of Sports Medicine, *Guidelines for Exercise Testing and Prescription*.
24. American College of Sports Medicine. *Guidelines for Exercise Testing and Prescription*.
25. American College of Sports Medicine, *Guidelines for Exercise Testing and Prescription*.
26. American College of Sports Medicine, *Guidelines for Exercise Testing and Prescription*.
27. Bray, 'Don't Throw the Baby Out'.
28. Hammersley and Atkinson, *Ethnography: Principles in Practice*; Tedlock, *Ethnography and Ethnogrphic Representation*.
29. Hammersley and Atkinson, *Ethnography: Principles in Practice*.
30. Hammersley, 'Whats Wrong with Ethnography?'; Richardson, 'Developing Support Mechanisms'; Sciarra, 'The Role of the Qualitative Researcher'; Morrow, 'Qualitative research in counseling psychology'.
31. Hammersley, 'Whats Wrong with Ethnography?'; Richardson et al., 'Developing Support'.

32. Elo and Kyngäs, 'The Qualitative Content Analysis Process'.
33. Elo and Kyngäs, 'The Qualitative Content Analysis Process'.
34. World Health Organization. 'The Heidelberg Guidelines'.
35. World Health Organisation, *Global Recommendations on Physical Activity.*
36. Booth et al., 'Social and Cognitive and Perceived'; Mcauley, 'Self-efficacy and Maintenance of Exercise'; Hall et al., 'Change in Goal Ratings'.
37. Hammersley, 'Whats Wrong with Ethnography?'; Richardson et al., 'Developing Support Mechanisms'; Baker, 'The Relationship between Coaching Behaviours'.
38. Long, 'Complementary and Alternative Medicine'.
39. Stewart, 'Effective Physician–Patient Communication'.
40. Parnell, 'Monitoring and Evaluation'.
41. Parnell, 'Monitoring and Evaluation'.
42. Department of Health, *Healthy Weight, Healthy Lives.*
43. Hunt, 'It's given me a good kick up the backside … the first thing I do is put my pedometer on.'; Gray, 'Football fans in training: the development and optimization of an intervention delivered through professional sports clubs to help men lose weight, become more active and adopt healthier eating habits.'

References

Abraham, C., and S. Michie. 'A Taxonomy of Behavior Change Techniques Used in Interventions'. *Health Psychology* 27 (2008): 379–87.
Agarwal, S.K., A. Misra, P. Aggarwal, A. Bardia, R. Goel, N.K. Vikram, J.S. Wasir, et al. 'Waist Circumference Measurement by Site, Posture, Respiratory Phase, and Meal Time: Implications for Methodology'. *Obesity* 17 (2009): 1056–61.
Age UK. 'Fit as a Fiddle'. (2013). http://www.ageuk.org.uk/health-wellbeing/fit-as-a-fiddle/about-fit-as-a-fiddle/.
American College of Sports Medicine (ACSM). *ACSMs Guidelines for Exercise Testing and Prescription* 7th ed., London: Lippincott Williams & Wilkins, 2009.
Biddle, S.J.H., and N. Mutrie. *Psychology of Physical Activity: Determinants, Well-being and Interventions.* 2nd ed., London: Routledge, 2007.
Booth, M.L.N., Neville Owen, Adrian Bauman, and Ornella Clavisi. 'Social–Cognitive and Perceived Environment Influences Associated with Physical Activity in Older Australians'. *Preventive Medicine* 31 (2000): 15–22.
Bray, G.A. 'Don't Throw the Baby out with Bath Water'. *American Journal of Clinical Nutrition* 79 (2004): 347–9.
Brown, A., T. Crabbe, and G. Mellor. *Football and Its Communities: Final Report*, London and Manchester: Football Foundation and Manchester Metropolitan University, 2006.
Curran, K., D.D. Bingham, D. Richardson, and D. Parnell. 'What Works? Ethnographic Engagement Inside a Football in the Community Programme at an English Premier League Football Club'. *Soccer in Society* (2014).
Dale, G.A. 'Existential Phenomenology: Emphasizing the Experience of the Athlete in Sports Psychology Research'. *The Sports Psychologist* 10 (1996): 307–21.
Denzin, N.K., and Y.S. Lincoln, eds., *The Handbook of Qualitative Research*, 2nd ed., Thousand Oaks, CA: Sage, 2000.
Department for Culture, Media and Sport. *Report to the Social Exclusion Unit – Arts and Sports*, London, 1999.
Department of Health. *Healthy Weight, Healthy Lives. London*, London: HMSO, 2007.
Elo, S., and H. Kyngäs. 'The Qualitative Content Analysis Process'. *Journal of Advanced Nursing* 62 (2008): 107–15.
Expert Panel. 'Executive Summary of the Clinical Guidelines of the Identification, Evaluation, and Treatment of Overweight and Obesity in Adults'. *Archives of Internal Medicine* 158 (1998): 1855–67.
Football Association. *The Football Development Strategy 2001–2006*, London: Football Association, 2001.
Gidlow, C., and R. Murphy. 'Physical Activity Promotion in Primary Health Care'. In *Physical Activity and Health Promotion*, ed. L. Dugdill, D. Crone, and R. Murphy, 87–102. Oxford: Wiley-Blackwell, 2009.

Gray, C.M., K. Hunt, N. Mutrie, A.S. Anderson, J. Leishman, L. Dalgarno, and S. Wyke. 'Football Fans in Training: The Development and Optimization of an Intervention Delivered through Professional Sports Clubs to Help Men Lose Weight, Become More Active and Adopt Healthier Eating Habits'. *BMC Public Health* (2013).

Hall, K.S, G.M. Crowley, E.S. McConnell, H.B. Bosworth, R. Sloane, C.C. Ekelund, and M.C. Morey. 'Change in Goal Ratings as a Mediating Variable between Self-Efficacy and Physical Activity in Older Men'. *Annals of Behavioral Medicine* 39 (2010): 267–73.

Hammersley, M. *Whats Wrong with Ethnography? Methodological Explorations*, London: Routledge, 1992.

Hammersley, M., and P. Atkinson. *Ethnography: Principles in Practice*, London: Routledge, 1995.

Hunt, K., C. McCann, C. Gray, N. Mutrie, and S. Wyke. 'It's given Me a Good Kick up the Backside … the First Thing I Do is Put My Pedometer on. Men's Experiences of Graduated Physical Activity Advice as Part of a Gender Sensitised Weight Management Programme'. Poster Presented at the 7th Annual Scientific Meeting of the UK Society for Behavioural Medicine, Oxford, 2013.

Joseph, B., J. Cote, and R. Homes. 'The Relationship between Coaching Behaviours and Sport Anxiety in Athletes'. *Journal of Science and Medicine in Sport* 3 (2000): 110–19.

Krane, Vikki, and Shannon M. Baird. 'Using Ethnography in Applied Sport Psychology'. *Journal of Applied Sport Psychology* 17 (2005): 87–107.

Leon, D.A. 'Trends in European Life Expectancy: A Salutary View'. *International Journal of Epidemiology* (2011): 1–7.

Liverpool City Council. 'The Indices of Multiple Deprivation 2007'. (2007, 2012). http://liverpool.gov.uk/Images/IndicesDeprivation07.pdf.

Long, A.F. 'The Potential of Complementary and Alternative Medicine in Promoting Well-being and Critical Health Literacy: A Prospective Observational Study in Shiatsu'. *Alternative Medicine* 9 (2009): 19.

Mcauley, E. 'Self-efficacy and Maintenance of Exercise Participation in Older Adults'. *Journal of Behavioural Medicine* 16 (1996): 103–12.

McFee, G. 'Triangulation in Research: Two Confusions'. *Educational Research* 34 (1992): 173–83.

Morrow, Susan. 'Qualitative Research in Counseling Psychology: Conceptual Foundations'. *The Counseling Psychologist* 35 (2007): 209–35.

National High Blood Pressure Education Programme (NHBEP). *The Seventh Report of the Joint National Committee on Prevention, Detection, Evaluation and Treatment of High Blood Pressure*, Washington, DC, 2003.

Parnell, D., G. Stratton, B. Drust, and D. Richardson. 'Implementing Monitoring and Evaluation' Techniques within a Premier League Football in the Community Programme: A Case Study Involving Everton in the Community'. *Routledge Handbook of Sport and Corporate Social Responsibility* 7 (2013): 326–43.

Priest, N.R.A., J. Doyle, and E. Waters. 'Policy Interventions Implemented through Sporting Organisations for Promoting Healthy Behaviour Change (Review)'. In *The Cochrane Collaboration*, Wiley, 2005a.

Priest, N.R.A., J. Doyle, and E. Waters. 'Interventions Implemented through Sporting Organisations for Increasing Participation in Sport (Review)'. In *The Cochrane Collaboration*, Wiley, 2005b.

Pringle, A., S. Zwolinsky, A. Smith, S. Robertson, J. McKenna, and A. White. 'The Pre-adoption Demographic and Health Profiles of Men Participating in a Programme of Men's Health Delivered in English Premier League Football Clubs'. *Public Health* 125 (2011): 411–16.

Pringle, A., S. Zwolinsky, J. McKenna, A. Daly-Smith, S. Robertson, and A. White. 'Effect of a National Programme of Men's Health Delivered in English Premier League Football Clubs'. *Public Health* 127 (2013): 18–26.

Richardson, D., D. Gilbourne, and M. Littlewood. 'Developing Support Mechanisms for Elite Young Players in a Professional Soccer Academy: Creative Reflections in Action Research'. *European Sport Management Quarterly* 4 (2004): 195–214.

Schorr, Lisbeth B. *Common Purpose: Strengthening Families and Neighbourhoods to Rebuild America*, New York: Anchor Books, 1997.

Sciarra. 'The Role of the Qualitative Researcher'. In *Using Qualitative Methods in Psychology*, ed. M. Kopala and L.A. Suzuki, 37–48. Thousand Oaks, CA: Sage, 1999.

Sparkes, A.C. 'Narrative Analysis: Exploring the Whats and Hows of Personal Stories'. In *Qualitative Research in Health Care*, ed. I. Holloway, 79–99. Maidenhead: Open University Press, 2005.

Stewart, M.A. 'Effective Physician–Patient Communication and Health Outcomes: A Review'. *Canadian Medical Association Journal* 152 (1995): 1423–33.

Tacon, R. 'Football and Social Inclusion: Evaluating Social Policy'. *Managing Leisure* 12 (2007): 1–23.

Tedlock, B. 'Ethnography and ethnographic representation'. In Handbook of Qualitative Research, ed. Norman K. Denzin, Vol. 2, 455–86. London: Sage, 2000. ISBN 0761915125.

United Kingdom Government. 'Change for Life'. (2013). http://www.nhs.uk/change4life/Pages/change-for-life.aspx.

White, A., and Karl Witty. 'Men's under Use of Health Services – Finding Alternative Approaches'. *Journal of Men's Health* 6 (2009): 95–7.

White, A., S. Zwolinsky, A. Pringle, J. McKenna, A. Daly-Smith, S. Robertson, and R. Berry. *Premier League Health: A National Programme of Men's Health Promotion Delivered in/by Professional Football Clubs. Final Report 2012*, Leeds: Centre for Men's Health and Centre for Active Lifestyles, Leeds Metropolitan University, 2012.

World Health Organisation. *Global Recommendations on Physical Activity for Health*, Geneva: WHO, 2010.

World Health Organization. 'The Heidelberg Guidelines for Promoting Physical Activity among Older Persons'. *Journal of Aging and Physical Activity* 5 (1997): 2–8.

Effect of a health-improvement pilot programme for older adults delivered by a professional football club: the Burton Albion case study

Andy Pringle, Daniel Parnell[1], Stephen Zwolinsky, Jackie Hargreaves and Jim McKenna

Carnegie Faculty, Centre for Active Lifestyles, Leeds Metropolitan University, Leeds, UK

Older adults are a priority within policy designed to facilitate healthy lifestyles through physical activities. Golden Goal is a pilot programme of physical activity-led health improvement for older adults, 55 years and older. Activities were delivered at Burton Albion Football Club. Sessions involved weekly moderate to vigorous intensity exercise sessions including exer-gaming (exercise-orientated video-games), indoor bowls, cricket, new age curling, walking football, and traditional board games and skittles. Secondary analysis of data collected through the original programme evaluation of Golden Goal investigated the impact of the intervention on participants. Older adults completed self-reports for demographics, health screening/complications and quality of life. Attendees, $n = 23$ males (42.6%) and $n = 31$ females (57.4%) with a mean age of 69.38 (±5.87) ($n = 40$), ranging from 55–85 years took part. The mean attendance was 7.73 (±3.12) sessions for all participants, ($n = 51$). Older adults with two or more health complications ($n = 22$, 42.3%) attended fewer sessions on average (6.91 ± 3.322) compared to those reporting less than two health complications (8.65 ± 2.694). Self-rated health was higher for women (87.32 ± 9.573) vs. men (80.16 ± 18.557), although this was not statistically significant ($U = 223.500$, $p = 0.350$). Results support the potential of football-led health interventions for recruiting older adults, including those reporting health problems.

Introduction

Older adults (OA) have been identified as being at risk from a range of chronic conditions.[1] It has been suggested that physical activity (PA) interventions have the potential to reduce the impact of these conditions on OA,[2] and this is reflected in key PA policy and guidance.[3] In doing so, this guidance highlights the importance of adopting a multi-sectorial approach in providing PA opportunities for OA. With those thoughts in mind, professional sports clubs have been recommended as one vehicle for providing lifestyle-based health-improvement programmes. Johnman, and colleagues have suggested that delivering lifestyle programmes in professional football clubs for fans and local people are an important contribution to the social and public health of individuals and communities.[4] This includes OA, who have been specifically targeted through health-improvement programmes delivered in, Premier and Football League clubs.[5]

---

[1]Original lead evaluator.

Chronological definitions of ageing do not always accurately reflect the diversity that exists amongst OA. Variations in functional capability and a host of complex needs mean there is a multiplicity of categorization possible across the OA spectrum. Yet OA have previously been referred to as 'adults over the age of 50 years'.[6] More recently, definitions have shifted to embrace a relative component of ageing and guidance[7] provides a more helpful and detailed framework for defining OA based on their PA needs and does so using three categories. (1) *Entering old age/Making activity choices* – where the aim is to promote a healthy and active life and compress morbidity. (2) *Transitional phase/Increasing the circle of life* – where the aim is to maintain independence, social networks and reduce dependency. (3) *Frail older people/Moving in the later years* – where the aim is to maintain independence, functional capacity and quality of life. This framework is especially important, given the range and complexity of health issues and determinants that OA participants can encounter when initiating and maintaining PA.[8]

Deteriorations in cardiovascular and metabolic health,[9] low functional capacity,[10] social isolation, poor mental health[11] and cognitive decline[12] represent potentially injurious health consequences of unhealthy ageing which can restrict PA. Yet, a persuasive evidence-base supports the role that PA can play in preventing and/or managing the effects of these conditions.[13] Despite the compelling case made for PA in both research and policy, at times, it remains challenging to deliver PA-based programmes within the National Health Service (NHS) as it attempts to deal with reductions in government funding[14] and rising healthcare costs.[15] Worse still, OA can now experience increasing financial pressure resulting from existing ill-health[16] and at the same time, some bespoke preventative health services have been withdrawn.[17] This holds particular consequences for many lone OA who report facing difficulties in finding and negotiating their own support to continue to live independently.[18]

Existing evidence highlights the beneficial effects of PA,[19] yet meeting recommended PA levels are rarely achieved.[20] OA are encouraged to accumulate at least 150 min of moderate intensity activity per week or around 30 min activity on most days of the week. This can be performed in sessions of 10 min or more. For OA who are habitually physically active, similar benefits can be achieved through 75 min of vigorous intensity PA or a combination of moderate and vigorous PA over the course of a week. Importantly, OA should also undertake activities that help to improve muscle strength on at least two days a week and reduce the amount of time they spend being sedentary.[21] However, current PA levels in OA are a matter for concern, with participation rates declining as age increases. Reports based on the previous PA recommendations indicate around 20% of men and 17% of women 65–74 met recommended guidelines.[22] Further, activity reports based on the accelerometery data collected from the 2008 Health Survey for England show that women aged 75+ achieve two minutes of moderate to vigorous physical activity per day. While for men aged 75+, the time spent in moderate to vigorous PA per day is as little as five minutes.[23]

Given the gap between the PA recommendations and existing behaviour, it is unsurprising that OA report facing significant challenges when attempting to adopt and/or sustain PA participation. Declining PA levels and poor diets make a significant contribution to unhealthy BMI; moreover, overweight OA can be significantly less active than their 'normal' weight counterparts.[24] Further, low self-efficacy, a lack of social support[25] and perceived environmental factors[26] can also combine – or act in isolation – to inhibit participation. Research shows that perceived barriers for outdoor PA participation precede a decline in the mobility levels in community-dwelling OA.[27] The same evidence base highlights the need to address the concerns of OA regarding safety, distance and access to PA facilities. Further research supports the notion that maintaining functional capacity is likely to be critical for the mental well-being of many OA,[28] as a degree of community mobility is essential for independent living.[29] This complex array – and interplay – of factors indicate the scale of the challenge faced by deliverers attempting to encourage OA to adopt and maintain PA.

OA have been 'targeted' as a group for health improvement through health and PA strategies, both in the UK[30] and globally.[31] Previous PA interventions have included walking schemes,[32] exercise referral programmes, exercise groups and peer mentoring[33] delivered by a range of public agencies. However, while it is important to identify suitable modes of PA, it is also important that the methods used to implement interventions are acceptable to participants.[34] A recent review of PA interventions with a sample of over 99,000 asymptomatic adults identified four key design characteristics for promoting PA.[35] Interventions should be: (1) delivered direct to the participant, (2) use local and familiar settings, (3) adopt behavioural change techniques and methods (4) involve key exercise leaders in the delivery of programmes. Moreover, contemporary public health guidance for OA compliments this knowledge base. Relevant guidance recommends that deliverers assess the needs of OA. Providers should also offer regular group and/or individual sessions which encourage OA to rehearse activities that support the maintenance of their active daily routines, as well as a flexible and varied menu of PA options to cater for the different needs of OA. Importantly, OA should be consulted on the design and delivery of provision.[36]

It is interesting that professional football clubs have been used as settings for the delivery of PA-led, health-improvement programmes for a number of groups,[37] including OA. Two bespoke PA-led interventions implemented in professional footballing settings are outlined below. Firstly, the *Extra Time* programme targeted OA aged 55 years and above with PA-led social inclusion and health-improvement projects delivered nationwide.[38] Interventions were offered to OA within Premier and Football League club community schemes using club and community facilities and centred on individual and group-based delivery designs. In particular, activities for both men and women, aimed to address key public health priorities, cardiovascular health, reducing social isolation and maintaining/improving physical/psychological functioning, three important outcomes for healthy ageing.[39] Secondly, and with the understanding that older men are at risk of poor health,[40] the Premier League Men's Health programme, was a national suite of 16 interventions delivered in English Premier League and Championship football clubs for adult men. Recruits also included males who were aged 55 years and older. Findings support that older men reached and adopted interventions. Further, men including, older males demonstrated statistically significant improvements for a range of cardiovascular disease (CVD) risk factors.[41] Importantly, some participants reported that they did not engage in health improvement interventions led and delivered in traditional healthcare settings.[42] These two examples demonstrate the potential of football-based, PA-led health-improvement programmes for reaching and facilitating changes in the health behaviours of OA.

National guidance recommends that behavioural health interventions are evaluated, in order that their impact is assessed and deliverers learn about the effects of such schemes.[43] This is particularly important, given that to the best of our knowledge, there is a paucity of peer-reviewed studies assessing the effect of football-led health-improvement programmes delivered in English football league clubs and aimed specifically at the engagement, PA promotion and health improvement of OA. With those thoughts in mind, this study set out to investigate the demographic and health profiles of participants attending Golden Goal (GG), a pilot programme of PA-led health improvement for OA delivered by Burton Albion FC. This case study of practice was undertaken using a secondary analysis of data collected as part of a previous local evaluation of the GG programme. In doing so, written permission was provided by the original lead evaluator, (who forms part of the authorship) for the secondary analysis of the data to take place.

Method
Intervention context
Burton Albion FC are located in the town of Burton in East Staffordshire in the English East Midlands and which has a population of 113,583; 19,131 (16.9%) are residents of retirement age (65+). Data on deprivation show that East Staffordshire has 70 lower layer super output areas (LSOAs – a measure of deprivation).[44] Consistent with this, adult male life expectancy is lower than the English average in 13 of the 21 wards within East Staffordshire,[45] while the numbers of hip fractures in the 65+ age group exceed the national average.[46] Further, local assessment of health needs highlighted a lack of awareness in OA, of the role of diet and PA in preventing and managing cognitive conditions such as dementia.[47] Local health plans for area over the next four years have endorsed the importance of PA promotion for the purposes of health improvement[48] including those linked to unhealthy ageing. In line with national guidance,[49] local health needs assessments supported the requirement for preventative health-improvement activities for OA and this was the basis for the GG programme.

Building on the governmental aspiration to generate strong local health partnerships, GG was conceived to address the health needs of OA identified locally. The programme resulted from the combined efforts of Burton Albion Community Trust (BACT) – (*the community arm and registered charity of Burton Albion Football Club*) – along with local partners and builds upon the concept and novel Extra Time project to reach OA.[50] To manage the often diverse and complex health needs of OA,[51] the GG programme aimed to promote positive physical and social opportunities to local participants through a diverse PA-based programme. Considering public health guidance,[52] which recommends that deliverers provide a range of mixed exercise programmes of moderate intensity in local venues, PA sessions were offered on a weekly basis at the Pirelli Stadium, home to Burton Albion FC. All activities were provided by BACT members of staff with a range of sports coaching qualifications and experience working on community engagement programmes. Activities included exer-gaming (*exercise orientated video-games*), indoor bowls, cricket, new age curling, walking football, alongside traditional board games, bingo, table tennis, zumba and skittles. A diverse range of PA options were provided to cater for participants with different interests, fitness levels and abilities. It should be remembered that it is possible for some OA to achieve moderate intensity PA through seemingly low intensity ambulation due to physiological changes over the life-course. As with other community PA interventions aimed at OA,[53] participants were recruited through a range of local partners and media, including healthcare agencies, the local authority sports development service, local elderly care homes and charities. Adverts were also placed in the local press and club media. The programme was funded by an *'Award for All'*, a National Lottery grant and forms part of the BACT community engagement plans.[54] To assess the impact of the programme, a service level evaluation was commissioned by the BACT from a local evaluator.

Instrumentation and ethics

Ethical clearance was secured from the research ethics committee at the Leeds Metropolitan University to perform a secondary analysis of the data that were collected as part of the original programme evaluation. OA had completed pre-intervention self-report measures at the first point of contact. These were usually performed at participant inductions to the programmes of GG events. Drawing on approaches and methods established for audiences with low health literacy,[55] questionnaires were completed for demographics (*age, gender and post code*) and for health screening. After the original lead evaluator secured the necessary permission, the EQ-5D quality of life questionnaire was used within this study, due to its applicability with older populations, providing a simple descriptive profile and a single index value for health status.[56] EQ-5D includes a vertical visual analogue scale (VAS), which shows 100 as a participant's 'best imaginable health state' and 0 as being their 'worst imaginable health state'. EQ-5D has been used widely,[57] including OA at risk of CVD[58] and OA with mobility impairments.[59] It has been reported that the measure compares favourably to other similar measures of quality of life.[60] In this study, EQ-5D was administered both pre- and post-12-week intervention. Registers were also used to measure attendance at the weekly sessions. All data were collected by the health coaches/instructors who led the activities, and who had been trained by the original evaluator on how to collect the data and to conform to ethical requirements.

Analysis of the data

Following data preparation, descriptive statistics were used to determine demographic breakdowns and pre-intervention profiles. Independent *t*-tests were used to assess the mean differences in attendance and EQ VAS scores by gender. Mann–Whitney *U* tests were used to examine differences between attendance rates in participants reporting less than two and two or more health complications. Pre vs. post intervention changes were assessed using cross-tabulation and analysed using Wilcoxon signed rank tests (*Z*). For all inferential tests, a *p* value of 0.05 or less was taken to be statistically significant. All analysis was performed using the Statistical Package for Social Science (SPSS) version 20.

Results

Demographic profile

Within this pilot project, disparities were found in the response rates to the questionnaire for the different variables, and Table 1 shows the extent of this loss of data. In

Table 1. The total number and percentage of participant's response rates to each variable.

	Total number of respondents	Percentage of total respondents (%)
Demographics		
Gender	$n = 54/54$	100
Age	$n = 40/54$	74
Attendance at sessions	$n = 51/54$	94
Health complications	$n = 52/54$	96
EQ 5D		
EQ 5D mobility pre-intervention	$n = 50/54$	93
EQ 5D mobility post-intervention	$n = 47/54$	87
EQ 5D self care pre-intervention	$n = 49/54$	91
EQ 5D self care post-intervention	$n = 49/54$	91
EQ 5D usual activities pre-intervention	$n = 49/54$	91
EQ 5D usual activities post-intervention	$n = 49/54$	91
EQ 5D pain/discomfort pre-intervention	$n = 47/54$	87
EQ 5D pain/discomfort post-intervention	$n = 49/54$	91
EQ 5D anxiety/depression pre-intervention	$n = 47/54$	87
EQ 5D anxiety/depression post-intervention	$n = 47/54$	87
EQ VAS		
EQ VAS pre-intervention	$n = 47/54$	87
EQ VAS post-intervention	$n = 47/54$	87

total, $N = 54$ participants engaged the evaluation of GG and provided data for analysis. The cohort contained $n = 23$ males (42.6%) and $n = 31$ females (57.4%). For demographics, data on age was provided by $n = 40$ participants, with a mean age of 69.38 (±5.87) years, ranging 55–85 years. Attendance data confirmed 51 active participants. Attendance at the weekly session ranged from 1 to all 12 occasions, with a mean attendance of 7.73 (±3.12) sessions. Mean male attendance was 7.90 (±3.35) sessions, and mean female attendance was 7.60 (±3.01) sessions. These differences were not statistically significant $t(49) = 0.333$, $p = 0.741$.

Pre-intervention health screening profiles

At pre-intervention screening, more participants reported having 'less than two' health complications (57.7%) compared to participants reporting 'two or more' (42.3%). Participants with 'two or more' health complications averaged fewer attendances (6.91 ± 3.322) than those reporting 'less than two' (8.65 ± 2.694). This difference was not significant ($U = 208.500$, $p = 0.073$).

EQ 5D questionnaire profiles

Results for the EQ 5D quality of life questionnaire are shown in the following tables. Table 2 shows that the majority of participants (83%) reported no problems with mobility at pre-intervention. This was mirrored at post intervention with 80.9%

Table 2. Pre- vs. post-intervention scores for EQ-5D for mobility.

		Post-intervention n (%)			
		No problems	Some problems	Extreme problems	Total
Pre-intervention n (%)	No problems	38 (97.4)	1 (2.6)	0 (0.0)	39 (83.0)
	Some problems	0 (0.0)	8 (100)	0 (0.0)	8 (17.0)
	Extreme problems	0 (0.0)	0 (0.0)	0 (0.0)	0 (0.0)
	Total	38 (80.9)	9 (19.9)	0 (0.0)	47 (100)

Table 3. Pre- vs. post-intervention scores for EQ-5D for self-care.

		Post-intervention n (%)			
		No problems	Some problems	Extreme problems	Total
Pre-intervention n (%)	No problems	45 (100)	0 (0.0)	0 (0.0)	45 (91.8)
	Some problems	0 (0.0)	4 (100)	0 (0.0)	4 (8.2)
	Extreme problems	0 (0.0)	0 (0.0)	0 (0.0)	0 (0.0)
	Total	45 (91.8)	4 (8.2)	0 (0.0)	49 (100)

reporting no problems with mobility. Statistical analysis revealed no significant changes from pre- to post-intervention ($Z = -1.000$, $p = 0.317$).

Table 3 shows that the majority of participants (91.8%) reported no problems with self-care at pre-intervention. There was no change in scores at post-intervention and statistical analysis revealed no significant changes from pre- to post-intervention ($Z = 0.000$, $p = 1.000$).

Table 4 shows that the majority of participants (87.8%) reported no problems undertaking usual activities at pre-intervention. There was little change in scores at post-intervention. Statistical analysis revealed no significant changes in ability to perform usual activities from pre- to post-intervention ($Z = -1.000$, $p = 0.317$).

Table 5 shows that the majority of participants (68.1%) reported no pain/discomfort at pre-intervention. At post-intervention, this figure dropped to 59.6%. Statistical analysis revealed no significant changes in pain/discomfort from pre- to post-intervention ($Z = -1.414$, $p = 0.157$).

Table 6 shows that the majority of participants (83%) reported no anxiety/depression at pre-intervention. At post-intervention, this figure improved to 87.2%. Statistical analysis revealed no significant changes in anxiety/depression from pre- to post-intervention ($Z = -1.414$, $p = 0.157$).

Table 4. Pre- vs. post-intervention scores for EQ-5D for usual activities.

		Post-intervention n (%)			
		No problems	Some problems	Extreme problems	Total
Pre-intervention n (%)	No problems	42 (97.7)	1 (2.3)	0 (0.0)	43 (87.8)
	Some problems	0 (0.0)	6 (100)	0 (0.0)	6 (12.2)
	Extreme problems	0 (0.0)	0 (0.0)	0 (0.0)	0 (0.0)
	Total	42 (85.7)	7 (14.3)	0 (0.0)	49 (100)

Table 5. Pre- vs. post-intervention scores for EQ-5D for pain/discomfort.

		Post-intervention n (%)			
		No problems	Some problems	Extreme problems	Total
Preintervention n (%)	No problems	26 (81.3)	6 (18.8)	0 (0.0)	32 (68.1)
	Some problems	2 (13.3)	13 (86.7)	0 (0.0)	15 (31.9)
	Extreme problems	0 (0.0)	0 (0.0)	0 (0.0)	0 (0.0)
	Total	28 (59.6)	19 (40.4)	0 (0.0)	47 (100)

Table 6. Pre- vs. post-intervention scores for EQ-5D for anxiety/depression.

		Post-intervention n (%)			
		No problems	Some problems	Extreme problems	Total
Pre-intervention n (%)	No problems	39 (100)	0 (0.0)	0 (0.0)	39 (83.0)
	Some problems	2 (25.0)	6 (75.0)	0 (0.0)	8 (17.0)
	Extreme problems	0 (0.0)	0 (0.0)	0 (0.0)	0 (0.0)
	Total	41 (87.2)	6 (12.8)	0 (0.0)	47 (100)

Results from the EQ VAS question suggest that pre-intervention scores were high (84.43 ± 14.183), especially considering the age of the participants. These scores remained high at post-intervention (84.51 ± 13.095), but there were no statistically significant intervention effects ($Z = -0.172$, $p = 0.864$). Although women (87.32 ± 9.573) self-rated their health as higher than men (80.16 ± 18.557) at pre-intervention, this difference was not statistically significant $t(45) = -1.736$ $p = 0.089$. At post-intervention, men reported slightly higher self-rated health scores compared to pre-intervention (81.16 ± 17.270). At post-intervention, women reported a slight decline (86.79 ± 8.946). The differences in EQ VAS scores at post-intervention by gender were not statistically significant $t(45) = -1.146$ $p = 0.150$. The men (mean change 1.00), showed a greater intervention effect on EQ VAS scores over the course of the intervention compared to women (mean change -0.54), but the difference in change was not statistically significant $t(45) = 0.750$ $p = 0.459$.

Discussion

Our case study investigated the impact of GG, a pilot programme of PA-led health improvement for OA delivered in Football League Division 2 club, Burton Albion FC.

Demographic and attendance profile of older-adults participating in Golden Goal

Key findings support the potential of professional football clubs for recruiting both male and female OA into health-improvement schemes, suggesting programmes centred in these settings can be acceptable to both men and women. The GG pilot project recruited a diverse age group with different health and PA needs, including, participants both *entering old age* and in the *transitional stage of ageing*.[61] Moreover, recruits attended almost two-thirds of the scheduled sessions. Adoption outcomes for GG are important, as both these categories of OA have been identified as important in public health guidance. Further, the GG programme of activities plays an important role in helping OA to initiate and/or maintain their existing activity levels as recommended in such guidance[62] as well as in local PA strategies.[63]

Concerns have been expressed over how to recruit older men into community health-improvement programmes[64] and research has shown that female attendees can outnumber their male counterparts as much as 2:1.[65] In comparison, attendance ratios at GG differed considerably. Notwithstanding a low level of overall recruitment from an evaluation perspective, once engaged, older male attendees were no less likely to miss a session than women. Importantly, male recruits reported lower initial self-rated health when compared to females, yet these outcomes were less divergent post-intervention. Results support the notion that older men will attend health-improvement programmes when these are deemed acceptable to them, including those delivered in professional football club settings as reported elsewhere.[66] Similarly, locating a programme of physical and social activities in a professional football club was not a barrier to the engagement of female attendees. PA provision similar to that shown in GG, may offer OA the opportunity to attend activities with their partners and/or in mixed gender groups of friends. Further, the supportive social networks that can be generated by such programmes are important in facilitating the maintenance of OA PA levels and recommended in guidance.[67]

Health profiles of older adults participating in Golden Goal

Results also indicate that the intervention attracted a relatively healthy cohort who typically reported few health complications. Those reporting fewest health complications were more likely to attend a greater number of activity sessions than those reporting multiple complications, which could imply that health problems can limit participation in PA. Existing guidance indicates that OA can be fearful that PA may act to worsen existing health conditions[68] and GG recruited a substantial minority of OA reporting health complications. Men also reported lower self-rated health when compared to their female counterparts. Given that PA can help manage a number of chronic conditions as previously discussed, the recruitment of these constituents to the programme is an important public health outcome. Owing to the absence of PA data, we have no means of confirming that GG-related PA initiated new activity or if the programme replaced the existing PA modes. This limitation means that the programme cannot confirm having reached the inactive priority groups identified that are highlighted in the local evidence base.[69] That said, there is Public Health value in maintaining the PA levels of 'already-active OA' and both National guidance[70] and local health strategies identify the importance of recruiting groups with a range of PA levels, not solely inactive OA into PA programmes.[71] This is because active participants not only create an activity group for others to join, but also can model PA participation for others and support those individuals who are new or returning to PA.[72]

Intervention design and impact on adoption profiles

Including a process evaluation that involved participants would have helped to confirm the extent to which the design of the programme influenced engagement profiles. In the absence of this, the deployment of four key, intervention design characteristics may help to explain the engagement profiles seen in this study.

Firstly, delivering activities within the Pirelli Stadium (*home of Burton Albion Football Club*) could have been considered to capitalize on its visibility and it being a local and familiar setting for local potential participants.[73] Secondly, providing a range of exercise modes and delivery options appears to offer an advantageous approach to recruiting and catering for a diverse range of OA with different PA interests and levels of ability.[74] Thirdly and contrastingly, more attention may have been paid to establishing informal social interaction, so as to enhance both levels of recruitment and engagement in the programme. This includes the use of captive audiences and social networks for reaching those hard-engaged OA, including sedentary and BME participants through 'word of mouth'. In the interventions we featured earlier, a number of clubs performed outreach work with BME groups and these offer potential routes for clubs to connect with these constituents.[75] Fourthly, the provision of PA in a fun, flexible and enjoyable form appears to influence recruitment and maintenance and is an important design consideration.[76] Finally, it is also important to reflect on the scale of this pilot intervention vs. the numbers of recruits achieved by the more prestigious clubs – and better funded health evaluation – associated with the Premier League Men's Health programme.[77] It is unclear whether the prestige, the 'club badge', funding or recruitment approaches were key issues in effecting lower level recruitment into the GG programme, even allowing for the widespread local need for improving the PA and health profiles of OA. As such, further investigations are needed and form the scope of future research activity on this intervention.

Important considerations for promoting physical activity with older-adults

Guidance informs us that OA participants are likely to have a diverse range of PA profiles and present with varied needs and to a degree, this has emerged in this study. New commissioning arrangements in Public Health raise the possibility that more commercial and not-for-profit providers, including professional football clubs will be seeking to offer health-improvement opportunities for specific groups with distinctive health needs linked to lack of PA. Considerable work may be needed to prepare these staff for ensuring that this work – and any investment that supports it – makes a genuine contribution to better Public Health.[78] Inactive and OA suffering from health problems face challenges in becoming active. As such, the recruitment of these individuals is likely to be challenging to both the participants and providers of health-improvement programmes. Those staff involved in the delivery of health-improvement programmes in football clubs will need to be well prepared to recruit and then cater for OA who present at interventions like GG. Going forward, training and education is an important component when enhancing the preparedness of the providers of health-improvement programmes for OA.

While lessons can be drawn for what helped the current group of participants to adopt the GG programme, Public Health guidance offers further considerations when planning and implementing PA interventions. One consideration of uppermost importance, is mapping the needs of different groups of OA[79] including, those sedentary and inactive participants. The needs of these individuals are likely to be different from those constituents who meet the PA recommendations, not least because they often have little behavioural success on which to build. It is recommended that the needs of different groups of OA are carefully plotted against the design and the delivery of interventions aimed at meeting these needs.[80] In doing so, it is fundamental to involve OA and where appropriate their careers and supporters in this process for a number of reasons.[81] Firstly, they will provide important insights on how to identify needs, plan, implement and evaluate PA and health-improvement interventions. Secondly, they can build a picture of the complex interplay between the determinants' PA participation. Many of these factors may seem unimportant to providers with limited experience, either in promoting PA or working with OA. Needs assessment is an on-going process and delivers should take the opportunity to consult with the captive audiences of OA as interventions 'get under way', as well as speaking to those whose attendance 'drops off'. In reality, such approaches provide invaluable information for shaping the delivery of bespoke health-improvement programmes for potential participants, including OA[82] and those groups reported as 'hard-to-engage' in health interventions.[83]

Limitations and strengths of this research

The limitations emerging from this study, including those inherent in the original programme evaluation strategy signal the need for further learning and provide important 'take away' messages. Earlier collaboration in the evaluation process would have reduced the impact of these factors. In line with guidance, findings endorse the importance of engaging appropriate evaluation skills at any early development stage. Nonetheless, these limitations provide valuable considerations for the development of future monitoring strategies, including those used in GG and other football-led health-improvement programmes. Limitations also include the use of self-report data, which were collected for a period of 12 weeks. A longer time period – closer to six months – is needed to identify the impact of the programme on sustaining both engagement and PA levels. Other limitations include the lack of 'blind' data collection (*where independent evaluators collect data*). While this is recommended, and will heighten data quality, it is not always possible in partnership evaluation designs which may predominate in community-based evaluations.[84] A further limitation was the absence of a measure of PA status, while the inclusion of a simple 'new or replacement' question would have allowed researchers to identify the extent to which recruits were new to PA or were transferring from existing PA participation. Further, the small sample size was also a limiting factor in this study. Strengths included the use of validated instrumentation and a strong desire and commitment on behalf of the club, to evaluate and learn from the outcomes emerging from this programme, so that delivery and evaluation strategies could be refined and enacted. As such, the outcomes emerging from this study provide helpful insights on what to do and what not to do.

Conclusion

Both male and female OA attended GG, a PA-led health-improvement pilot programme delivered in/by a professional football club. The sample appears to predominantly healthy, but those reporting health complexities were also engaged. Participants with two or more health complications attended fewer sessions on average compared to those reporting less than two health complications, while men had lower self-rated health when compared to women. Our paper highlights some of the considerations when planning, delivering and evaluating PA interventions delivered to OA in footballing settings. Further research is needed to explore the potential of professional football clubs in engaging inactive OA into health-improvement programmes, including changes in health profiles and an understanding of what makes such programmes acceptable to different groups of OA.

Acknowledgements

In preparing this manuscript, the authors most gratefully acknowledge the participants and staff of Burton Albion FC and their partners who generously contributed to and supported this research. The Centre for Active Lifestyles at Leeds Metropolitan University provided the resources to undertake the secondary analysis of the data in this study.

Notes

1. BHF, *Active for Later Life*.
2. Clark et al., 'Effectiveness of a Lifestyle Intervention in Promoting the Well-being of independently Living Older People'; and Pringle et al., 'Cost Effectiveness of Interventions to Improve Moderate Physical-Activity'.
3. Department of Health, *Start Active, Stay Active*.
4. Johnman et al., 'The Beautiful Game'.
5. Football Foundation, *Extra-Time: Evaluation Summary Report*.
6. WHO, *Health Statistics and Information*.
7. BHF, *Active for Later life*.
8. BHF, *Active for Later life*.
9. Kahn et al., 'The Impact of Prevention on Reducing the Burden of Cardiovascular Disease'.
10. Stathi, 'Populations: Older People and Physical Activity'.
11. Cornwell and Waite, 'Social Disconnectedness, Perceived Isolation and Health Among Older Adults'.
12. Wilson et al., 'Loneliness and Risk of Alzheimer Disease'.
13. Brown et al., 'Physical Activity and All-Cause Mortality in Older Women and Men'. Department of Health, Start Active, Stay Active.
14. Wray, 'The Impact of the Financial Crisis on Nurses and Nursing'.
15. Wang et al., 'Health and Economic Burden of the Projected Obesity Trends in the USA and the UK'.
16. Hill et al., *Managing Resources in Later Life*.
17. DCSM, *News Stories: Free Swimming Programme*.
18. Hill et al., *Managing Resources in Later Life*.
19. Department of Health, *Start Active, Stay Active*.
20. The Information Centre for Health and Social Care, *Statistics on Obesity, Physical Activity and Diet in England* 2010.
21. BHF, *Key Facts: Older People*.
22. BHF, *Current Physical Activity Levels in Older Adults*.
23. The Information Centre for Health and Social Care, *Health Survey for England. Physical activity and fitness*.
24. Davis et al., 'Objectively Measured Physical Activity in a Diverse Sample of Older Urban UK Adults'.
25. Marcus and Forsyth, *Motivating People to be Physically Active*.
26. Booth et al., 'Social-Cognitive and Perceived Environment Influences Associated with Physical Activity in Older Australians'.
27. Rantakokko et al., 'Perceived Barriers in the Outdoor Environment and Development of Walking Difficulties in Older People'.
28. Netz et al., 'Physical activity and psychological wellbeing in advanced age'.
29. Stathi, 'Populations: Older People and Physical Activity'.
30. DH, *Healthy Lives, Healthy People*.
31. WHO, *Global Strategy on Diet, Physical Activity and Health*.

32. Dawson et al., 'Perceived Barriers to Walking in the Neighbourhood Environment and Change in Physical Activity Levels Over 12 months'.
33. Pringle et al., 'Cost Effectiveness of Interventions to Improve Moderate Physical-Activity'.
34. Pringle et al., 'Delivering Men's Health Interventions in English Premier League Football Clubs'.
35. Conn et al., 'Interventions to Increase Physical Activity among Healthy Adults'.
36. NICE, *Occupational Therapy and Physical Activity Interventions*. BHF, *Active for Later Life*.
37. Parnell et al., 'Football in the Community Schemes'.
38. Football Foundation, *Extra Time*.
39. BHF, *Active for Later Life* and Department of Health. *Start Active, Stay Active*.
40. European Commission, *The State of Men's Health in Europe*.
41. Pringle et al., 'Effect of a National Programme of Men's Health Delivered in English Premier League Football Clubs' and Pringle et al., 'Health Improvement for Men and Hard-to-Engage-Men Delivered in English Premier League Football Clubs'.
42. Robertson et al., 'It's Fun, Fitness, Football Really'.
43. NICE, *Behaviour Change*.
44. East Staffordshire Borough Council, 2011 *Census Data: East Staffordshire*.
45. NHS East Staffordshire, Clinical Commissioning Group. *East Staffordshire, Enhanced Joint Strategic Needs Assessment*.
46. East Staffordshire Borough Council 2011, *Census Data: East Staffordshire*.
47. NHS East Staffordshire, Clinical Commissioning Group *East Staffordshire, Enhanced Joint Strategic Needs Assessment*.
48. NHS East Staffordshire Clinical Commissioning Group, *East Staffordshire Delivery of Change Plan: 2012–2016*.
49. NICE, *Occupational Therapy and Physical Activity Interventions*.
50. Football Foundation, *Extra Time*.
51. BHF, *Active for Later Life*.
52. BHF, *Active for Later Life*.
53. Sport England, *Learning from LEAP*.
54. Burton Albion Community Trust, *Golden Goal*.
55. Sport England, *Learning from LEAP*.
56. Euroqol. *EQ-5D^{TM}, A Standardised Instrument for use as a Measure of Health Outcome*.
57. Brook et al., 'The Measurement and Valuation of Health Status Using EQ-5D: A European Perspective'.
58. Sahlen et al., 'Health Coaching to Promote Healthier Lifestyle among Older People at Moderate Risk for Cardiovascular Diseases, Diabetes and Depression'.
59. Davis et al., 'Exploration of the Association between Quality of Life, Assessed by the EQ-5D and ICECAP-O, and Falls Risk, Cognitive Function and Daily Function, in Older Adults with Mobility Impairments'.
60. Barton et al., 'A Comparison of the Performance of the EQ-5D and SF-6D for Individuals aged >45 years'.
61. BHF, *Active for Later Life*.
62. BHF, *Active for Later Life*.
63. East Staffordshire Borough Council, *Community Sport and Physical Activity Network, 2012–2013 Action Plan*.
64. European Commission, *The State of Men's health in Europe*; and Pringle et al., 'Health Improvement for Men and Hard-to-Engage-Men Delivered in English Premier League Football Clubs'.
65. Pringle et al., 'Cost Effectiveness of Interventions to Improve Moderate Physical-activity'.
66. Football Foundation, *Extra Time*.
67. BHF, *Active for Later Life*.
68. BHF, *Active for Later Life*.
69. East Staffordshire Borough Council, *Community Sport and Physical Activity Network, 2012–2013 Action Plan*.
70. BHF, *Active for Later Life*.

71. East Staffordshire Borough Council, *Community Sport and Physical Activity Network*, 2012–2013 *Action Plan*.
72. Pringle et al., 'Cost Effectiveness of Interventions to Improve Moderate Physical-activity'.
73. Conn et al., 'Interventions to Increase Physical Activity among Healthy Adults'.
74. BHF, *Active for Later Life*.
75. Pringle et al., Effect of a National Programme of Men's Health Delivered in English Premier League Football Clubs'.
76. Robertson et al., 'It's Fun, Fitness, Football Really'; and BHF, *Active for Later Life*.
77. Pringle et al., 'Effect of a National Programme of Men's Health Delivered in English Premier League Football Clubs'.
78. Pringle et al., 'Health Improvement and Professional Football: Players on the Same Side'.
79. NICE, *Occupational Therapy and Physical Activity Interventions*.
80. Ransdell et al., *Developing Effective Physical Activity Programmes*.
81. NICE, *Occupational Therapy and Physical Activity Interventions*; and BHF, *Active for Later Life*.
82. Pringle et al., 'Working with Black and minority ethic elders in planning a DVD resource to promote physical activity'.
83. Pringle et al., 'Health Improvement for Men and Hard-to-Engage-Men Delivered in English Premier League Football Clubs'.
84. Pringle et al., 'Health Improvement for Men and Hard-to-Engage-Men Delivered in English Premier League Football Clubs'.

References

Barton, G.R., T.H. Sach, A.J. Avery, C. Jenkinson, M. Doherty, and D.K. Whynes. 'A Comparison of the Performance of the EQ-5D and SF-6D for Individuals Aged >45 Years'. *Health Economics* 17 (2008): 815–32.

Booth, M., N. Owen, A. Bauman, O. Clavisi, and E. Leslie. 'Social–cognitive and Perceived Environment Influences Associated with Physical Activity in Older Australians'. *Preventive Medicine* 31 (2000): 15–22.

British Heart Foundation. *Active for Later Life*. London: BHF, 2009, http://www.bhfactive.org.uk/older-adults-resources-and-publications-item/78/index.html (accessed August 1, 2013).

British Heart Foundation. 'Current Physical Activity Levels in Older Adults: Fact Sheet, 2012, file:///C:/Users/Pringl02/Downloads/Physical%20Activity%20Older%20Adults%20AW%20(1).pdf (accessed March 17, 2014).

British Heart Foundation National Centre. *Key Facts: Older People*. Loughborough: British Heart Foundation, 2013, http://www.bhfactive.org.uk/older-adults-key-facts/index.html (accessed August 1, 2013).

Brook, R., R.F. Rabin, and F. Charro *The Measurement and Valuation of Health Status using EQ-5D: A European perspective*. Dordrecht: Kluwer Academic Publishers, 2003.

Brown, W.D., D. McLaughlin, J. Leung, K. McCaul, L. Flicker, O. Almeida, G. Hankey, D. Lopez, and A. Dobson. 'Physical Activity and All-cause Mortality in Older Women and Men'. *British Journal of Sports Medicine* 46 (2012): 664–8.

Burton Albion Community Trust. *Golden Goal*. BACT: Burton, 2013, http://burtonalbioncommunitytrust.co.uk/courses/golden-goal-over-50s-activity-programme/ (accessed August 1, 2013).

Clark, F., J. Jackson, M. Carlson, C.P. Chou, B. Cherry, M. Jordan-Marsh, B. Knight, et al., 'Effectiveness of a Lifestyle Intervention in Promoting the Well-being of Independently Living Older People: Results of the Well Elderly 2 Randomised Controlled Trial'. *Journal of Epidemiology & Community Health* 66 (2012): 782–90.

Conn, V., A. Hafdahl, and D. Mehr 'Interventions to Increase Physical Activity among Healthy Adults: Meta-Analysis of Outcomes'. *American Journal of Public Health* 101 (2011): 751–58.

Cornwell, E., and L. Waite. 'Social Disconnectedness, Perceived Isolation, and Health among Older Adults'. *Journal of Health and Social Behavior* 50 (2009): 31–48.

Davis, M., K. Fox, M. Hillsdon, D. Sharp, J. Coulson, and J. Thompson. 'Objectively Measured Physical Activity in a Diverse Sample of Older Urban UK Adults'. *Medicine & Science in Sports & Exercise* 4 (2011): 647–54.

Davis, J.C., S. Bryan, R. McLeod, J. Rogers, K. Khan, and T. Liu-Ambrose. 'Exploration of the Association between Quality of Life, Assessed by the EQ-5D and ICECAP-O, and Falls Risk, Cognitive Function and Daily Function, in Older Adults with Mobility Impairments'. *BMC Geriatrics* 12 (2012), http://www.biomedcentral.com/1471-2318/12/65 (accessed 24 September, 2013).

Dawson, J., M. Hillsdon, I. Boller, and C. Foster. 'Perceived Barriers to Walking in the Neighbourhood Environment and Change in Physical Activity Levels over 12 months'. *British Journal of Sports Medicine* 41 (2007): 562–8.

Department for Culture, Media and Sport. *News Stories: Free Swimming Programme.* London: Department for Culture, Media and Sport, 2013, http://www.culture.gov.uk/news/news_stories/7193.aspx (accessed September 24, 2013).

Department of Health. *Healthy Lives, Healthy People: Our Strategy for Public Health in England.* London: Department of Health, 2011, http://www.dh.gov.uk/en/Publicationsandstatistics/Publications/PublicationsPolicyAndGuidance/DH_121941. (accessed August 1, 2013).

Department of Health. *Start Active, Stay Active: A Report on Physical Activity for Health from the Four Home Countries Chief Medical Officers.* London: Crown, 2011, http://www.dh.gov.uk/prod_consum_dh/groups/dh_digitalassets/documents/digitalasset/dh_128210.pdf (accessed September 24, 2013).

East Staffordshire Borough Council. *Census Data.* East Staffordshire: East Staffordshire Borough Council, 2011, http://www.eaststaffsbc.gov.uk/Services/2011%20Census/2011CensusSecondReleaseEastStaffsPopulationSummary.pdf (accessed September 23, 2013).

East Staffordshire Borough Council. *Community Sport and Physical Activity Network, 2012–13 Action Plan.* East Staffordshire Borough Council, 2013, http://www.eaststaffsbc.gov.uk/Services/SportEastStaffs/Pages/CommunitySportandPhysicalActivityNetwork.aspx (accessed September 9, 2013).

European Commission. *The State of Men's Health in Europe.* Luxembourg: European Commission, 2011, http://ec.europa.eu/health/population_groups/docs/men_health_report_en.pdf. (accessed January 24, 2012).

Euroqol. EQ-5D™, 'A Standardised Instrument for Use as a Measure of Health Outcome', http://www.euroqol.org/home.html (accessed September 24, 2013).

Football Foundation. *Extra-Time: Evaluation Summary Report*, 2011. http://www.footballfoundation.org.uk/our-schemes/extra-time/extra-time-summary-report/?assetdet240618=29315 (accessed August 1, 2013).

Hill, K., L. Sutton, and L. Cox. *Managing Resources in Later Life: Older People's Experience of Change and Continuity.* York: Joseph Rowntree Foundation, http://www.jrf.org.uk/system/files/older-people-resourcesFULL.pdf (accessed September 12, 2013).

Johnman, C., P. Mackie, and F. Sim. 'The Beautiful Game'. *Public Health* 127 (2013): 697–98, http://www.publichealthjrnl.com/article/PIIS0033350613002448/fulltext (accessed September 10, 2013).

Kahn, R., R.M. Robertson, R. Smith, and D. Eddy. 'The Impact of Prevention on Reducing the Burden of Cardiovascular Disease'. *Circulation* 118 (2008): 576–85, http://circ.ahajournals.org/cgi/content/full/118/5/576 (accessed September 9, 2013).

Marcus, B., and L. Forsyth. *Motivating People to be Physically Active* 2nd ed. Champaign, IL: Human Kinetics, 2009.

National Institute of Health and Clinical Excellence. *Occupational Therapy and Physical Activity Interventions to Promote the Mental Wellbeing of Older Adults in Primary Care and Residential Care.* London: National Institute of Health and Clinical Excellence, 2004, http://www.nice.org.uk/nicemedia/pdf/ph16guidance.pdf (accessed September 24, 2013).

National Institute of Health and Clinical Excellence. *The Most Appropriate Means of Generic and Specific Interventions to Support Attitude Behavioural Change at Population and Community Levels.* London: National Institute of Health and Clinical Excellence, 2013, http://www.nice.org.uk/PH6 (accessed September 24, 2013).

Netz, Y., M. Wu, B. Becker, and G. Tenenbaum. 'Physical Activity and Psychological Well-being in Advanced Age: A Meta-analysis of Intervention Studies'. *Psychology and Aging* 20 (2005): 272–84.

NHS East Staffordshire Clinical Commissioning Group, *East Staffordshire Delivery of Change Plan: 2012–16*. NHS East Staffordshire, 2012, http://www.eaststaffsccg.nhs.uk/strategies (accessed September 24, 2013).

NHS East Staffordshire, Clinical Commissioning Group, 'East Staffordshire, Enhanced Joint Strategic Needs Assessment (e-JSNA) Submission, 2012'. http://www.eaststaffsccg.nhs.uk/search?term=joint+strategic+needs&search=Search&searchType=all (accessed September 24, 2013).

Parnell, D., G. Stratton, B. Drust, and D. Richardson. 'Football in the Community Schemes: Exploring the Effectiveness of an Intervention in Promoting Healthful Behaviour Change'. *Soccer & Society* 14 (2013): 35–51.

Pringle, A., C. Cooke, N. Gilson, K. Marsh, and J. McKenna. 'Cost-effectiveness of Interventions To Improve Moderate Physical Activity: A Study in Nine UK Sites'. *Health Education Journal* 69 (2010): 211–24.

Pringle, A., J. McKenna, and A. Smith. 'Working with Black and Minority Ethic Elders in Planning a DVD Resource to Promote Physical Activity'. *Journal of Sport and Exercise Science* 27 (2010): S59–60.

Pringle, A., J. McKenna, and S. Zwolinsky. 'Health Improvement and Professional Football: Players on the Same Side?' *Journal of Policy Research in Tourism, Leisure and Events* 5 (2013): 207–12.

Pringle, A., S. Zwolinsky, J. McKenna, A. Daly-Smith, S. Robertson, and A. White. 'Effect of a National Programme of Men's Health Delivered in English Premier League Football Clubs'. *Public Health* 127 (2013): 18–26.

Pringle, A., S. Zwolinsky, J. McKenna, A. Daly-Smith, S. Robertson, and A. White. 'Delivering men's Health Interventions in English Premier League Football Clubs: Key Design Characteristics'. *Public Health* 127 (2013): 717–26.

Pringle, A., S. Zwolinsky, J. McKenna, A. Daly-Smith, S. Robertson, and A. White. 'Health Improvement for Men and Hard-to-Engage-Men Delivered in English Premier League Football Clubs'. *Health Education Research* (2014). doi:10.1093/her/cyu009.

Ransdell, B., K. Dinger, J. Huberty, and K. Miller. *Planning and Evaluating Physical Activity Programmes*, Developing Effective Physical Activity Programmes, 13–21. Champaign, IL: Human Kinetics, 2009.

Rantakokko, M., S. Iwarsson, M. Manty, R. Leinonen, and T. Rantanen. 'Perceived Barriers in the Outdoor Environment and Development of Walking Difficulties in Older People'. *Age and Ageing* 41 (2012): 118–21.

Robertson, S., S. Zwolinsky, A. Pringle, J. McKenna, A. Daly-Smith, and A. White. "It is Fun, Fitness And Football Really': A Process Evaluation of a Football-based Health Intervention for Men'. *Qualitative Research in Sport, Exercise and Health* 5, no. 3 (2013): 419–39.

Sahlen, K.-G., H. Johansson, L. Nyström, and L. Lindholm. 'Health Coaching to Promote Healthier Lifestyle Among Older People at Moderate Risk for Cardiovascular Diseases, Diabetes and Depression: A Study Protocol for a Randomized Controlled Trial in Sweden'. *BMC Public Health* 13 (2013): 199, http://www.biomedcentral.com/1471-2458/13/199 (accessed September 25, 2013).

Sport England. *Learning from LEAP*. London: Sport England, 2006, http://webarchive.nationalarchives.gov.uk/20130107105354/http://www.dh.gov.uk/prod_consum_dh/groups/dh_digitalassets/@dh/@en/documents/digitalasset/dh_063822.pdf (accessed February 4, 2014).

Stathi, A. 'Populations: Older People and Physical Activity'. In *Physical Activity and Health Promotion: Evidence Based Approaches to Practice*, ed. L. Dugdill, D. Crone and R. Murphy, 174–97. London: Wiley-Blackwell, 2009.

The Information Centre for Health and Social Care. *Health Survey for England. Physical Activity and Fitness: Summary of Key Findings, 2008*, London: The Information Centre for Health and Social Care, 2008, https://catalogue.ic.nhs.uk/publications/public-health/surveys/heal-surv-phys-acti-fitn-eng-2008/heal-surv-phys-acti-fitn-eng-2008-rep-v1.pdf (accessed September 24, 2013).

The Information Centre for Health and Social Care. *Statistics on Obesity, Physical Activity and Diet in England 2010*, London: The Information Centre for Health and Social Care, 2010, http://www.ic.nhs.uk/webfiles/publications/opad10/Statistics_on_Obesity_Physical_Activity_and_Diet_England_2010.pdf (accessed February 20, 2013).

Wang, Y., K. McPherson, T. Marsh, S. Gortmaker, and M. Brown. 'Health and Economic Burden of the Projected Obesity Trends in the USA and the UK'. *The Lancet* 378 (2011): 815–25.

Wilson, R., K. Krueger, S. Arnold, J. Schneider, J. Kelly, L. Barnes, Y. Tang, and D. Bennett. 'Loneliness and Risk of Alzheimer Disease'. *JAMA Psychiatry* 64 (2007): 234–40, http://archpsyc.jamanetwork.com/article.aspx?articleid=482179 (accessed September 24, 2013).

World Health Organisation. *Global Strategy on Diet, Physical Activity and Health*, Geneva: World Health Organisation, 2004, http://www.who.int/dietphysicalactivity/strategy/eb11344/strategy_english_web.pdf (accessed August 24, 2013).

World Health Organisation. *Health Statistics and Information. Definitions of an Older Person*, World Health Organisation: Geneva, 2013, http://www.who.int/healthinfo/survey/ageingdefnolder/en/ (accessed September 24, 2013).

Wray, J. 'The Impact of the Financial Crisis on Nurses and Nursing'. *Journal of Advanced Nursing* 69 (2013): 497–99.

'I just want to watch the match': a practitioner's reflective account of men's health themed match day events at an English Premier League football club

Kathryn Curran[a], Barry Drust[b] and Dave Richardson[b]

[a]Academic Group of Engineering, Sports and Sciences, University of Bolton, Bolton, UK; [b]The Football Exchange, Research Institute for Sport and Exercise Sciences, Liverpool John Moores University, Liverpool, UK

> This study reflects on the effectiveness and delivery of a series of health themed match day events at an English Premier League Football Club which aimed to create awareness and motivate men to adopt recommended health behaviours. A range of marketing techniques and activities were adopted within a targeted space and time to increase men's exposure to health information. The first author adopted a practitioner-cum-researcher role and was immersed in the planning and delivery of the events utilising the principles of ethnography. Data were predominately collated through observations and personal reflections logged via autobiographical field notes. Data were analysed through abductive reasoning. In general, men were reluctant to engage in health-related behaviours on match days. However, subtle, non-invasive approaches were deemed successful. Positive outcomes and case studies from the latter techniques are presented and suggestions for effective strategies that will better engage men in health information and behaviours are made.

Introduction

In the UK, there is a particular concern regarding the physical activity and health behaviours of men. National statistics indicate that the health of men in the UK is poor. A recent and comprehensive report by White et al.,[1] entitled *The State of Men's Health in Europe,* highlighted that more than 100,000 men in the UK die prematurely (i.e. under the age of 75 years) each year and many of these deaths are a result of non-communicable lifestyle diseases such as fat-related cancers, diabetes and cardiovascular disease. Compared to women, men in the UK have a lower life expectancy (i.e. 77.4 years for men compared to 81.6 years for women), are three times more likely to become dependent on alcohol, more likely to commit suicide and twice as likely to die from a circulatory disease.[2] Furthermore, 65% of men in the UK are currently classified as overweight or obese (BMI over 25) and only 39% of the male population are currently meeting the Chief Medical Officers recommendations for physical activity.[3]

The poor state of men's health in the UK is further exacerbated by the apparent reluctance of men to frequently engage with traditional community health services. Although evidence suggests that men are no less likely than women to consult their General Practitioner at a given level of severity for a given condition type,[4] White et al.[5] reported that men are less likely than women to access health services frequently. There is a large body of empirical research to support the concept that men are reluctant to seek preventative help from health professionals.[6] The reasons cited for this poor level of engagement include the limited opening hours of health services, excessive delays for appointments and/or a lack of vocabulary required to discuss sensitive issues.[7] Social constructions of masculinity have also been implicated as explanations for men's poor uptake of health services. The writings of Harrison,[8] Courtney,[9] Robertson[10] and Gough and Robertson[11], for example, highlight the negative impact that masculinity and male role socialization can have on influencing men's health behaviours and thus, men's health status. For example, Gough[12] reported that concealing vulnerability is often associated with male role socialization with men not wishing to appear weak by seeking help and engaging with health services. Furthermore, Gough[13] identified that traditional health care and health advice is typically dominated by women-friendly practices and therefore men can be regarded, and often regard themselves, as intruders in a female land.

As men's uptake of traditional health services has been highlighted as an area of concern, it has been argued that health services need to reach out to men using alternative health intervention techniques.[14] White and Witty[15] proposed that the setting in which 'male targeted' interventions are delivered is an important factor in engaging men with health. The UK Government's White Paper *Healthy People, Healthy Lives*,[16] identified the *community* as an appropriate setting to engage men in positive health behaviours. Wilkins and Baker[17] suggested that the most appropriate community settings to deliver health messages are in places that men already go and where they are more likely to feel comfortable. Examples of such places include community groups or forums and groups associated with sport, sports events and/or sports stadia.

Targeting men's health during their leisure time has been successfully achieved through associations with professional sports teams.[18] The Tackling Men's Health intervention[19] is a recent example of a health promoting intervention targeting men with health improvement schemes at large UK sports stadia. The intervention targeted men attending popular rugby league matches, with the aim of promoting men's engagement with community health services and thus, promoting improved health and well-being. The intervention achieved strong rates of engagement with the target group and received positive feedback from attendees of the stadium.

More recently, the Premier League Health programme funded by the UK Football Pools (2009–2012) targeted male football supporters (and other men who lived in the local community). This programme was delivered by 16 English Premier League Football Clubs through their Football in the Community schemes (FitC). The Premier League Health programme used the unique opportunity that football offers to reach some of the most marginalized individuals in the community.[20] Premier League Health aimed to raise men's awareness, and subsequently engage men, in health-related behaviours at their respective football clubs both on match days and non-match days (i.e. through organized physical activity sessions and access to health services). Awareness and engagement in health behaviours was achieved through a variety of approaches with engagement tools being primarily based on the assumption that men will respond to health messages offered in places that they feel comfortable.[21]

It can be argued that the findings of the Tackling Men's Health intervention and the Premier League Health programme demonstrate that men are willing to engage in health behaviours if the services provided are sensitive to their needs and masculine identities. Whilst this evidence is useful for building evidence-base in, and advancing, men's health initiatives, academics have argued that more needs to be done. White and Witty[22] argued that there is a need to further examine the effectiveness of such programmes in order to better understand how we can engage men in health information and behaviours. Furthermore, it has been suggested that men will only achieve the highest level of well-being when health promotion programmes are built on an understanding of the social factors underpinning men's health-related decision-making practices.[23] It would appear necessary, therefore, to undertake further evaluation of what aspects of a community health promotion activity work for men and why, and conversely identify activities that do not work and why. It has been argued that generating evidence from local practice will provide valuable insights into overall best practice which can therefore translate into grassroots health promotion programmes for men.[24] Carmichael and Miller[25] suggested that novel methodologies (i.e. those that allow for plunging into the culture and environment of research setting) such as practitioner-researcher approaches, allow for truthful and powerful evidence to be generated.

With these thoughts in mind, this paper focuses on the accounts and personal reflections of the first author (practitioner-cum-researcher) during the development and delivery of a series of community-based health themed match day events through Everton Football Club's Premier League Health programme. Each match day event aimed to engage men in health-related information and behaviours in a community setting, during their leisure time. The study examines the effectiveness of, and barriers to, promoting and engaging male football fans in positive health-related behaviours and messages at an English Premier League football stadium (i.e. a community setting) on match days. Moreover, this study aims to provide valuable insights into the best ways to communicate health messages to men and offer suggestions for effective strategies that will better engage men in health information and behaviours in a community setting.

Profiling the researcher

At this point it appears relevant to identity to the reader that throughout the duration of this research, the first author was employed as a full-time member of staff by Liverpool John Moores University (LJMU), School of Sport and Exercise Sciences but was based as the men's health practitioner within the grounds of Goodison Park, home of Everton Football Club. It was here that the author worked full time with/for Everton in the Community (Everton Football Club's FitC scheme) co-ordinating their Premier League Health project and conducting immersed practitioner research. The author's role as a practitioner-researcher involved the day-to-day management and continuous development of the Premier League Health programme. Furthermore, this role encouraged the author to examine the current men's health and FitC-based literature and design and conduct appropriate research to address the gaps in knowledge.

It is anticipated that by setting the scene and clarifying the author's position at this point, the reader can travel through this paper with the knowledge of the author's set up and operational role during this research.

Methods

During this study, six health promoting match day events were organized by the author over a period of eight months. The match day events took place both in and around Everton Football Club (an English Premier League football club) as part of Everton in the Community's Premier League Health programme. The match day events all aimed to create awareness of a particular health theme and motivate men to consider adopting and/or engaging in recommended health behaviours. Health themes were dictated by the programme funding body and included physical activity, cancer, sexual health, mental health, alcohol awareness and smoking cessation. Where possible, match day health themes were chosen to align with regional and national health awareness days, for example national alcohol awareness week, national no smoking day and World cancer day. During each event, project staff worked alongside community health service providers and key organizations working in relevant fields in order to promote appropriate local health services.

In order to increase the awareness of a particular health message, a range of marketing techniques were adopted within a targeted space and time. According to Walsh et al.[26] marketing has been advocated as a powerful tool for segmenting, profiling and targeting specific populations in public health messages. Information on the health themed match day event were uploaded onto the official football club website, independent fan websites and a variety of social networking websites, approximately one week prior to the event. Simultaneously, an email was distributed to season ticket holders and a targeted press release was produced for the local media by the football club communications department. It was envisaged that by increasing the awareness of the event and the aligned health message, acceptance and engagement in health behaviours and messages on the match day would be amplified.

On the day of each of the match day events, dissemination of the health messages occurred both in and around the stadium through a range of promotional materials such as the distribution of leaflets and health themed car air fresheners, a series of health themed awareness bathroom stickers installed into the male toilets throughout the stadium and a page of health literature was contained in the official match day programme. Additionally, specific health information were transmitted pre, post and during the match day in a series of multifaceted multimedia outputs including Bluetooth messages to mobile phones, large visual screen images and verbal health information relayed by the announcer both pre match and during the half-time interval. Such techniques were based on the premise that men will engage in health behaviours in places that they already go and feel comfortable.[27] As a direct result of the marketing and promotion of the event, and the gender sensitive approach adopted, it was expected that men would wish to engage with health information on match days. In anticipation of the demand for health services, health experts from relevant national and local organizations were available on the day for male fans to engage with. These health partners were based at a *health station* inside the grounds of the stadium at each match day event.

Research design

In order to become immersed in the culture and environment of the research setting and to allow for truthful and powerful evidence to be generated,[28] the first author adopted a practitioner-cum-researcher role throughout the study.[29] The first author was responsible for the planning and delivery of all health themed match day events and for the collection of data. Carmichael and Miller[30] suggested that the use of practitioner-researchers is an appropriate and powerful method of getting closer to the culture and environment of the research setting in ways that would be very difficult to achieve otherwise.

Prior to data collection, ethical consent was sought and granted by LJMU ethics board. Furthermore, written consent was gained from Everton Football Club that permitted the use of the club name in all related dissemination and publication of the work. Furthermore, any publication of such material resulting from the work was subject to final 'proof' approval from an appropriate representative of the football club. During each match day event, the author adopted principles of ethnography and observational research.[31] Specifically, data were collected through observations and reflections logged via autobiographical field notes.[32] Typically, field notes were made in the first author's office after the events of the day had ceased. These initial field notes were then used to form the framework of further reflective accounts.[33] Data were also collected via emails received from match day attendees and health service staff. This relaxed and informal reflective methodology allowed for *sense making* and encouraged the practitioner to learn from the knowledge gained *in action*. In essence, the researcher was able to comprehend a greater understanding of the situation, and place specific encounters and events into fuller and more meaningful contexts that were useful for explaining human behaviour.[34]

In this study, knowledge was predominately gained from the first-hand experiences of the first author within a community setting. The author learnt from and reflected upon these experiences through the construction of autobiographical field notes using principles of autoethnography.[35] In line with a constructivist approach,[36] I (the first author) endeavour to show you (the reader) what I know, what I saw and how I saw it.[37]

Data analysis and representation

The author engaged in a period of close reading in order to become immersed in the data.[38] At this stage, initial ideas and thoughts were recorded. Following this, principles of content analysis were adopted by the researcher in order to identify and categorize themes arising from the data.[39] Data were analysed through abductive reasoning.[40] Deductive analysis (based on presented evidence) followed by inductive analysis ensured that relevant theoretical and contextual themes and categories emerged from the data. The data and themes were then presented by the author to the co-authors by means of cooperative triangulation.[41] The co-authors critically questioned the analysis and cross-examined the data and themes. This process allowed for alternative interpretations of the data to be offered and for a consensus to be reached. The author and co-authors discussed the data and emergent themes until an acceptable consensus had been reached. This process allowed the first author to refine the specifics of each theme and generate clear definitions and names for each theme.

Data are represented through a series of themed narrative accounts in order to capture 'moments' from applied observations and reflections to give the reader a greater understanding of the lived experiences of the author. The first author's field note extracts and personal reflections are presented as single-spaced lines within the text.

Furthermore, the voice of the football fan and health practitioner (captured via emails received from match day attendees and health service staff) are also utilized in this study to illustrate the personal experiences of others. This data are represented through verbatim citations and are also identified as single-spaced lines within the text. Pseudonyms are used throughout the results section. Finally, a number of images are presented in order to help bring-to-life aspects of the data and supplement the text. The following results and discussion sections outline what the authors perceive to be the relevant issues emerging from the expansive data collected.

Results

Avoidance and lack of engagement with health service staff

In contrast to existing research,[42] only a small number of men engaged with health services at the stadium on match days. In order to increase men's awareness of, and engagement in, health messages, a range of services were deliberately placed in areas where men frequently attend and feel comfortable (i.e. an English Premier League football match). However, whilst information on the health themed match day event was advertised through a range of different mediums in the lead up to the event, it appeared that this had little or no effect on the 'engagement behaviour' of the male football supporters. To put this into context, approximately 32,000 male fans attended each football match; therefore, a total of roughly 192,000 male bodies were present over the six health themed match day events. Whilst this figure includes the possible repeat attendances of the 26,048 male season ticket holders, it is still a vast number of men that were potentially exposed to the match day health themes. However, the health experts present on each of the match days only engaged with a total of 14 men.

The following reflection captures the frustrations of the author in relation to the male football fans' lack of engagement with health service staff and their lack of interest in the health stations:

Practitioner reflection 16/02/2010, 14:05:

The health stations at the match day events just don't seem to be working. It seemed like such a good idea; men aren't going out of their way to access health services so we'll put health experts in a place where they are already going! Thousands of men are passing by our health stations in the hours leading up to kick off and it's [the health station] right there under their noses and yet they just don't want to know. When I watch them [the male football fans], they mostly seem to be in a rush. It's like they know where they are heading to and they don't want anything, or anyone, to interrupt them. It was the same a couple of hours before the match kicked off, when it's less busy and more chilled out. But they (the men we are trying to engage with) would rather go and watch the players park their cars than stop and talk to us about their health. It's hard to put into words just how frustrated and disappointed I am with this outcome. It took a lot of hard work to get these health stations accepted by the Club and I think I've even put a strain on some professional relationships whilst arguing the case for them.

Figure 1 (below) epitomizes the men's behaviour on a typical match day. Specifically, the scene captures the first author's frustrations (highlighted in the reflection above) as we see hoards of men preferring to loiter around the area where the first team players park their cars rather than stop and talk to health professionals about their health in the hours leading up to kick-off.

Figure 1. Male football fans gather round to watch football players park their cars and bypass smoking cessation health station.

The dissemination of health messages through the distribution of leaflets also had little impact on the men's engagement with health messages and health services. Leaflets were generally disregarded and when approached, many men verbalized such comments as, 'Not now love/girl' and 'No thanks, I just want to watch the match'.

Branded freebies and subliminal messages; a step in the right direction

Football club-branded health themed car air fresheners, however, had a greater acceptance than health themed leaflets and information stations and appeared to be a step in the right direction for engaging men in health messages at on match days. Car air fresheners were designed in the profile of a football shirt, printed in the corresponding colour of the home team and displayed printed signs and symptoms of bowel cancer (see Figure 2 below). Over 5000 air fresheners were distributed to male fans during one match day event in various locations in and around the stadium grounds, with men appearing content to receive them.

The thoughts of the author following the cancer awareness match day event are captured in the following reflection:

Figure 2. Car air fresheners displaying printed signs and symptoms of bowel cancer.

Practitioner reflection 05/12/2009, 16:30:

Today was interesting! A couple of weeks ago we handed out health information leaflets and not many men took them. Those that did take a leaflet tended to stuff them in their pockets very quickly or threw them on the floor. Today we handed out health information again, but this time it was printed on car air fresheners. I was amazed by the difference in response! Not only did everyone want one, but men even came up asking if they could have another couple for their mates. I know it's not because of the health messages that people want them, but that doesn't matter, as soon as they are dangling in front of them in the car, they won't be able to escape the health messages printed on them. It's only one small step for health promotion but perhaps one giant leap for health promotion with men?

This finding highlights the power of the football club brand[43] and suggests that health practitioners are able to disseminate health information material to men on match days. However, in order to create interest and acceptance, the health messages/material need to be in a form that is tangible; it must be complimentary and it is advisable that it reflects the brand of the football club (i.e. colours and logo) without infringing upon it. It is also important that the health messages do not drown the merchandize. Instead, subtle subliminal messages seemed more appropriate for these products so that they are still deemed *masculine* and therefore appealing to our target audience.

Engagement 'inside' the stadium

Specific health information transmitted both pre match and during the half-time interval via a series of multifaceted multimedia outputs (including Bluetooth messages to mobile phones, large visual screen images, verbal health information relayed by the stadium announcer and health literature in the official match day programme) were generally considered welcome by the target population in comparison to invasive engagement approaches (i.e. stopping men to talk and handing them health information leaflets). These methods of engagement also appeared not to impose on, nor contaminate, the men's match day experience. Furthermore, these methods of engagement occurred within the confines of the football stadium. It could be argued that, when the men were inside the stadium, they became a more captive audience. Once inside, the stadium the men appeared more settled and were (generally) more likely to connect with health information than when they were outside the stadium (i.e. get me now I'm in). Typically, the experience outside of the stadium before the match involved the intricate navigation through large crowds in order to get inside the ground, get to your seat and get settled before kick-off. It appears that such a hectic environment is not conducive to the promotion and/or receipt of health-related information.

Another example of the non-invasive and more subliminal approach to engaging the men inside the ground was the use of the cancer awareness vinyl bathroom stickers (see Figure 3). These health awareness raising stickers were provided by the local cancer network service (stickers were produced for a larger social marketing campaign) and were installed into the male toilets throughout the stadium by the first author prior to a cancer awareness health themed match day event. The stickers aimed to raise awareness of the signs and symptoms of prostate and bowel cancer in an informal male-dominated setting.

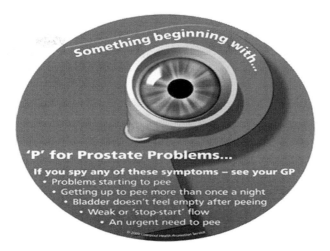

Figure 3. Cancer awareness bathroom stickers.

In the subsequent months, the first author received the following feedback via email.

E-mail received 01/02/2010, 09:17:

Dear Kathryn, After going to the bathroom in the Park End of the Goodison Stadium my awareness was raised by the large sticker in relation to prostate and bowel cancer. I already had a slight problem with my prostate, but after reading the symptoms in relation to the bowel problems, I realised that I had some of the symptoms. I have since been to the doctors, had a CAT scan, been diagnosed with bowel cancer and had an operation to remove the problem. I feel that most males of my age and generation are not aware of the risks in relation to both bowel and prostrate problems and, like myself, would probably not go to seek advice from there General Practitioner, I feel that the Premier League Health bathroom sticker campaign alerts people and makes them far more aware of the potential risks to them. Peter, Male, 51, Liverpool

The following reflection captures the thoughts and feelings of the author upon receiving this information;

Practitioner reflection 25/01/2010, 10.00:

This week I received an e-mail from a man who had realised that he had significant cancer symptoms after reading one of our cancer awareness bathroom stickers. I was quite emotional after receiving this information. The day I put the stickers up in the male toilets throughout the stadium, was a freezing cold December day and nobody wanted to help me with it (I don't blame them!). I was freezing cold, my fingers were red raw, the toilets were pretty unpleasant and I felt really lonely. I have always recalled this day as one of the only days that I haven't enjoyed since starting this project. Yet now I know that my actions on this day may have contributed to saving this man's life. This just shows that we can make a difference and men are actually taking notice of some of the things we have been doing. I have a very different feeling about that cold lonely day in December now.

This data reinforce the concept that health promotion within an English Premier League Football Club is possible and that it can be both efficient and effective if the correct methods are adopted for capturing the attention of your target audience.

A take-home message

Following each match day awareness event, an email was sent by the first author to health service staff that had been involved in the match day event. The purpose of the email was to determine the usefulness and impact of the event to their organization. An unanticipated finding emerged that the majority of organizations reported significantly higher traffic on their website and/or phone line in the one to two weeks following the match day event. The following email extract is an example of this finding:

> E-mail received 20/02/2010, 13:45:
>
> Hi Kathryn, We had a great time on Wednesday, especially as the Blues won too!!! The following day we received 16 requests for postal chlamydia kits via our website or text system which is a significant increase on the average daily number of testing requests. If anyone else mentions that they heard about us via the match day awareness event we will be sure to let you know. Regards, Rachel.

As the organization's website and phone number were predominantly advertised through a series of branded multifaceted multimedia outputs, this finding again supports the concept that non-invasive health promotion messages that are branded with the football club logo were better received, and thus more successful. This finding also supports the theory that men live in the *now*[44]) and so when we market health information to men we should take into account that men will typically concentrate on what is currently happening (in this regard, a football match) and are more likely to take on-board information targeted at them in their downtime. Therefore, a 'take home' health message is likely to be more successful than a message that men must attend to whilst other stimuli are taking place.

Discussion

In 2009, White and Witty[45] asserted that more evidence of the impact of sport and sports stadia on men's health engagement was needed. This study aimed to contribute to this call for research by understanding the effectiveness of, and barriers associated with, promoting and engaging male football fans in health-related behaviours and messages at an English Premier League football stadium on match days. Through the use of reflective methodologies, this study has provided contextual real-life information which offers valuable insights into men's engagement with health messages and behaviours on a match day at an English Premier League football club. The findings also formulate a number of important messages and future directions for men's health practitioners-researchers to take into consideration.

White and Witty[46] and Robertson et al.[47] proposed that the setting where male-targeted interventions are delivered is an important factor in men's engagement with health services. Moreover, Wilkins and Baker[48] suggested that men will respond to health messages offered in places that they already go and feel comfortable such as sports stadia. This finding was supported by the Tackling Men's Health intervention which concluded that the delivery of a men's health intervention at large UK Rugby stadia was feasible and achieved good levels of engagement. In contrast, the Premier League Health 'health' themed match day awareness events at this large UK football club did not appear to achieve such levels of engagement with men in and around the stadium. It would appear that whilst there is an appeal to use sport, and sports stadia in particular, for engaging men in health messages, *one size may not fit all*.

Specifically, we cannot assume that male supporters will absorb health messages in and around all sport stadia on match days.

Importantly, this study revealed that whilst one approach may not be successful in all stadia settings, there is a case for engaging men in health issues in the community setting, during their leisure time and more specifically at an English Premier League football club and on a match day. In this instance, health-related awareness and engagement methods that encroached on men's match day experiences (i.e. health stations and leaflets) were not successful as the majority of male football fans appeared to have a *match day ritual* (i.e. catch a glimpse of the players as they park their cars, meet with friends, navigate their way inside the stadium, place a bet, buy a programme, get their pie and/or drink and take their seat) during which they did not like to be disturbed. Having said this, it would appear that practitioners and researchers can be successful in communicating with and engaging men in health information in this, or similar settings, both at the event and after the event (via 'take home' messages). The findings of this research unravelled important implications which provide guidance for good practice. They are presented below.

Implications for practice

The findings of this research suggest that in order to successfully promote health behaviours and messages to male football fans on an English Premier League match day, practitioners should aim to adopt a range of subtle, non-invasive approaches that may include multimedia messages or the development of tangible, masculine, club-branded promotional materials that allude to published health messages. Furthermore, this research highlighted that men became a more captive audience once settled *inside* the stadium setting. Therefore, in order to engage male football fans in health behaviours and messages on an English Premier League match day (i.e. a high volume context), practitioners and researchers should seek to engage with men within the confines of the football stadium rather than outside the stadium where it is typically busy and distracting.

Conclusion and future research

Through the interpretation of the first-hand experiences of the first author within a community setting, this study has identified what aspects of a FitC health promotion activity worked for men on a match day, and conversely what did not work, and why. Furthermore, this study has offered suggestions for effective strategies that will better engage men in health information and behaviours in similar settings. By doing so, this study contributes to an underserved area within health promotion and men's health literature and offers a potential solution to the concerns raised regarding men's under use of health services.[49] However, there still remains a lack of accessible, research-based evidence examining the effectiveness of different types of innovative approaches to health promotion among men.[50] Therefore, it can be argued that more contextual evidence is required in order to build a more informed understanding of men's engagement with health services in community settings and subsequently assist in the advancement and creation of future men's health promotion initiatives and interventions.

Acknowledgements

The authors would like to thank the staff of Everton Football Club and Everton in the Community for their support with this research and permission to identify the club explicitly in this publication.

Notes

1. White et al., *The State of Men's Health in Europe*.
2. White et al., *The State of Men's Health in Europe*.
3. Townsend et al., *Physical Activity Statistics 2012*.
4. Hunt et al., 'Gender Differences in Family Practitioner Consultation for Common Chronic Conditions'.
5. White et al., 'Men's Health in Europe'.
6. Addis and Mahalik, 'Men, Masculinity, and the Contexts of Help Seeking'.
7. White et al., *The State of Men's Health in Europe*.
8. Harrison, 'Warning: The Male Sex Role May Be Dangerous to Your Health'.
9. Courtenay, 'Constructions of Masculinity and Their Influence on Men's Wellbeing'.
10. Robertson, *Understanding Men and Health*.
11. Gough and Robertson, *Men, Masculinities and Health*.
12. Gough, 'The Psychology of Men's Health'.
13. Gough, 'The Psychology of Men's Health'.
14. White and Witty, 'Men's under Use of Health Services – Finding Alternative Approaches'.
15. White and Witty, 'Men's under Use of Health Services – Finding Alternative Approaches'.
16. Department of Health, *Healthy People, Healthy Lives*.
17. Wilkins and Baker, *Getting It Sorted*.
18. White et al., *The State of Men's Health in Europe*.
19. Witty and White, *The Tackling Men's Health Evaluation Study*.
20. Pringle et al., 'The Pre-adoption Demographic and Health Profiles of Men Participating in a Programme of Men's Health Delivered in English Premier League Football Clubs'.
21. Dunn et al., 'Kicking the Habit'; Pringle et al., 'The Pre-adoption Demographic and Health Profiles of Men Participating in a Programme of Men's Health Delivered in English Premier League Football Clubs; Robertson et al., 'It's Fun, Fitness and Football Really'.
22. White and Witty, 'Men's Health and Sporting Venues'.
23. Robinson et al., 'Working towards Men's Health'.
24. Robertson and Williamson, 'Men and Health Promotion in the UK'.
25. Carmichael and Miller, 'The Challenges of Practitioner Research'.
26. Walsh et al., 'Social Marketing for Public Health'.
27. Wilkins and Baker, *Getting It Sorted*.
28. Carmichael and Miller, 'The Challenges of Practitioner Research'.
29. Robson, *Real World Research*; Jarvis, 'The Practitioner–Researcher in Nursing' and Gray, *Doing Research in the Real World*.
30. Carmichael and Miller, 'The Challenges of Practitioner Research'.
31. Tedlock, 'Ethnography and Ethnographic Representation'.
32. Atkinson and Hammersley, 'Ethnography and Participant Observation'; Clandinin and Connelly, *Narrative Inquiry*.
33. Knowles and Telfer, 'The Where, What, Why of Reflective Practice'; Schinke et al., 'Toward Cultural Praxis and Cultural Sensitivity'; Knowles et al., *Reflective Practice in the Sport and Exercise Sciences*.
34. Polkinghorne, *Narrative Knowing and the Human Science*; Tedlock, 'Ethnography and Ethnographic Representation'; Knowles et al., 'Developing the Reflective Sports Coach'.
35. Heider, 'What Do People Do? Dani Auto-ethnography'.
36. Crotty, *The Foundations of Social Research*.

37. Mitchell and Charmaz, 'Telling Tales and Writing Stories – Postmodern Visions and Realist Images in Ethnographic Writing'.
38. Sparkes, 'Narrative Analysis'.
39. Elo and Kyngäs, 'The Qualitative Content Analysis Process'.
40. Ryba et al., 'Towards a Conceptual Understanding of Acute Cultural Adaptation'.
41. Shenton, 'Strategies for Ensuring Trustworthiness in Qualitative Research Projects'.
42. Witty and White, *The Tackling Men's Health Evaluation Study*.
43. Richardson and O'Dwyer, 'Football Supporters and Football Team Brands'.
44. Deutsch, 'Gender Differences in Cognition'.
45. White and Witty, 'Men's Health and Sporting Venues'.
46. White and Witty, 'Men's under Use of Health Services – Finding Alternative Approaches'.
47. Robertson et al., 'It's Fun, Fitness and Football Really'.
48. Wilkins and Baker, *Getting It Sorted*.
49. Gough, 'The Psychology of Men's Health'.
50. Robinson et al., 'Working towards Men's Health'.

References

Addis, M., and J. Mahalik. 'Men, Masculinity, and the Contexts of Help Seeking'. *American Psychologist* 58 (2003): 5–14.
Atkinson, P., and M. Hammersley. 'Ethnography and Participant Observation'. In *Strategies of Qualitative Inquiry*, ed. N. Denzin and Y. Lincoln, 111–36. London: Sage, 1994.
Carmichael, J., and K. Miller. 'The Challenges of Practitioner Research: Some Insights into Collaboration between Higher and Further Education in the LfLFE Project'. In *What a Difference a Pedagogy Makes: Researching Lifelong Learning and Teaching. Proceedings of 3rd International CRLL Conference*, eds. J. Caldwell, 700–2. Glasgow: Centre for Research in Lifelong Learning, 2006.
Clandinin, D., and F. Connelly. *Narrative Inquiry: Experience and Story in Qualitative Research*. San Francisco, CA: Jossey-Bass, 2000.
Courtenay, W. 'Constructions of Masculinity and Their Influence on Men's Well-being: A Theory of Gender and Health'. *Social Science and Medicine* 50 (2000): 1385–401.
Crotty, M. *The Foundations of Social Research: Meaning and Perspective in the Research Process*. London: Sage, 1998.
Department of Health. *Healthy People, Healthy Lives: Our Strategy for Public Health in England*. London: Department of Health, 2010.
Deutsch, R. 'Gender Differences in Cognition'. Presentation, Ad Club of New York, October 29, 2009.
Dunn, K., B. Drust, D. Flower, and D. Richardson. 'Kicking the Habit: A Biopsychosocial Account of Engaging Men Recovering from Drug Misuse in Regular Recreational Football'. *Journal of Men's Health* 8 (2011): 233.
Elo, S., and H. Kyngäs. 'The Qualitative Content Analysis Process'. *Journal of Advanced Nursing* 62 (2008): 107–15.
Gilbourne, D., and D. Richardson. 'Tales from the Field: Personal Reflections on the Provision of Psychological Support in Professional Soccer'. *Psychology of Sport and Exercise* 7 (2006): 325–37.
Gough, B. 'The Psychology of Men's Health: Maximizing Masculine Capital'. *Health Psychology* 32 (2013): 1–4.
Gough, B., and S. Robertson. *Men, Masculinities and Health: Critical Perspectives*. Hampshire: Palgrave Macmillan, 2010.
Gray, D. *Doing Research in the Real World*. London: Sage, 2004.
Harrison, J. 'Warning: The Male Sex Role May Be Dangerous to Your Health'. *Journal of Social Issues* 34 (1978): 65–86.
Heider, K. 'What Do People Do? Dani Auto-ethnography'. *Journal of Anthropological Research* 31 (1975): 3–17.
Hunt, K., G. Ford, L. Harkins, and S. Wyke. 'Are Women More Ready to Consult than Men? Gender Differences in Family Practitioner Consultation for Common Chronic Conditions'. *Journal of Health Services Research and Policy* 4 (1999): 96–100.

Jarvis, P. 'The Practitioner–Researcher in Nursing'. *Nurse Education Today* 20 (1998): 30–5.

Jones, G. 'Performance Excellence: A Personal Perspective on the Link between Sport and Business'. *Journal of Applied Sport Psychology* 14 (2002): 268–81.

Knowles, Z., D. Gilbourne, B. Cropley, and L. Dugdill. *Reflective Practice in the Sport and Exercise Sciences: Contemporary Issues*. London: Routledge, 2013.

Knowles, Z., D. Gilbourne, and V. Tomlinson. 'Reflections of the Application of Reflective Practice for Supervision in Applied Sport Psychology'. *The Sport Psychologist* 21 (2007): 109–22.

Knowles, Z., and T. Telfer. 'The Where, What, Why of Reflective Practice'. In *Exploring Sport and Fitness*, ed. C. Heaney, B. Oakley, and S. Rea, 22–36. London: Routledge, 2009.

Lee, C., and R. Owens. *The Psychology of Men's Health*. Buckingham: Open University Press, 2002.

Mitchell, R., and K. Charmaz. 'Telling Tales and Writing Stories – Postmodern Visions and Realist Images in Ethnographic Writing'. In *Doing Ethnographic Research – Fieldwork Settings*, ed. S. Grills, 228–48. London: Sage, 1996.

Polkinghorne, D. *Narrative Knowing and the Human Sciences*. Albany: University of New York Press, 1988.

Pringle, A., S. Zwolinsky, A. Smith, S. Robertson, J. McKenna, and A. White. 'The Pre-adoption Demographic and Health Profiles of Men Participating in a Programme of Men's Health Delivered in English Premier League Football Clubs'. *Public Health* 125 (2011): 411–6.

Richardson, B., and E. O'Dwyer. 'Football Supporters and Football Team Brands: A Study in Consumer Brand Loyalty'. *Irish Marketing Review* 16 (2003): 43–51.

Robertson, S. *Understanding Men and Health. Masculinities, Identity and Well-being*. Berkshire: Open University Press, 2007.

Robertson, S., and R. Williams. 'Men: Showing Willing'. *Community Practitioner* 82 (2009): 34–5.

Robertson, S., and P. Williamson. 'Men and Health Promotion in the UK: Ten Years Further on?' *Health Education Journal* 64 (2005): 293–301.

Robertson, S., S. Zwolinsky, A. Pringle, J. McKenna, A. Daly-Smith, and A. White. "It is Fun, Fitness and Football Really': A Process Evaluation of a Football-based Health Intervention for Men'. *Qualitative Research in Sport, Exercise and Health* 5 (2013): 419–39.

Robinson, M., S. Robertson, J. McCullagh, and S. Hacking. 'Working towards Men's Health: Findings from the Sefton Men's Health Project'. *Health Education Journal* 69 (2010): 139–49.

Robson, C. *Real World Research: A Resource for Social Scientists and Practitioner Researchers*. Oxford: Blackwell, 1993.

Ryba, T., S. Haapanen, S. Mosek, and K. Ng. 'Towards a Conceptual Understanding of Acute Cultural Adaptation: A Preliminary Examination of ACA in Female Swimming'. *Qualitative Research in Sport, Exercise and Health* 4 (2012): 80–97.

Schinke, R., K. McGannon, W. Parham, and A. Lane. 'Toward Cultural Praxis and Cultural Sensitivity: Strategies for Self-reflexive Sport Psychology Practice'. *Quest* 64 (2012): 34–46.

Shenton, A. 'Strategies for Ensuring Trustworthiness in Qualitative Research Projects'. *Education for Information* 22 (2004): 63–75.

Sparkes, A. 'Narrative Analysis: Exploring the Whats and Hows of Personal Stories'. In *Qualitative Research in Health Care*, ed. I. Holloway, 191–209. Maidenhead: Open University Press, 2005.

Tedlock, B. 'Ethnography and Ethnographic Representation'. In *The Handbook of Qualitative Research*, ed. N. Denzin and Y. Lincoln, 455–86. Thousand Oaks, CA: Sage, 2000.

Townsend, N., P. Bhatnagar, K. Wickramasinghe, P. Scarborough, C. Foster, and M. Rayner. *Physical Activity Statistics 2012*. London: British Heart Foundation, 2012.

Walsh, D., R. Rudd, B. Moeykens, and T. Moloney. 'Social Marketing for Public Health'. *Health Affairs* 12 (1993): 104–19.

White, A., B. De Sousa, R. De Visser, R. Hogston, S. Madsen, P. Makara, M. McKee, et al. 'Men's Health in Europe'. *Journal of Men's Health* 8 (2011): 192–201.

White, A., B. De Sousa, R. De Visser, R. Hogston, S. Madsen, P. Makara, N. Richardson, and W. Zatonski. *The State of Men's Health in Europe*. Luxembourg: European Commission, 2011.

White, A., and K. Witty. 'Men's under Use of Health Services – Finding Alternative Approaches'. *Journal of Men's Health* 6 (2009a): 95–7.

White, A., and K. Witty. 'Men's Health and Sporting Venues'. *Journal of Men's Health* 6 (2009b): 273.

White, A., S. Zwolinsky, A. Pringle, J. McKenna, A. Daly-Smith, S. Robertson, and R. Berry. *Premier League Health: A National Programme of Men's Health Promotion Delivered in/by Professional Football Clubs. Final Report 2012*. Leeds: Centre for Men's Health and Centre for Active Lifestyles, Leeds Metropolitan University, 2012.

Wilkins, D., and P. Baker. *Getting It Sorted: A Policy Programme for Men's Health*. London: Men's Health Forum, 2004.

Witty, K., and A. White. *The Tackling Men's Health Evaluation Study*. Leeds: Centre for Men's Health, Leeds Metropolitan University, 2010.

Ethnographic engagement from within a Football in the Community programme at an English Premier League football club

Kathryn Curran[a], Daniel David Bingham[b,c], David Richardson[d] and Daniel Parnell[e]

[a]*Academic Group of Engineering, Sport and Sciences, University of Bolton, Bolton, UK;* [b]*Bradford Institute for Health Research, Bradford, UK;* [c]*School of Sport, Exercise and Health Sciences, Loughborough University, Loughborough, UK;* [d]*The Football Exchange, Research Institute of Sport and Exercise Sciences, Liverpool John Moores University, Liverpool, UK;* [e]*Carnegie Faculty, Centre for Active Lifestyles, Leeds Metropolitan University, Leeds, UK*

> The present paper draws upon six years of applied practitioner research experience of the authors who were based within a Football in the Community (FitC) programme at an English Premier League football club in a deprived community in the UK. The paper explores the critical emergent issues concerned with participant recruitment, engagement and retention within a range of FitC physical activity, health improvement interventions with the following populations; primary school children, families, men aged 18–35 years and men aged 55 years and above. Results are drawn from a range of ethnographic, reflective and observational data collection and analysis techniques undertaken by the authors. A first person writing style is used alongside creative non-fiction vignettes. Results relating to the effectiveness of a range of behaviour and lifestyle change interventions are discussed. The authors conclude with a series of proposed operational and strategic ways forward for FitC schemes.

Introduction

In England, Football in the Community (FitC) programmes was formally established in 1986 by the Footballers' Further Education and Vocational Training Society. At this time, English football was suffering from serious economic and social problems (e.g. the height of hooliganism) and FitC programmes were established to 'do good' in the community and, in part, help to reconnect professional football clubs with their local communities.[1] FitC programmes (typically registered charities and the community arm of football clubs) are now found in the majority of professional football clubs in England and Wales.[2] FitC schemes often use the 'brand' of the football club as a powerful tool for engagement,[3] however they are (typically) run as a separate (organizational) entity to the football club, with many having their own staff and independent funding streams (excluding some payments in-kind from the host club).[4] Initially, FitC programmes concentrated on the provision of grassroots football coaching with children, however, in 1997 the New Labour government identified football as a potential key deliverer of a range of policy objectives in areas as diverse as health, education, community cohesion, regeneration and crime reduction.[5]

In recent years, football's potential 'power' has also been increasingly utilized by the UK coalition government to assist in attending to social agendas resulting in an increasing amount of community work being undertaken by FitC programmes and an increasing amount of financial support being provided. However, despite this investment, FitC interventions appear to lack monitoring and/or evaluation into their effectiveness and/or an understanding of, 'what works'.[6] With this issue in mind, a formal collaboration between Liverpool John Moores University, School of Sport and Exercise Sciences (LJMU SPS) and Everton EitC was established in June 2007.

Everton in the Community is a financially independent charity that is based within an English Premier League football club; Everton Football Club. Like many current football clubs, Everton Football Club is an institution which plays a key role in its local community.[7] Everton in the Community aims to motivate, educate and inspire diverse communities in the North-west of England and North Wales through the programmes that it delivers. EitC has undertaken community work (in a formal capacity) since 1988, was formalized as a registered charity in 2004, and has since become one of the most successful sporting charities in the UK; boasting awards such as the prestigious 'Community Mark', a national standard from Business in the Community (patron HRH Prince of Wales) through to more recent Global Business Excellence Awards, 2011, the Football Business Awards, 'Best Club Community Scheme', 2012 and a Big Society Award in 2013.[8] The charity currently employs a specialist team of 32 full-time members of staff, 45 casual staff and more than 175 volunteers, with an annual turnover of approximately £1.6 m.

Despite Everton in the Community's award winning work, the community it serves still suffers from significant health inequalities. Everton in the Community is based in the ward of Everton which is located within the City and North Neighbourhood Management Area in Liverpool, a region which falls within the most deprived 10% in the country.[9] Long-term unemployment in this area is high[10] and life expectancy is amongst the lowest in Liverpool.[11] Furthermore, over 50% of the adult population are classified as overweight or obese, and smoking prevalence and hospital admissions for alcohol-related conditions amongst adults are amongst the highest in the city.[12]

Despite a growing number of health initiatives operated by Everton in the Community, there was (at the time) little evaluation of health-related programmes and a lack of dissemination of 'what works'. Taylor[13] highlighted the danger of committing to highly favourable outcomes and the risks of someone actually holding them to their commitments. In this regard, EitC were (at the time) claiming to improve quality of life however there was no empirical evidence to support such a claim and no prior intention (i.e. understanding or ability) to begin to measure whether such a claim was valid. EitC recognized that they could be doing more to evaluate the real impact of their initiatives and that developing a collaborative partnership to conduct monitoring and evaluation could help them to improve the efficacy of their practices. The formal collaboration between LJMU SPS and Everton in the Community therefore had a consensus to develop an understanding of the 'real' impact of EitC physical activity, health and behaviour change programmes through immersed practitioner–research and an integrated programme of monitoring and evaluation.

The collaboration endeavoured to use practitioner involved research as a means to establish whether or not the programmes delivered by EitC 'made a difference' and subsequently improve the quality of life of those within the local community.[14] The partnership's philosophy was as follows:

> to deliver quality programmes that aim to promote 'real' positive behaviour and lifestyle change improving the quality of life and the well being of people within our community across a range of social agendas via a plethora of projects, programmes, initiatives and campaigns.

Through the collaboration, the 'Everton Active Family Centre' (EAFC) was developed, established and operated from June 2008 to August 2012. EAFC was a bespoke outward-facing centre within the grounds of Goodison Park and acted as hub for immersed community-based health research in the heart of a professional football club based within a deprived community. EAFC was equipped with gym and fitness equipment (see Figure 1), bathroom and showering facilities, and a furnished common room/office. EAFC was the base of the authors' and a number of EitC's physical activity and health improvement interventions.

EAFC was funded via a collaboration including internal capital funds from Liverpool John Moores University, in-kind funding from Everton Football Club, in-kind equipment provision by Liverpool Lifestyles (through Liverpool City Council leisure services), Liverpool Active City and from several small grants including one from Liverpool Primary Care Trust. The authors acted as programme managers and practitioner-cum-researchers within EitC. They were involved in the development, day-to-day management and delivery of a range of physical activity, health and lifestyle

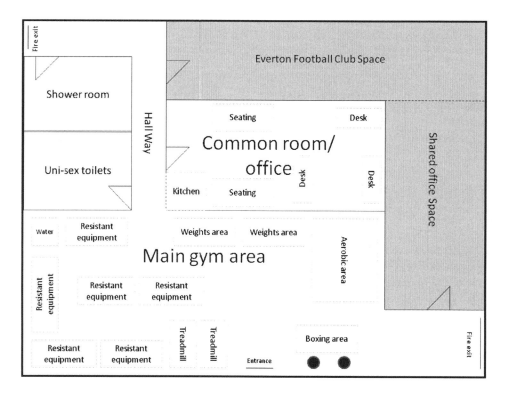

Figure 1. An outline of floor plan of the EAFC facility.

change interventions which operated from within EAFC. Interventions were targeted at, and engaged, the following populations; primary school children, families, men aged 18–35 years and men aged 55 years plus, on a weekly basis.

This paper focuses on the personal accounts and reflections of the authors (i.e. practitioner-cum-researchers) who, through qualitative techniques, recount the effectiveness of the development and delivery of a range of FitC-based physical activity and health improvement interventions. Specifically, the authors explore 'what worked?' when attempting to engage 'at risk' community populations (i.e. those at risk of developing non-communicable diseases) in positive health behaviours. Furthermore, the role of the researcher-cum-practitioners was to provide a platform for these populations to sustain positive behaviour change. By exploring the critical emergent issues within six years of applied research and practice, this paper aims to provide insights into effective approaches to engaging and sustaining positive health behaviours amongst 'at risk' community populations. Furthermore, in order to build on, and improve current practice, this paper proposes a number of operational and strategic ways forward for FitC programmes.

Method

After obtaining ethical approval, participants (i.e. primary school children, families, men aged 18–35 years and men aged 55+ years) were recruited for participation in weekly physical activity programmes of moderate intensity which formed part of Everton in the Community's EAFC-based health improvement programmes. Services hosting these particular populations (i.e. health care agencies, the local authority, local elderly care homes and sport development agencies within the City of Liverpool, UK) were then contacted. Participants were continuously recruited over a rolling period of three years using a variety of mechanisms including face-to-face engagement, phone calls, referrals from service staff and word of mouth. Enrolment on all EAFC programmes was voluntary and participants were free to withdraw at any point. Informed consent was given by all participants and/or gatekeepers. Table 1 outlines participant figures and demographics over the three year period.

The nature of delivery of EAFC programmes was to provide bespoke physical activity and exercise support alongside personalized goal setting to all participants on a weekly basis. Figure 2 outlines the overarching process adopted by practitioners operating within EAFC. Sessions were typically delivered one to one or within small groups (i.e. no more than 1:5 ratio, practitioner to participant), lasted approximately 1–1.5 h and were delivered on a weekly basis. Initially, participants were enrolled on a six-week programme. Activities would be led by the participants and

Table 1. Participant engagement figures (August 2009–2012) and broad demographics.

	Numbers recruited by programme year				
Participant numbers	2009	2010	2011	2012	Total
Families (all ages)	2	4	5	4	15
Men (18–35 years)	23	35	46	43	147
Men (55 years+)	5	13	17	5	40
Children (10–11 years)	8	8	9	5	30

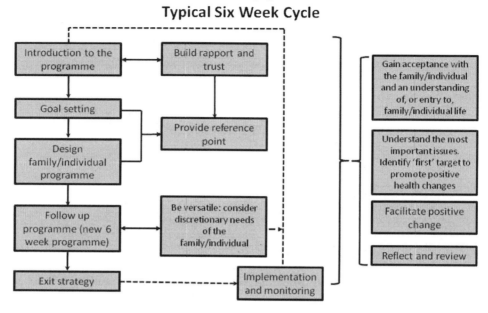

Figure 2. An outline of the overarching process adopted by EAFC practitioners.

would typically include a number of resistant and aerobic exercises within EAFC such as boxing-oriented workouts, walks and/or short runs (around the stadium and a local public park), exergaming and football or games in the stadium car park outside of the EAFC. Following completion of the six-week programme, practitioners and participants would review progress together and mutually agree the 'next steps' for the participant/s. This typically involved a structured exit strategy or continued support and engagement through the EAFC programme.

Research design

Throughout the research the authors adopted principles of ethnography[15] in order to undertake prolonged fieldwork with extensive observation in the natural setting (i.e. within EAFC, typically 4 days per week). The authors attempted to develop a clear understanding of what daily life was like for the participants, become accustomed to and understand the physical and institutional settings in which they lived, the daily routine of activities, the beliefs that guided their actions and the linguistic and other semiotic systems that mediated all their contexts and activities.[16] In order to balance the notions of engagement and trust, whilst adopting an (initially) objective lens, participant observations were utilized in a variety of settings throughout the study.[17] The authors actively engaged in both observation and participation, and participant observation throughout their time as practitioner-cum-researchers.[18] As practitioner-cum-researchers we were immersed in the planning and delivery of all the physical activity and health improvement interventions.[19] Engagement and immersion within all physical activity and health promotion sessions allowed the authors to adopt a range of informal, open and relaxed approaches (e.g. conversations) to data collection. Such an approach enabled the researcher(s) to explore issues as they evolved 'on the ground' and to develop closeness, trust and familiarization with the programme participants. Carmichael and Miller[20] suggested that the use of practitioner–researchers is an appropriate and powerful method of understanding the deeper cultural, situational and environmental context of the applied research setting in ways that would be very difficult to achieve otherwise. The research process, aligned, and hostage to, culture and circumstance, is inevitably slower and more complex. Whilst a simpler and more direct research methodology would be quicker and easier to undertake, it would be lacking in richness and the 'thick contextual description' that this method is aimed at developing.[21]

The authors' personal reflections and observations were recorded through informal field notes and reflective diaries.[22] The informal field notes were continually developed in an attempt to capture the context, culture and practice of EitC.[23] When the researchers felt a more flexible method of data collection was needed (e.g. where visible note taking may jeopardize the quality of conversation) mental notes were made.[24] These mental notes were typically keywords and quotes from participants (i.e. children, parents, families, men and other practitioners) which were jotted on a note pad, at an appropriate time and developed at the end of the day in detailed reflective field notes.[25] This relaxed and informal reflective methodology allowed for *sense making* and encouraged the practitioner-cum-researchers to learn from the knowledge gained *in action*.[26]

Data analysis and representation

Following the completion of all of the EAFC programmes each author prepared their respective field notes and reflections, before engaging in a period of close reading in order to become immersed in the data.[27] At this stage initial ideas and thoughts were recorded. Following this, principles of content analysis were adopted by the researchers in order to identify and code themes arising from the data.[28] The analysis was then read and re-read by each author in isolation from the research team following this coding process, which is considered both practical and preferred in circumstances of prolonged engagement and a developed researcher-cum-practitioner relationship.[29]

Throughout the results and discussion the authors aim to highlight the key issues that emerged during this research. The key emerging themes from the extensive data collected are presented within the results section. Verbatim citations (identified as single space text) are utilized to illustrate the contextual features of the participants, that serve to illuminate the rich detail of the collected data.

In order to 'bring to life' pertinent 'moments' recorded by the researchers during the extensive ethnographic and engagement phase of this research, it seems appropriate to include the researcher's personal reflections. The authors reflections are represented as a series of creative non-fiction narrative vignettes and evidenced through indented (0.5) single-spaced lines. This approach of author involved text is a genre championed by Gilbourne and Richardson,[30] in which the researcher is presented as the narrator using a first person writing style[31] in order to contextualize the data collected and move the story on for the reader.[32] Field note extracts (i.e. the voice of the participants) are also evidenced as indented (0.5), single spaced within the text. Pseudonyms are used for all participants involved in the research.

Results and discussion

There were two key themes that emerged from the expansive data collected. The following results and discussion section outline what the authors perceive to be the relevant, but not exhaustive, issues in participant recruitment, engagement and retention.

Brand of the football club: 'I was interested as soon as they mentioned Everton'

Much of the support for football as a vehicle for health engagement is that it can offer a 'hook' to engage those most 'at risk'. With football being one of the largest sports globally and the most popular sport within the United Kingdom,[33] its widespread appeal to the masses has contributed to this belief.[34] In line with these beliefs, it became apparent that the 'brand' of the football club acted as the major catalyst for attracting our participants to EAFC physical activity and health interventions.

When one author asked Claire a 38-year-old single mum of two teenagers what the most important thing for her and her children's continued engagement at EAFC, she replied:

> The most important thing for me is that Adam and Chloe [her son & daughter] enjoy it. They love coming here. I think if they didn't it would make things difficult for me to come!! To be honest I think Adam likes telling his mates he gets to walk to Goodison Park after school for training.

Here, Claire is highlighting the 'glitz' or 'wow factor' that surrounds a professional football club. On reflection one author highlighted:

> The families come to the Centre regardless of colour (or club) allegiance, so we have both Everton and Liverpool supporters, however the children tell us being able to say 'I train in Goodison Park' is something the children boast about in the playground ... It's powerful. Everyone in this city lives and breathes football. For some people it's their meaning of life day-to-day. I know the dads love coming here for that reason; it's up there with taking their children to the match ... However, the football 'pull' is just that. The rest is the safe, enclosed, intimate, private environment and subsequent bespoke support and guidance we offer in the Centre [EAFC] – this wouldn't work if we operated like a commercial gym.

The following reflection of another author highlights the influence that the football club brand had on EAFC programme engagement for a participant of the EAFC family engagement programme:

> Andy is a 37 year old male, father of two young teenagers, who, along with their brother in-law/uncle (29 year old) attended weekly sessions as a family. Andy and his family had within the recent past had to deal the most awful of circumstances, one of which was the death of Andy's wife and the two boys' mother. Andy was struggling to deal with the problems of being a widower and a single parent. His main support network was his brother in-law. When I asked Andy about his involvement in the EAFC families programme, the response he gave spoke volumes:

> I got involved mainly because of the lads (two sons), they are getting older and I don't want them walking the streets or getting into trouble. They love footie and finding out about coming here was ace. I mean all of the lads friends are jealous that they go to Goodison Park every week to train. Also to be honest I knew I was overweight and eating shit [unhealthy foods]every day, which ain't fair on the kids is it? So coming here has been great; I mean coming every week getting a buzz walking through those gates, seeing Dixie Dean [Everton Legend], getting ready for me and all the tribe [family] to be active and healthy is great. The kids love it now because they can show off to their friends about going to Goodison Park. But I know that when they are old men like me, they will look back and think of coming here every week as being great time in their life.

The lure of the professional sport club was also highlighted by the older (55+) men engaged in activities within EAFC. During some activity sessions men would meet at EAFC (see Figure 3 below) before engaging within a warm up in the main stadium car park, followed by a run around the circumference of the Goodison Park stadium. During a run the following unfolded between an author and participant:

> The weather was mild so we warmed up in the car park with a few stretches, but I guess this was also important for the men to speak, meet and catch up with one another. Before long, we shot off on a light jog around the stadium. I wasn't leading the session so I stuck towards the back. Quite quickly a couple of the guys dropped off and fell behind the main group. I decided to drop back and check on one of the men that had stopped to walk ... I asked 'How are you doing? They've started on quite a pace aven't they?' said a breathless Tommo. 'Tell me about it, am goosed [tired] too!!!' As we slowed, we talked a little about football. Tommo was a blue [Everton FC fan]. I asked Tommo about why he joined the EAFC programme and what he thought about it, 'I need to get fit, simple as that. But I haven't got into any gyms, they are not for me.' 'Why the Everton Family Centre then?' I inquired, Tommo responded 'where

Figure 3. A photograph depicting the location of EAFC within the grounds of Goodison Park.

else would you want to train? I get to come to Goodison after work and train. I just tell the lads, yeh, I am off to Goodison tonight, to train. I just laughits quality'.

Similarly, Mick a 58-year-old man who was out of work due to suffering from anxiety and depression, described to the authors that seeing a 'lifestyle programme' for men aged 55 and over taking place at Everton football club 'spoke out to him.' When asked whether the football club was the main reason behind his regular attendance, Mick described that he had tried to attend a 'normal' gym but the anxiety he got was 'crippling'. Mick described that while attending his local doctor's surgery he saw an advertisement for EAFC, and seeing this appeared to be the catalyst for him to become more active and healthier:

> I had just seen the doctor who was telling me again about how important diet, and particularly exercise, can be in treating psychological illness, but also just in all round health. When I left the doctor's office I saw the card (advertisement) saying that weekly sessions were taking place for 55 years plus at Everton Football Club. I thought if there is going to be place that I am going to start to take care of myself it's going to be there. So I picked up the phone and called the number on the advert.

Being able to say that participants could come to a professional football club to improve their health and fitness also appeared to be a major factor for male participants aged 18–35 years. Colin, an avid and lifelong Everton Football Club supporter told one author:

> That was big [finding out the programme was delivered by Everton Football Club], that was a big, big, big thing that. That was just like winnin' the World Cup, the Champions League an everything all in one; it really was.

Similarly, Gary (34 years) and Simon (32 years) expressed the importance of the football club brand, as a 'hook' for capturing their interest in the programme:

> I was interested as soon as they mentioned Everton. (Gary)

> … when they mentioned it [the programme] and it was to do with Everton, I was like yeah it's to do with Everton being an Everton fan … anything to do with Everton I was interested, you know what I mean. (Simon)

The power of the brand is interesting within sport, however generally very little is known about how effective or compelling the brand is and/or how it works with respect to disseminating a positive health message or capturing participants in health-oriented concepts or projects. Witty and White[35] found within the 'Tackling Men's Health' intervention that many participants had joined the health project due to the tangible connection with the rugby club. This finding was echoed within football, in research that highlighted the importance of club-related branding and activities in the recruitment of men across the 16 Premier League Health football club programmes.[36] Gray et al.[37] in their research across the Scottish Premier League football clubs found that men reported that they would not have attended the health improvement activities had they been delivered by the National Health Service. Furthermore, 'Extra Time', a national project to promote health and social opportunities for older people through football reported that 78% participants across the 24 professional football clubs highlighted that the connection with the club made Extra Time more appealing.[38] Our findings support and enhance the emerging discourse that the brand of professional football clubs has an important role to play in reaching, attracting and engaging participants in health improvement activities.

Skill base of practitioners: 'You are a top lad: You listen to what I have say ...'

Players and coaches are significant figures within a Premier League football club. In the professional football environment, the coach plays an important role in the development of 'the player'. They are key protagonists in shaping their character and identity (e.g. values, beliefs and attitude).[39] Whilst this is also the case in non-professional sport and physical activity settings, in this environment the (community) coach–participant relationship is particularly crucial in aiding participation and engagement levels.[40] Further, the practitioner/coach–participant relationship is critical when promoting health to such individuals.[41]

In the final report of the Premier League Health evaluation, White et al.[42] asserted that the project staff and their ability to interact with the participants on a personal and social level was as key factor in facilitating participant adoption to the Premier League Health programme. Consistent with these findings, it appeared that the nature of the programme delivery staff was a key factor influencing continuous engagement in EAFC programmes. The following quote captures Gary's (male, aged 34) (colloquial) view on the nature of the programme staff as facilitators for programme adoption and maintenance:

> Even though it's not that good round here like but [laughs] I couldn't see meself living anywhere else, but ... like youse, youse [practitioners] have all been alright with us ... That makes it easier as well, it's like, well say youse are teachers like aren't youse really, you know what I mean, tutors sort of thing. So like if youse are alright then that's half the battle. Coz if you get a little shit (or up-start) or something or someone you can't relate to, they can put people off from goin', an people just won't enjoy it, people won't go.

This finding was supported by Brian and Colin (two EAFC participants, male 18–35 years) who also made reference to the welcoming and supportive nature of the programme staff as a motivator for engagement:

> I'd say you and Drew [EitC coach/practitioner], as a team, you were very welcomin', there was no individuals, everyone was treated the same, so it was good. It was good and professional the way youse all are, the welcome side of it ... but then it was always maintained as well, very well throughout. If there was any problems youse were always there. Drew always helped ya, yourself always helped us, youse were there to help throughout the entire course and that was what I really liked about it. It was run professionally, it wasn't arsed about, youse were there, and because youse were there, we said we would be there, so we had to be there. (Brian)

> At first when I first was goin' in for the operation I was petrified, but with you and Drew sayin', you know, I've got that support and then, you know but that was a big weight off me shoulders, you know what I mean ... being able to come and talk about like anything, you know what I mean is was good like. (Colin)

The skill base of the practitioner and their ability to interact with the participants on a personal and social level was also highlighted during one of the older men's (55+ years) sessions. Mick (58-year-old male) made a comment to one author about the expertise of the practitioner and what it meant to him:

> Its ace to think this all on my door step, at me club and best of all it run by no amateurs. I mean you lad [researcher] are a personal trainer but also from a university. I know you know your stuff and you're not blaggin [making it up] it lad, when I hear some news story on this new diet, I think this is utter shite. Dan [researcher] told me the other day what a healthy diet is and this other person [on the news] is telling me to never eat carbohydrates!

When asked whether it was just the prestige of working with someone with high academic credentials that made a difference, Mick commented:

> It helps, but also you are a top lad, you listen to what I have say ... you don't talk down to me and make me feel like an old man. I come out of this place feeling top of the world!

This notion of the empathic and caring practitioner is noted by Hillsdon,[43] who noted that the knowledge base of practitioners is central in gaining trust and cooperation from patients. Similarly, Bogdan-Lovis et al.[44] noted that the ability to emphasize practitioner control over the exercise supported the cooperation and trust issues that brought about adherence and therefore life changes in this instance occurring within participants of EAFC.

In an attempt to capture the complexity of interventions, interactions and challenges emerging from working within EAFC, one author reflected:

> EAFC wasn't for the typical or traditional coach. By this I mean a Football Association coaching qualification would not prepare you for this work. You are more than just a physical activity instructor, you are involved as a make shift counsellor, life coach, supporting diet and health choices, providing lifestyle advice on drugs and alcohol and engaging in brief interventions for smoking cessation. And you have to do all of this through informal and personal conversational support mechanisms. These interactions that were regular, informal and friendly helped participants feel happier, better able to achieve their personal targets and provided a pair of ears [listened] to people. This was far more than what any General Practitioner (local doctor) surgery or mainstream health intervention does, or would offer.

Research suggests that as FitC programmes are growing, they are becoming overstretched and unable to keep pace with projects and staff development (i.e. the emergence of skills shortages).[45] As a result, serious consideration must be given to exploring the role, and support provided for the community coaches working within FitC schemes.

Applied recommendations and ways forward for FitC

By exploring the critical emergent issues within applied research and practice, this paper has highlighted the 'power' and 'pull' of a professional football club brand for attracting participants to physical activity and health engagement programmes. Therefore, it is recommended that stadia-based physical activity and health programme managers capitalize on the use of the club including the brand (i.e. the imagery and icons that reflect the club) and the people (i.e. senior players, former players, management and coaching staff) in order to develop a marketing strategy for the promotion, implementation and dissemination of any aligned health information and messages.

The findings of this research also suggest that FitC practitioners need to be trained beyond 'the typical' Football Association Level 2 or UEFA B qualification in order to deal with the increasing demands of FitC schemes for addressing government agendas and social ills.[46] The outcomes of this research lead to the recommendation that FitC physical activity and health practitioners should be qualified or trained in additional skills such as counselling and behaviour change management[47] in order to deal with, successfully manage and support the increasing needs of the 'new age' of FitC programme participants. FitC schemes therefore need to execute relevant professional development and enhanced recruitment procedures. Furthermore, the findings of this research highlighted that participant engagement in EAFC programmes was influenced by positive perceptions and opinions of the programme practitioner/s. It is recommended therefore that personable, respectful, empathic, supportive and caring practitioners[48] are employed into such positions of responsibility.

Role of the researcher

This research has relied heavily on the field notes and personal reflections of the practitioner–researcher for learning 'on the job', for understanding the contextual experiences of the EAFC programme participants and for the subsequent development of the EAFC programmes based on an understanding of 'what works'. Reflective practice plays a vital role in enabling professionals to learn and understand the impact of their actions.[49] Therefore, it is recommended that FitC programme managers and practitioners should continually seek to gather data from 'the field' and reflect on practice in order to learn from their applied work in the field and develop FitC programmes and initiatives accordingly.

Limitations and strengths

This research has a number of strengths and limitations. The main strengths of this research lie in the prolonged and immersed nature of the research methodology that was adopted that has led to the richness and quality of the data collected. According to Lee,[50] negotiating access to research participants and the subsequent collection of good quality data depends on the quality of interpersonal relationships between researchers and participants. Gaining access to the research participants in this research was achieved due to the embedded nature of the authors within the fabric of the EAFC. Being 'there' and being 'seen'[51] was particularly important in this research to get as close as possible to the participants, to build relationships, trust and rapport, and subsequently to understand the participants day-to-day lives, norms and behaviours. The quality and richness of the data collected therefore is a direct reflection of the qualitative methods adopted and afforded by the practitioner-cum-researcher role and the strength of the participant–researcher relationships.

These methods are not without the challenges. Throughout this research, the authors adopted, maintained and attempted to balance the responsibilities associated with a practitioner-cum-researcher role.[52] Whilst this was a particularly useful approach for the researcher in this context and for the collection of rich data 'in the field', there were many occasions where this dual role became difficult to balance. It should be noted that a huge investment in time and emotional energy was required on the part of the researchers in order to achieve the aims of this research through the qualitative methods employed. However, we strongly believe that without adopting this dual role, a true picture of the intricacies associated with promoting and engaging 'at risk' populations in behaviour change programmes could not have been captured.

Conclusion

This research aimed to develop a greater understanding of 'what worked' in a FitC physical activity and health improvement intervention. More specifically, how effective its development and intimate and flexible approaches to delivery were at engaging 'at risk' community populations (i.e. those at risk of developing non-communicable diseases), encouraging positive health behaviours and sustaining positive behaviour change. Our findings support and enhance the emerging discourse that the brand of professional football clubs has an important role in reaching, attracting and engaging participants in health improvement activities. Furthermore, our research has placed a lens firmly on the need to recognize the eclectic skill base and nature required of FitC practitioners for continued and sustained participant engagement.

This research is unique both in method and focus and the results make an important contribution to our understanding of professional football clubs as a vehicle for health engagement and behaviour change. However, the findings highlight the need for additional research into the delivery and practice of FitC programmes. Given that football is a global concept and that most football clubs have an obligation to care for their community, it is hoped that the nature and role of this qualitative work will act as a catalyst to assist in the understanding of the effectiveness of football in the community programmes worldwide.

Acknowledgements

The authors gratefully acknowledge the contribution of all those individuals involved with this research and the agencies who partnered with the Everton Active Family Centre, including the participants, staff and volunteers of Everton in the Community and Everton Football Club. The authors would also like to express their gratitude to all students from Liverpool John Moores University that have been involved with, and supported, EAFC programmes and research.

Notes

1. Brown et al., *Football and Community in the Global Context*.
2. McGuire and Fenogilo, 'Football in the Community'.
3. Richardson et al., 'Football as an Agent for Social Change'.
4. Jenkins and James, 'It's Not Just a Game'.
5. Brown et al., *Football and Community in the Global Context* and Parnell et al., 'Implementing Monitoring and Evaluation Techniques within a Premier League Football in the Community Programme'.
6. Watson, 'Football in the Community'; Jackson et al., 'Policy Interventions Implemented Through Sporting Organizations'; Tacon, 'Football and Social Inclusion'; and Jenkins and James, 'It's Not Just a Game'.
7. Bale, 'The Changing Face of Football'.
8. Everton Football Club, *Everton in the Community*.
9. Liverpool City Council, 'Ward Profile of Everton 2012'.
10. Liverpool Primary Care Trust, *Public Health Annual Report 2009–2010*.
11. Liverpool City Council, 'Key Statistics and Data 2010'.
12. Liverpool City Council, 'Ward Profile of Everton 2012'.
13. Taylor, 'Multi-paradigmatic Research Design Spaces for Cultural Studies Researchers Embodying Postcolonial Theorising'.
14. Parnell et al., 'Implementing Monitoring and Evaluation Techniques within a Premier League Football in the Community Programme'.

15. Atkinson and Hammersley, 'Ethnography and Participant Observation' and Eder and Corsaro, 'Ethnographic Studies of Young Children and Youth'.
16. Eder and Corsaro, 'Ethnographic Studies of Young Children and Youth'.
17. Lofland and Lofland, *Analysing Social Settings*; Atkinson and Hammersley, 'Ethnography and Participant Observation'; and Tedlock, 'Ethnography and Ethnographic Representation'.
18. Hong and Duff, 'Modulated Participant-observation'.
19. Robson, *Real World Research*; Jarvis, 'The Practitioner–Researcher in Nursing'; and Gray, *Doing Research in the Real World*.
20. Carmichael and Miller, 'The Challenges of Practitioner Research'.
21. Carmichael and Miller, 'The Challenges of Practitioner Research'.
22. Atkinson and Hammersley, 'Ethnography and Participant Observation'.
23. McFee, 'Triangulation in Research' and Krane and Baird, 'Using Ethnography in Applied Sport Psychology'.
24. Lofland, *Doing Social Life*.
25. Sanjeck, *Fieldnotes* and Lofland, *Doing Social Life*.
26. Polkinghorne, *Narrative Knowing and the Human Science*; Tedlock, 'Ethnography and Ethnographic Representation'; and Knowles et al., 'Developing the Reflective Sports Coach'.
27. Sparkes, 'Narrative Analysis'.
28. Elo and Kyngäs, 'The Qualitative Content Analysis Process'.
29. Janesick, 'The Choreography of Qualitative Research'.
30. Gilbourne and Richardson, 'Tales from the Field'.
31. Jones, 'Performance Excellence'.
32. Tierney, 'Get Real' and Gilbourne and Richardson, 'Tales from the Field'.
33. Jenkins and James, 'It's Not Just a Game'.
34. Vigor et al., 'A Good Game? The Role of Sport in Society'.
35. Witty and White, *The Tackling Men's Health Evaluation Study*.
36. Pringle et al., 'The Pre-adoption Demographic and Health Profiles of Men Participating in a Programme of Men's Health Delivered in English Premier League Football Clubs' and White et al., *Premier League Health: A National Programme of Men's Health Promotion Delivered in/by Professional Football Clubs*.
37. Gray et al., 'Can the Draw of Professional Football Clubs Help Promote Weight Loss in Overweight and Obese Men?'.
38. Football Foundation, 'Monitoring and Evaluation Report'.
39. Wylleman et al., 'Career Transitions in Sport'.
40. Jowett, 'On Repairing and Enhancing the Coach–Athlete Relationship' and Dwyer et al., 'Adolescent Girls' Perceived Barriers to Participation in Physical Activity'.
41. Parnell et al., 'Football in the Community Schemes'.
42. White et al., *Premier League Health: A National Programme of Men's Health Promotion Delivered in/by Professional Football Clubs*.
43. Hillsdon, 'Promoting Physical Activity'.
44. Bogdan-Lovis and Sousa, 'The Contextual Influence of Professional Culture'.
45. McGuire and Fenogilo, 'Football in the Community'.
46. Parnell et al., 'Implementing Monitoring and Evaluation Techniques within a Premier League Football in the Community Programme'.
47. White et al., *Premier League Health: A National Programme of Men's Health Promotion Delivered in/by Professional Football clubs*.
48. Gilbert, 'Why are we Interested in Emotions'; Rager, 'Compassion Stress and the Qualitative Researcher'; and Coy, 'This Morning I'm a Researcher, this Afternoon I'm an Outreach Worker'.
49. Knowles et al., 'Developing the Reflective Sports Coach'; Dugdill et al., 'Developing New Community Health Roles' and Parnell et al., 'Football in the Community Schemes'.
50. Lee, *Doing Research on Sensitive Topics*.
51. Sixsmith et al., 'Accessing the Community'.
52. Robson, *Real World Research*.

References

Atkinson, P., and M. Hammersley. 'Ethnography and Participant Observation'. In *Strategies of Qualitative Inquiry*, ed. N. Denzin and Y. Lincoln, 111–36. London: Sage, 1994.
Bale, J. 'The Changing Face of Football: Stadiums and Communities'. In *The Future of Football: Challenges for the Twenty-first Century*, ed. J. Garland, D. Malcolm, and M. Rowe, 91–101. London: Frank Cass, 2000.
Bogdan-Lovis, E., and A. Sousa. 'The Contextual Influence of Professional Culture: Certified Nurse-midwives' Knowledge of and Reliance on Evidence-based Practice'. *Social Science & Medicine* 62 (2006): 2681–93.
Brown, A., T. Crabbe, and G. Mellor. *Football and Community in the Global Context. Studies in Theory and Practice*. Oxon: Routledge, 2009.
Carmichael, J., and K. Miller. 'The Challenges of Practitioner Research: Some Insights into Collaboration between Higher and Further Education in the LfLFE Project'. In *What a Difference a Pedagogy Makes: Researching Lifelong Learning and Teaching. Proceedings of 3rd International CRLL Conference*, 700–2. Glasgow: Centre for Research in Lifelong Learning, 2006.
Coy, M. 'This Morning I'm a Researcher, This Afternoon I'm an Outreach Worker: Ethical Dilemmas in Practitioner Research'. *International Journal of Social Research Methodology* 9 (2006): 419–31.
Dugdill, L., M. Coffey, A. Coufopoulos, K. Byrne, and L. Porcellato. 'Developing New Community Health Roles: Can Reflective Learning Drive Professional Practice?' *Reflective Practice* 10 (2009): 121–30.
Dwyer, J., K. Allison, E. Goldenberg, A. Fein, K. Yoshida, and M. Boutilier. 'Adolescent Girls' Perceived Barriers to Participation in Physical Activity'. *Adolescence* 41 (2006): 75–89.
Eder, D., and W. Corsaro. 'Ethnographic Studies of Children and Youth: Theoretical and Ethical Issues'. *Journal of Contemporary Ethnography* 28 (1999): 520–31.
Elo, S., and H. Kyngäs. 'The Qualitative Content Analysis Process'. *Journal of Advanced Nursing* 62 (2008): 107–15.
Everton Football Club. *Everton in the Community*. Everton Football Club. http://community.evertonfc.com/ (accessed October 17, 2012).
Football Foundation. *Monitoring and Evaluation Report*. http://www.footballfoundation.org.uk/digitalpublications/other%20publications/monitoring%20and%20evaluation%20report%202011/files/assets/seo/page26.html (accessed August 01, 2013).
Gilbert, K. 'Why are We Interested in Emotions?' In *The Emotional Nature of Qualitative Research*, ed. K. Gilbert, 3–14. Florida: CRC Press LCD, 2001.
Gilbourne, D., and D. Richardson. 'Tales from the Field: Personal Reflections on the Provision of Psychological Support in Professional Soccer'. *Psychology of Sport and Exercise* 7 (2006): 325–37.
Gray, D. *Doing Research in the Real World*. London: Sage, 2004.
Gray, C., K. Hunt, N. Mutrie, A. Anderson, S. Treweek, and S. Wyke. 'Can the Draw of Professional Football Clubs Help Promote Weight Loss in Overweight and Obese Men? A Feasibility Study of the Football Fans in Training Programme Delivered through the Scottish Premier League'. *Epidemiology and Community Health* 65 (2011): A37–8.
Hillsdon, M. 'Promoting Physical Activity: Issues in Primary Health Care'. *International Journal of Obesity* 22 (1998): S52–4.
Hong, L., and R. Duff. 'Modulated Participant-observation: Managing the Dilemma of Distance in Field Research'. *Field Methods* 14 (2002): 190–6.
Jackson, N., F. Howes, S. Gupta, J. Doyle, and E. Waters. 'Policy Interventions Implemented through Sporting Organizations for Promoting Healthy Behaviour Change'. *The Cochrane Database of Systematic Reviews*, no. 2 (2005). http://www.ncbi.nlm.nih.gov/pubmed/15846732
Janesick, V. 'The Choreography of Qualitative Research: Minuets, Improvisations, and Crystallization'. In *Strategies of Qualitative Inquiry*, ed. N. Denzin and Y. Lincoln, 379–400. Thousand Oaks, CA: Sage, 2004.
Jarvis, P. 'The Practitioner–Researcher in Nursing'. *Nurse Education Today* 20 (1998): 30–5.

Jenkins, H., and L. James. *It's Not Just a Game: Community Work in the UK Football Industry and Approaches to Corporate Social Responsibility*. Word Press, 2011. http://davidcoethica.files.wordpress.com/2012/09/its-not-just-a-game1.pdf (accessed April 01, 2012).

Jones, G. 'Performance Excellence: A Personal Perspective on the Link between Sport and Business'. *Journal of Applied Sport Psychology* 14 (2002): 268–81.

Jowett, S. 'On Repairing and Enhancing the Coach–Athlete Relationship'. In *The Psychology of Coaching*, ed. S. Jowett and M. Jones, 14–26. Leicester: The British Psychological Society, Sport and Exercise Psychology Division, 2005.

Knowles, Z., D. Gilbourne, A. Borrie, and A. Nevill. 'Developing the Reflective Sports Coach: A Study Exploring the Processes of Reflective Practice within a Higher Education Coaching Programme'. *Reflective Practice* 2 (2001): 185–207.

Krane, V., and S. Baird. 'Using Ethnography in Applied Sport Psychology'. *Journal of Applied Sport Psychology* 17 (2005): 87–107.

Lee, R. *Doing Research on Sensitive Topics*. Newbury Park, CA: Sage, 1993.

Liverpool City Council. *Key Statistics and Data 2010*, 2011. http://liverpool.gov.uk/council/key-statistics-and-data/data/ (accessed March 17, 2011).

Liverpool City Council. *Ward Profile of Everton 2012*, 2012. http://liverpool.gov.uk/council/key-statistics-and-data/ward-profiles/ward-map/ (accessed May 20, 2012).

Liverpool Primary Care Trust. *Public Health Annual Report 2009–2010*. Liverpool: Liverpool Primary Care Trust, 2011.

Lofland, J. *Doing Social Life*. New York: John Wiley, 1976.

Lofland, J., and L. Lofland. *Analysing Social Settings: A Guide to Qualitative Observation and Analysis*. 2nd ed. Belmont, CA: Wadsworth, 1984.

McFee, G. 'Triangulation in Research: Two Confusions'. *Educational Research* 34 (1992): 173–83.

McGuire, B., and R. Fenogilo. 'Football in the Community: Still "The Game's Best Kept Secret"?' *Soccer & Society* 9 (2008): 439–54.

Parnell, D., G. Stratton, B. Drust, and D. Richardson. 'Football in the Community Schemes: Exploring the Effectiveness of an Intervention in Promoting Healthful Behaviour Change'. *Soccer & Society* 14 (2013): 35–51.

Parnell, D., G. Stratton, B. Drust, and D. Richardson. 'Implementing Monitoring and Evaluation Techniques within a Premier League Football in the Community Programme: A Case Study Involving Everton in the Community'. In *The Routledge Handbook of Sport and Corporate Social Responsibility*, ed. J. Salcines, K. Babiak, and G. Walters, 326–43. London: Routledge, 2013.

Polkinghorne, D. *Narrative Knowing and the Human Sciences*. Albany, NY: State University of New York Press, 1988.

Pringle, A., S. Zwolinsky, A. Smith, S. Robertson, J. McKenna, and A. White. 'The Pre-adoption Demographic and Health Profiles of Men Participating in a Programme of Men's Health Delivered in English Premier League Football Clubs'. *Public Health* 125 (2011): 411–6.

Rager, K. 'Compassion Stress and the Qualitative Researcher'. *Qualitative Health Research* 15 (2005): 423.

Richardson, D., T. Burgess, A. Newland, L. Watson, D. Bingham, and D. Parnell. 'Football as an Agent for Social Change'. Paper Presented at European College of Sport Science 16th Annual Conference, Liverpool (UK), July 9, 2011.

Robson, C. *Real World Research: A Resource for Social Scientists and Practitioner Researchers*. Oxford: Blackwell, 1993.

Sanjeck, R. *Fieldnotes: The Makings of Anthropology*. New York: Cornell University Press, 1990.

Sixsmith, J., M. Boneham, and J. Goldring. 'Accessing the Community: Gaining Insider Perspectives from the Outside'. *Qualitative Health Research* 13 (2003): 4578–89.

Sparkes, A. 'Narrative Analysis: Exploring the Whats and Hows of Personal Stories'. In *Qualitative Research in Health Care*, ed. I. Holloway, 191–209. Maidenhead: Open University Press, 2005.

Tacon, R. 'Football and Social Inclusion: Evaluating Social Policy'. *Managing Leisure* 12 (2007): 1–23.

Taylor, P. 'Multi-paradigmatic Research Design Spaces for Cultural Studies Researchers Embodying Postcolonial Theorising'. *Cultural Studies of Science Education* 3 (2008): 881–90.

Tedlock, B. 'Ethnography and Ethnographic Representation'. In *The Handbook of Qualitative Research*, ed. N. Denzin and Y. Lincoln, 455–86. Thousand Oaks, CA: Sage, 2000.

Tierney, W.G. 'Get Real: Representing Reality'. *International Journal of Qualitative Studies in Education* 15 (2002): 385–98.

Vigor, A., K. Hallam, and M. Jackson. 'A Good Game? The Role of Sport in Society: A Scoping Study'. Draft Report Presented to Football Association, 2006.

Watson, N. 'Football in the Community: 'What's the Score?'' *Soccer & Society* 1 (2000): 114–25.

White, A., S. Zwolinsky, A. Pringle, J. McKenna, A. Daly-Smith, S. Robertson, and R. Berry. *Premier League Health: A National Programme of Men's Health Promotion Delivered in/by Professional Football Clubs. Final Report 2012*. Leeds: Centre for Men's Health and Centre for Active Lifestyles, Leeds Metropolitan University, 2012.

Witty, K., and A. White. *The Tackling Men's Health Evaluation Study*. Leeds: Centre for Men's Health, Leeds Metropolitan University, 2010.

Wylleman, P., D. Alfermann, and D. Lavallee. 'Career Transitions in Sport: European Perspectives'. *Psychology of Sport and Exercise* 5 (2004): 7–20.

'Motivate': the effect of a Football in the Community delivered weight loss programme on over 35-year old men and women's cardiovascular risk factors

Zoe Rutherford[a], Brendan Gough[b], Sarah Seymour-Smith[c], Christopher R Matthews[d], John Wilcox[e], Dan Parnell[a] and Andy Pringle[a]

[a]Centre for Active Lifestyles, Carnegie Faculty, Leeds Metropolitan University, Leeds, UK; [b]Centre for Men's Health, Faculty of Health, Leeds Metropolitan University, Leeds, UK; [c]School of Social Sciences, Nottingham Trent University, Nottingham, UK; [d]School of Sport and Service Management, University of Brighton, Brighton, UK; [e]Public Health, Nottingham City Council, Nottingham, UK

> The purpose of this study was to examine whether an innovative, inclusive and integrated 12-week exercise, behaviour change and nutrition advice-based weight management programme could significantly improve the cardiovascular risk factors of overweight and obese men and women over the age of 35. One hundred and ninety-four men and 98 women (mean age = 52.28 ± 9.74 and 51.19 ± 9.04) attending a community-based intervention delivered by Notts County Football in the Community over one year, took part in the study. Height (m), weight (kg), fitness (meters covered during a 6 min walk) and waist circumference (cm) were measured at weeks 1 and 12 as part of the intervention. Changes in body weight, waist circumference and fitness for men and women were measured by a 2-way repeated measures ANOVA, with significance set to $p < 0.05$. Weight, waist circumference and fitness significantly improved over time in both men (4.96 kg, 6.29 cm, 70.22 m; $p < 0.05$) and women (4.26 kg, 5.90 cm, 35.29 m; $p < 0.05$). The results demonstrated that the FITC lead weight loss intervention was successful in significantly improving cardiovascular risk factors in both men and women. In particular, the weight loss reductions achieved were comparable to those seen in similar, more costly men-only programmes. This is the first study to demonstrate the efficacy of such an intervention in an inclusive, mixed gender programme and more specifically, in women.

Introduction

The World Health Organization has described obesity as a global epidemic.[1] Obesity has 'escalated' over the last four decades[2] and the prevalence in UK men is amongst the highest in Europe.[3] Moreover, there is a higher prevalence of total overweight and obesity (BMI ≥ 25 kg m^2) amongst men than women in the UK[4] and although a greater proportion of women are obese/morbidly obese, more men than women will be obese in the future: indeed, it is predicted that by 2050, the proportion of the population that is obese will be 60% of males and 50% of females.[5] Nottingham, located in the English Midlands (United Kingdom), it is estimated that around 25% of men (37,000) are obese (with a BMI ≥ 30 kg m^2). Applying projections set out in Foresight indicates that the predicted number of obese men in the city is likely to reach 41% (55,020) by 2020, thus overtaking the number of obese women.[6] Moreover, obesity results in considerable costs to health services in the UK (forecast to reach £50billion by 2050).[7]

There is considerable international evidence that demonstrates the serious health consequences of excess body weight.[8] Illnesses associated with obesity include coronary artery disease, stroke, type 2 diabetes, anxiety and depression, and some cancers.[9] In particular, cardiovascular disease (CVD) is responsible for the majority of morbidity and mortality of both men and woman in the UK, with obese men at 40 years of age likely to reduce their life expectancy by 5.8 years.[10] While these obesity-associated co-morbidities contribute to gender and socio-economic inequalities and premature mortality, they may also affect individual men's and women's concerns about their own bodies and health status. It is for these reasons that weight management in relation to CVD risk has been identified as a public health priority globally.[11] This emphasises the importance of designing interventions that are acceptable to populations effected by obesity.[12] Such interventions require imaginative solutions that are innovative and capable of baring sustainable services.

Since as early as the mid-1980s, a joint initiative by the Football League (FL) and the Professional Footballers' Association saw the majority of professional football clubs in the country, through their Football in The Community (FITC) departments, delivering mainly coaching-based programmes, with the primary aim of tackling the issue of hooliganism.[13] By the mid-1990s, football's potential had been elevated to be a position as a 'key' deliverer of policy objective for a range of social welfare issues, notable health.[14] This belief for football (alongside sport) was championed (by many with sport, policy-making and politics) in what Perkins (113,[15]) encapsulated as, 'what football … can be used for almost has no bounds these days given the huge public interest in sport'. Despite this widespread belief, there is little empirical evidence to support the role of football and sport in delivering on these key social welfare issues.

Numerous authors argue that there is a lack of robust evidence to support the impact of sport and physical activity on key issues including health and call for more rigorous and sustained testing.[16] Coalter argues further that the outcomes of such sport-based interventions are too vague and/or far too ambitious.[17] This situation appears to be worsened by that fact FITC schemes lack the resources or skill base to collect research and evaluation[18] and the understanding of health improvement.[19] There is strong recommendation for rigorous, controlled evaluations to be conducted on health promotion interventions delivered by professional sport clubs.[20] A body of literature has begun to emerge more recently with authors contributing to the evidence of the role football has in health improvement.

The potential of professional sports organizations to attract participants to participate in a range of health promotion initiatives has been recognized.[21] Through capitalizing on the powerful social and psychological connections to professional football and specific clubs (e.g. loyalty, identity, validation, belonging) that 'being a fan' creates.[22] Using professional sport clubs for weight management,[23] weight loss[24] and more recently as a 'key' deliverer in health improvement policy.[25] This research has mainly focused on the role of football-led health improvement in men. There is little research into the role of football in health improvement in adult women; however, a recreational football-based intervention for women has been shown to be more valuable at developing social capital (than running).[26] This literature continues to support the need for further research and evaluation, which has been echoed by authors who have called for a culture change in FITC,[27] greater learning and development opportunities for practitioners[28] and the development of meaningful partnerships with higher education departments to improve research and evaluation and practice.[29]

The aims of the present study were to examine whether the FITC lead 'Motivate' programme could significantly improve >35-year old men and women's cardiovascular risk and to see if there was any significant difference in these changes over time between men and women.

Methods
Participants and settings

Notts County Football in the Community (NCFIT) was established in 1989. NCFIT have a track record of success within FITC having won a FLs Trusts Best Community Initiative for working with young men with mental health issues in 2008, whilst also receiving the Best Community Project for Health in 2010 for their Active Schools initiative (Hindley and Williamson 2013). In response to the City's health inequalities, the 'Motivate' programme was designed by NCFIT, in order to improve cardiovascular health in overweight (BMI ≥ 25 kg m^2) men over 35 years old in Nottingham City. The programme was piloted by NCFITC and developed with the support of researchers from Nottingham Trent University and as a result, was subsequently commissioned by NHS Nottingham city as a service for any overweight adult city resident to take up for reducing their weight.

Participants were volunteers and recruited onto the Motivate programme via a telephone-based lifestyle behaviour change and referral service, provided by NHS Direct and commissioned by Nottingham City Council[30], or via self-referral following a city-wide promotion campaign employed by NCFITC. This included displaying posters in various community sites (e.g. Notts County FC, community centres, workplaces, libraries, pubs, barbers, betting shops), distributing flyers and through media coverage (e.g. local press and radio, use of social media such as twitter).Participants were accepted onto the Motivate programme if they were over the age of 18, classed as overweight (with a BMI of > 25 kg m^2) and permanently lived or worked in the City of Nottingham. Only participants who were 35+ were included in the present study, as this is the population identified as at risk of CVD by the health commissioners and the population most likely to benefit their health.[31] Upon acceptance onto the programme, participants were invited to take part in the present study via an information sheet. Consent was provided by 194 men and 98 women (Table 1; 23% BME). Ethical approval was obtained from the College of Business Law and Social Science Ethics Committee at Nottingham Trent University and all participants consented to their participation in the research.

Intervention context

The Motivate programme is a free 12-week weight loss intervention that aims to encourage and facilitate overweight individuals to increase their levels of physical activity, improve their diet and improve their lifestyle risk factors related to CVD. The service was delivered in community leisure centres across Nottingham City, offering an integrated approach to weight loss. Individual weekly sessions lasting 1.5 h, combining behaviour change and dietary information delivered by NHS dietetics staff (approx. half of the session); and high intensity exercise by NCFITC

Table 1. Mean (±SD) minutes and session percentage of physical activity by category of intensity during six different exercise sessions ($n = 12$).

Physical Activity Intensity

Week	Moderate Minutes	Moderate %	Vigorous Minutes	Vigorous %	V. Vigorous Minutes	V. Vigorous %	Total MVPA Minutes	Total MVPA %
3	6.19 (2.66)	15.5–17.7	1.54 (0.81)	3.9–4.4	2.36 (1.35)	5.9–6.7	10.08 (4.44)	25.2–28.8
4	8.68 (2.93)	21.7–24.8	5.53 (2.54)	13.8–15.8	6.62 (3.20)	16.6–18.9	20.82 (3.81)	52.0–59.5
5	7.84 (2.89)	19.6–22.4	2.69 (2.45)	6.7–7.7	3.64 (3.11)	9.1–10.4	14.18 (3.20)	35.5–40.5
7	4.81 (1.38)	12.0–13.7	2.62 (0.72)	6.6–7.5	3.99 (1.39)	10.0–11.4	11.42 (2.32)	28.6–32.6
8	8.40 (2.91)	21.0–24.0	4.06 (2.70)	10.2–11.6	6.06 (3.52)	15.2–17.3	18.52 (6.69)	46.3–53.0
9	6.81 (1.75)	17.0–19.5	2.01 (0.20)	5.0–5.7	3.97 (1.03)	9.9–10.8	12.79 (1.67)	32.0–36.5

coaches (a little less than half of the session after transition from classroom to sports hall; 35–40 min), were supplemented by reduced cost membership to leisure services within the City (Figure 1).

The approach to the design, delivery and content of Motivate is similar to that of the Football Fans in Training (FFIT) intervention outlined by Gray et al.[32] Process analysis of the FFIT intervention (a men-only weight management programme delivered through Scottish Premier League (SPL) clubs) revealed that such an approach to a weight loss programme was acceptable to 35–65-year old male participants. However, distinctive from Motivate, the FFIT programme used existing football club coaches (i.e. non-specialists in weight loss) to deliver both the nutrition and behaviour change aspects of the intervention. This aspect of the process evaluation was highlighted as a point for future consideration, as some coaching staff found it difficult to adequately prepare for these sessions; some of the calculations of calorific intake for weight loss proved difficult and therefore some coaches were unable to deliver the sessions as they were intended.[33] To that end, commissioners and the research team felt that using expertise from a commissioned NHS service to deliver this aspect of the Motivate strengthened the programme and in line with recommendations in the NICE guidance.[34]

During the pilot phase of the Motivate programme development, accelerometers were used to determine the intensity of the physical activity accumulated in a sample during the exercise sessions. The same 12 men wore an Actigraph uni-dimensional accelerometer (Model GT1M, ActiGraph, LLC, Fort Walton Beach, FL) on an elastic belt provided by the manufacturer, on the waistband above their right hip, for the duration of the exercise session on six separate occasions (Table 1). Accelerometers

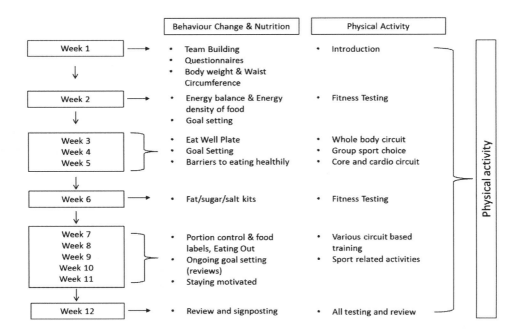

Figure 1. Schematic showing the content of the Motivate 12-week programme including behaviour change, nutrition and physical activity.

were chosen to measure physical activity as they provide a reliable, valid and objective field measure of physical activity.[35] To ensure that high and very high intensity physical activity was captured, 5 s measurement epochs were used.[36] After each session, data were downloaded from the ActiGraph and uploaded to the MAHUffe software (http://www.mrc-epid.cam.ac.uk/Research/PA/Downloads.html) for data reduction. The amount of time the men engaged in moderate, vigorous and moderate-to-vigorous intensity physical activity (MVPA) was calculated using cut-points determined by Freedson et al.[37] As women were only accepted onto the programme following the city-wide roll out of the Motivate, accelerometer data were unavailable for women during the pilot.

As an incentive to increase participants' physical activity beyond the weekly sessions, reduced cost gym memberships (including exercise classes) and courses of free swimming were offered. This incentive aimed to reduce the barrier of cost to participants, many of whom came from deprived communities within the city.[38]

Procedures

All measures (height, weight, BMI, waist circumference and cardiovascular fitness) were performed at week 1 and 12 of the programme within the physical activity sessions and were used as part of the monitoring and goal setting tasks to aid behaviour change within Motivate. Height was measured to the nearest 0.1 cm using a Leicester Height Measure (Birmingham, England[39]), with the participant stood upright and barefoot. Body mass was calculated to the nearest 0.1 kg using Seca weighing scales (Birmingham, England), and Body mass index (BMI) was calculated as $kg \cdot m^2$.

Waist circumference has been acknowledged as a substitute technique for the precise assessment of visceral fat around the abdomen.[40] Welborn and Dhaliwal[41] suggest that waist circumference is superior to BMI in predicting CVD risk, with the World Health Organization's cut-points of 102 cm in men and 88 cm in women used to denote high cadriometabolic risk within normal weight, overweight and obese BMI categories.[42] There are a number of anatomical landmarks used to measure waist circumference such as the umbilicus, the midpoint between the lowest rib and the iliac crest, and just above the iliac crest. In a study by Ross et al.[43] authors demonstrated that each of these waist circumference landmarks was equally effective in identifying all-cause mortality, CVD and diabetes risk. In order to maximise the reliability of the measurement across the different measurement sights, NCFITC coaches were trained in measuring waist circumference at the umbilicus to the nearest 0.1 cm, directly on the landmarked skin with a flexible, inelastic measuring tape.[44]

During the pilot phase of the 'Motivate' development, the Multi Stage Fitness Test was used as a submaximal estimate of cardiovascular fitness in men. However, due to the limited fitness of participants, many were unable complete the first shuttle of the test and it was observed and reported that this 'failure' had a negative effect on participants' self-confidence and was attributed to a number of individuals dropping out of the programme. While demonstrating that the programme was targeting those most at need of intervention, upon review, it was considered that a walking test would be a more inclusive and appropriate means of providing an estimate of cardiovascular fitness and indeed functional capacity.[45] The 6 Minute Walk Test (6MWT) was chosen because of its adaptability and acceptability.[46] In this case, it was easier to administer, better tolerated and better reflects activities of daily living than other walk tests performed in similar populations.[47]

To standardize the 6 min walk across each of the Motivate delivery sites, the leisure centre sports hall area was used and a 25 m track was marked out using plastic cones. Participants were required to complete as many laps of a 25 m track during the 6 min as possible, picking up a counter after each 4 lap cycle. Standardized encouragement was provided during the 6 min walk as follows:

- At minute one: 'One minute gone. Well done!'
- At minute two: 'Two minutes done. You're doing well – keep it up!'
- At minute three: 'Half way point. Three minutes remaining. Really well done!'
- At minute four: 'Last two minutes. You're doing well – keep it up!'
- At minute five: 'One minute remaining. Keep it up, you've done so well!'

At the end of the 6 min, participants were asked to stop and stand still. A tape measure was used to measure the distance from where each individual stopped in relation to the end of the lap. The distance was added to the distance denoted by the number of cones collected to calculate the total distance covered.

Statistical analysis

All data were first checked for normality using the Shapiro-Wilk test and any outliers were checked for faulty measurement. To examine whether there was a significant change in CVD risk by gender, 2-way repeated measures Analysis of Variance (ANOVA) were conducted for body mass, waist circumference and 6 min walk distance. Greenhouse-Geisser correction factors were applied where appropriate. All analyses were conducted using IBM SPSS Statistics 19 (IBM Corp.: Armonk, NY) and statistical significance was set to $p < 0.05$. The number of men and women meeting the criterion of 5% weight loss were also calculated.

Results

Table 2 demonstrates the mean (±SD) CVD risk factor scores for men and women at weeks 1 and 12 of the programme. Shapiro-Wilk analyses revealed that all data were normally distributed ($p > 0.05$). The 2-way repeated measures ANOVAs revealed a significant improvement in body weight ($F_{(1,147)} = 178.13$, $p = 0.000$), waist circumference ($F_{(1,129)} = 110.58$, $p = 0.000$) and cardiovascular fitness ($F_{(1, 94)} = 22.07$, $p = 0.000$) over time. Men were significantly heavier ($F_{(1,147)} = 9.91$, $p = 0.002$), had significantly larger waist circumferences ($F_{(1,94)} = 19.48$, $p = 0.000$) and covered significantly more meters during the 6 min walk test than women. However, no significant interaction was found between time and gender for any of the CVD risk factors, suggesting that the programme was as effective for both men and women.

Ten per cent of men and 18% of women were classified as overweight (90% and 82% classed as obese, respectively) at the beginning of the programme. While 25% men remained overweight, the percentage of men classified as obese reduced to 75% at the end of 12 weeks. Three women were able to reduce their BMI to become normal weight, with fewer classified as overweight (15%) and obese (78%) at the end of the programme. Forty-nine per cent of men ($n = 50$) and 37% of women ($n = 17$) who completed the 12-week programme achieved the target 5% weight loss. On

Table 2. Mean (±SD) anthropometric and CVD risk factor measures of men and women who took part in the Motivate programme.

	Men				Women		
	N	Week 1	Week 12	N	Week 1	Week 12
Age (years)	194	52.28 (9.74)	–	98	51.19 (9.04)	–
Height (m)	98	1.75 (0.07)	–	40	1.62 (0.07)	–
Weight (kg)	98	106.05 (17.07)*	101.09 (16.09)†	40	96.38 (17.88)*	92.11 (16.85)†
BMI (kg m^2)	98	35.27 (4.67)	33.44 (4.10)	40	36.77 (7.44)	35.12 (6.98)
Waist Circumference (cm)	92	116.89 (12.59)*	110.60 (12.06)†	39	111.23 (12.69)*	105.33 (12.06)†
6 Minute Walk (m)	64	773.30 (168.06)*	843.52 (149.96)†	32	661.14 (113.60)*	696.43 (109.19)†

*Denotes a significant main effect for gender $p < 0.05$. †Denotes a significant main effect for time $p < 0.01$.

average, men and women reduced their waist circumference by and 6.2 cm and 5.9 cm and improved the distance covered during the 6 min walk by 70.22m and 35.29 m, respectively.

Discussion

The aims of this study were to examine whether the FITC delivered Motivate weight management programme could significantly improve > 35-year old men and women's CVD risk and to determine if there was any significant difference in health risk improvement between men and women. The findings of the study show that the 12-week intervention, funded by a city council's Public Health Grant, delivered in partnership in the community was successful in achieving significant improvements in body weight, waist circumference and cardiovascular fitness in both men and women with a BMI over 25 kg m^2.

The key performance indicator of the Motivate programme from a commissioning point of view was that participants should reduce their body weight by 5% by the end of the programme. While there was a significant reduction in body mass over the 12 weeks ($p = 0.000$; 5.04 kg in men, 4.62 kg in women), 49% of men and 37% of women achieved this target. These results were less than the desired outcome set by commissioners at the outset of funding, but similar weight loss has been reported in professional Rugby settings,[48] and more recently by Hunt et al., who's RCT of the gender-sensitised FFIT healthy living programme reported 47% of men achieving a 5% weight loss.[49] When examining mean weight loss percentage, authors determined that the 4.97% weight loss of their participants was likely to be clinically beneficial. To that end, participants in the present study may also have experienced a clinical benefit to their weight loss (4.68% in men and 4.43% in women). Because of the novelty of this type of intervention for women, comparative data are unavailable. However, in an examination of a range of commercial- and primary care-led weight reduction programmes, Jolly et al. found that weight loss in women over a 12-week intervention ranged from 1.4 (±4.1 kg) and 4.4 (±4.3 kg), suggesting that women in the present study were as successful (4.27 kg) in reducing their body weight.[50] While there was not a significant reduction in BMI, 15% of men moved from the obese to a lower risk category (overweight; 4% of women) and three women were able to move from the overweight to normal weight category, significantly reducing their CVD risk.

Understanding why participants may have struggled to reduce their overall body weight is important, especially when interpreting the success of the programme for individuals and ultimately, the commissioner. Indeed, one of the possible reasons could be that participants demonstrated an overall increase in lean mass, which would underestimate weight loss. One for the possible reasons identified for this was the intensity of the physical activities performed during the exercise sessions. Accelerometer measured intensity of the physical activity sessions demonstrated that on average, half of the time spent in MVPA was of at least a vigorous intensity. This is supported by Randers et al. in their study exploring the activity profile and physiological response to football training for untrained males and females.[51] Authors demonstrated that small-sided football had the potential to create physiological adaptations and improve performance with regular training.[52] Furthermore, in their study on the physiological improvements of untrained premenopausal women undergoing a 16-week recreational football intervention, Bangsbo et al. also demonstrated that as with men, women were able to increase their muscle strength, lean mass and fitness.[53] Another stimulus for the possible improvement of lean mass in Motivate participants could be the enrolment of individuals to discounted leisure facilities offered by the local authority.

A different measure of body fatness and a more accurate measure of the distribution of fat is waist circumference.[54] Waist circumference is an independent risk factor for CVD as it represents visceral fat stored in the abdomen.[55] Abdominal fat stores occur primarily in men and are likely to be more reactive than peripheral fat stores on the basis of lipolytic activity.[56] Jensky et al. demonstrated that a standard deviation increment in the ratio of abdominal fat is significantly associated with significant increases in thoracic artery calcification[57] and in large meta analyses have demonstrated that measures of central adiposity and not BMI are significantly related to cardiovascular mortality.[58] Furthermore, research by Fujioka et al., in their study of effects of reducing intra-abdominal adiposity on glucose and lipid metabolism following a low calorie diet, found that women reduced their visceral fat to a greater extent than abdominal subcutaneous fat and that this was associated with significant metabolic improvements, when controlling for adipose tissue volume.[59] Results from the present study show a significant reduction in waist circumference over the 12 weeks, with men losing on average 6.29 and women 5.90 cm, suggesting that participants on the Motivate programme are likely to have significant metabolic improvements.

When considering waist circumference as a possible performance indicator of weight loss programmes, Egger and Dobson suggest that a 1 cm waist loss within men was equivalent to an average weight loss of approximately 0.75 kg.[60] They recommend that neither weight nor waist circumference alone is sufficient to provide a true reflection of fat loss in men. Indeed, the use of both these measures may be necessary at different stages of a programme to get a true indication of relative success in men and women, although the greater emphasis may still be put on the more potentially dangerous abdominal fat stores through waist circumference measures. Since paradoxical weight changes are more likely to occur in the early stages of a programme, research has shown that after baseline weight and waist measurements are taken, weight should not be measured again for some time, possibly 4 ± 6 weeks for best results.[61] An exception to this may be as a check where no waist loss appears to be occurring in this time. Use of both weight and waist measures in the sequence allows for individual variations in the reactivity of fat depots between men and women and may also support individuals with their weight loss goals, especially if no change is seen in relation to weight loss.

Another independent risk factor for CVD is cardiovascular fitness.[62] During the 12 weeks, participants significantly increased the distance covered in the 6 min walk, with men covering 70.22 m and women 35.29 m on average. While the 6 min walk is a somewhat crude estimate of cardiovascular fitness, it is sensitive enough to detect change over time. Most other studies have looked at football specific fitness tests such as the YoYo test[63] or a VO_{2max} test. The 6 min walk allows non-experts collect fitness data in the field with minimal and non-specialist equipment.[64] Furthermore, Enright suggests that the minimum clinically important difference (i.e. improvement) in the distance walked in a 6MWT has been estimated as 54 m (with 95% confidence limits of 37 to 71 m),[65] suggesting that men on the Motivate programme were able to increase their cardiovascular fitness to a level that would clinically improve their health. This improvement may be more important to health as well as from a motivational point of view when thinking about maintenance. As suggested by Egger and Dobson, people need to feel they are progressing even if progress falls short of the guidelines and it is therefore important to view change as a process requiring ongoing support.[66] Using feedback such as fitness improvements and waist circumference reduction may act as such.[67] To that end, follow on exit routes like the leisure card are important, especially in the maintenance of any weight loss or behaviour change post intervention.

Football remains a popular activity with men in health improvement programmes.[68] Indeed, in this intervention males were plentiful and not hard-to-engage, when recruitment was focused on their interests and delivered in non-clinical settings. While it has been reported that the complex lives of the participants can hinder retention in football-based interventions, the engagement and positive changes observed suggest that this project was able to overcome such barriers with the participants.[69] Activities were packaged in the male friendly language, which promoted sport and fitness as opposed to health. Further activities were delivered in local community venues vs. clinical settings which have been shown to be important in reaching men.[70] The successful engagement of women within the intervention is a unique and interesting finding, as there is very little research concerning this in health improvement interventions delivered by professional football clubs. Whilst gender-specific interventions have attracted 'non-fans',[71] suggesting other outcomes other than the draw of the football club may be influential in engaging 'non-fans'. The attraction of women suggests others factors may be in play. In fact, women's participation in football has increased exponentially over the past 15 years and it has overtaken netball as England's most popular female sport. There is a growing consensus belief that women and girls are gaining greater prominence in football culture and it is becoming a more normalised part of many girls' lives.[72] Consideration must be given to whether participating in football, a sport recognized as male,[73] can provide girls with the opportunity to resist traditional gender norms and perform alternative scripts of femininity.[74] This particular finding requires further research to better understand gendered identity and female participation in football club-based health improvement interventions.

Limitations and strengths

Compared to studies such as that of Hunt et al.[75] the sample size in the present study is relatively small with a high dropout rate (compared to the number of people who first enrolled onto the programme). Despite this, the population reflects the true nature of the intervention taken place in a real-world setting. While no process data were reported in this instance, qualitative data were captured from a sample of men from Motivate and will be used to better understand the reasons for dropout to help inform future programmes. However, due to the focus of the study, no process data were obtained from women and future research should include this to better understand women's reasons for engaging in a traditionally male-orientated programme. A number of studies have shown this context to be successful in improving health risk factors in men, but to the authors' knowledge, this is the first to evaluate a programme aimed to target men and women.

In terms of commissioners expectations, but in line with similar studies, there were relatively low numbers meeting 5% target (especially women), but this may be due to an increase in lean mass as a result of the high-intensity exercise programme.

In addition, despite training being provided by researchers, there may have been possible issues with measurement error associated with inexperienced and multiple testers.

Conclusion

Innovative and inclusive weight loss interventions designed and lead by Football in the Community and supported by a multidisciplinary team can be successful in significantly reducing body weight and waist circumference, improving cardiovascular fitness and reducing cardiovascular risk in overweight adults over 35 years old. The present study provides support to previous studies that have shown FITC lead programmes to improve health in men, but is the first to demonstrate that they can be as effective in women and in an inclusive mixed gender setting. When combining behaviour change, dietary information and high intensity exercise in a weight loss programme to reduce cardiovascular risk, commissioners should look beyond a 5% weight loss as the main measure of success of a programme, as body weight alone is unlikely to provide an accurate assessment of cardiovascular risk change. Future research should examine the reasons why women attend football-lead weight loss programmes and the possible impact of mixed exercise and dietary advice-based weight loss sessions on men and women's attendance and retention.

Acknowledgements

Notts County Football in the Community.

Notes

1. World Health Organization, *Global Strategy on Diet, Physical Activity and Health*.
2. Gortmaker et al., 'Changing the Future of Obesity: Science, Policy, and Action'.
3. International Association for the Study of Obesity, *International Obesity Taskforce Prevalence Data*.
4. NHS Information Centre, *Health Survey for England -2008 Trend Tables*.
5. Foresight, *The Foresight Report, Tackling Obesities: Future Choices – Modelling Future Trends in Obesity and the Impact on Health*.
6. Nottingham City Council, *Nottingham City JSNA Adult Obesity Chapter*.
7. Nottingham City Council, *Nottingham City JSNA Adult Obesity Chapter*.
8. Haslam and James, 'Obesity'; Ezzati et al., 'Selected Major Risk Factors and Global and Regional Burden of Disease'; Brown et al., 'Physical Activity and All-cause Mortality in Older Women and Men'.
9. Kopelman, 'Health Risks Associated with Overweight and Obesity'.
10. Logue et al., 'Management of Obesity: Summary of SIGN Guideline'.
11. Kahn et al., 'The Impact of Prevention on Reducing the Burden of Cardiovascular Disease'; Wang et al., 'Health and Economic Burden of the Projected Obesity Trends in the USA and the UK'.
12. Conn, Hafdahl, and Mehr, 'Interventions to Increase Physical Activity among Healthy Adults: Meta-analysis of Outcomes'; Gray et al., 'Football Fans in Training: The Development and Optimization of an Intervention Delivered Through Professional Sports Clubs to Help Men Lose Weight Become More Active and Adopt Healthier Eating Habits'; Pringle et al., 'Effect of a National Programme of Men's Health Delivered in English Premier League Football Clubs'.
13. Walters and Chadwick, 'Corporate Citizenship in Football: Delivering Strategic Benefits Through Stakeholder Engagement'; Anagnostopoulos and Shilbury, 'Implementing Corporate Social Responsibility in English Football: Towards Multi-theoretical Integration'.

14. Department for Culture, Media and Sport, *Report to the Social Exclusion Unit – Arts and Sports*; Mellor, 'Politics, Theory and Practice: "The Janus-faced Sport" English Football Community and Legacy of the "Third Way"'; Tacon, 'Football and Social Inclusion: Evaluating Social Policy'; Coalter, 'Sports Clubs, Social Capital and Social Regeneration: "Ill-defined Interventions with Hard to Follow Outcomes?"'; Bloyce and Smith, *Sport Policy and Development: An Introduction*.
15. Perkins, 'Exploring Future Relationships Between Football Clubs and Local Government'.
16. Collins and Kay, *Sport and Social Exclusion*; Spaaij, 'The Social Impact of Sport: Diversities, Complexities and Contexts'; Priest et al., 'Policy Interventions Implemented Through Sporting Organisations for Promoting Healthy Behaviour Change'.
17. Priest et al., 'Policy Interventions Implemented Through Sporting Organisations for Promoting Healthy Behaviour Change'.
18. McGuire and Fenoglio, *Football in the Community: Resources and Opportunities*; Nichols, *Sport and Crime Reduction: The Role of Sports in Tackling Youth Crime*; Parnell et al., 'Football in the Community Schemes: Exploring the Effectiveness of an Intervention in Promoting Positive Healthful Behaviour Change'.
19. Parnell et al., *Implementing Monitoring and Evaluation' Techniques within a Premier League Football in the Community Programme: A Case Study Involving Everton in the Community*.
20. Priest et al., 'Interventions Implemented Through Sporting Organisations for Increasing Participation in Sport'; 'Policy Interventions Implemented Through Sporting Organisations for Promoting Healthy Behaviour Change'.
21. Gray et al., 'Football Fans in Training: The Development and Optimization of an Intervention Delivered Through Professional Sports Clubs to Help Men Lose Weight Become More Active and Adopt Healthier Eating Habits'; Witty and White, *The Tackling Men's Health Evaluation Study*; Pringle, 'The Growing Role of Football as a Vehicle for Interventions in Mental Health Care'; Pringle et al., 'The Pre-adoption Demographic and Health Profiles of Men Participating in a Programme of Men's Health Delivered in English Premier League Football Clubs'; Brady et al., 'Sustained Benefits of a Health Project for Middle Aged Football Supporters at Glasgow Celtic and Glasgow Rangers Football Clubs'.
22. Hirt and Clarkson, 'The Psychology of Fandom: Understanding the Etiology, Motives, and Implications of Fanship'.
23. Witty and White, 'The Tackling Men's Health Evaluation Study'; Brady et al., 'Sustained Benefits of a Health Project for Middle Aged Football Supporters at Glasgow Celtic and Glasgow Rangers Football Clubs'.
24. Brady et al., 'Sustained Benefits of a Health Project for Middle Aged Football Supporters at Glasgow Celtic and Glasgow Rangers Football Clubs'.
25. Pringle, McKenna, and Zwolinsky, 'Health Improvement and Professional Football: Players on the Same Side'.
26. Ottesen, Jeppesen, and Krustrup, 'The Development of Social Capital Through Football and Running: Studying an Intervention Program for Inactive Women'.
27. Coalter, *Realising the Potential of Cultural Services: The Case for Sport*.
28. Hindley and Williamson, *Measuring and Evaluating Community Sport Projects: Notts County Football in the Community*.
29. Parnell et al., *Implementing Monitoring and Evaluation' Techniques within a Premier League Football in the Community Programme: A Case Study Involving Everton in the Community*.
30. Wilcox, Doherty, and Thompson, *Evaluation of Healthy Change – A Telephone Based Behaviour Change Service to Address CVD Risk Factors*.
31. Grey et al., 'Football Fans in Training: The Development and Optimization of an Intervention Delivered Through Professional Sports Clubs to Help Men Lose Weight Become More Active and Adopt Healthier Eating Habits'.
32. Gray et al., 'Football Fans in Training: The Development and Optimization of an Intervention Delivered Through Professional Sports Clubs to Help Men Lose Weight Become More Active and Adopt Healthier Eating Habits'.

33. Gray et al., 'Football Fans in Training: The Development and Optimization of an Intervention Delivered Through Professional Sports Clubs to Help Men Lose Weight Become More Active and Adopt Healthier Eating Habits'; Parnell et al., 'Football in the Community Schemes: Exploring the Effectiveness of an Intervention in Promoting Positive Healthful Behaviour Change'.
34. National Institute of Health and Clinical Excellence, *The Most Appropriate Means of Generic and Specific Interventions to Support Attitude Behavioural Change at Population and Community Levels*.
35. Nichols et al., 'Validity, Reliability, and Calibration of the Tritrac Accelerometer as a Measure of Physical Activity'; Brage et al. 'Re-examination of Validity and Reliability of the CSA Monitor in Walking and Running'; Trost, Mciver, and Pate, 'Conducting Accelerometer-based Activity Assessments in Field-based Research'; Welk, 'Principles of Design and Analyses for the Calibration of Accelerometry-based Activity Monitors'.
36. Welk, 'Principles of Design and Analyses for the Calibration of Accelerometry-based Activity Monitors'.
37. Freedson, Melanson, and Sirard, 'Calibration of the Computer Science and Applications, Inc. Accelerometer'.
38. Nottingham City Council, *Nottingham City JSNA Adult Obesity Chapter*; Seefeldt, Malina and Clark, 'Factors Affecting Levels of Physical Activity in Adults'.
39. Lohman, Roche, and Martorell, *Anthropometric Standardization Reference Manual*.
40. Janssen et al., 'Body Mass Index and Waist Circumference Independently Contribute to the Prediction of, Abdominal Subcutaneous and Visceral Fat'; Bigaard et al., 'Influence if Lifestyle Aspects on the Association of Body Size and Shape with All-cause Mortality in Middle Aged Men and Women'; Dagan et al., 'Waist Circumference vs. Body Mass Index in Association with Cardiorespiratory Fitness in Healthy Men and Women: A Cross Sectional Analysis of 403 Subjects'.
41. Welborn and Dhaliwal, 'Preferred Clinical Measures of Central Obesity for Predicting Mortality'.
42. Ness-Abramof and Apovian, 'Waist Circumference Measurement in Clinical Practice'.
43. Ross et al., 'Does the Relationship Between Waist Circumference, Morbidity and Mortality Depend on Measurement Protocol for Waist Circumference?'.
44. Ross et al., 'Does the Relationship Between Waist Circumference, Morbidity and Mortality Depend on Measurement Protocol for Waist Circumference?'.
45. Solway et al., 'A Qualitative Systematic Overview of the Measurement Properties of Functional Walk Tests used in the Cardiorespiratory Domain'.
46. Pringle, McKenna, and Zwolinsky, 'Health Improvement and Professional Football: Players on the Same Side'.
47. Enright, 'The 6 Minute Walk Test'.
48. Witty and White, *The Tackling Men's Health Evaluation Study*; Brady et al., 'Sustained Benefits of a Health Project for Middle Aged Football Supporters at Glasgow Celtic and Glasgow Rangers Football Clubs'.
49. Hunt et al., 'A Gender-sensitised Weight Loss and Healthy Living Programme for Overweight and Obese Men Delivered by Scottish Premier League Football Clubs (FFIT): A Pragmatic Randomised Controlled Trial'.
50. Jolly et al., 'Comparison of Range of Commercial or Primary Care Led Weight Reduction Programmes with Minimal Intervention Control for Weight Loss in Obesity: Lighten Up Randomised Controlled Trial'.
51. Randers et al., 'Activity Profile and Physiological Response to Football Training for Untrained Males and Females, Elderly and Youngsters: Influence of the Number of Players'.
52. Randers et al., 'Activity Profile and Physiological Response to Football Training for Untrained Males and Females, Elderly and Youngsters: Influence of the Number of Players'.
53. Bangsbo et al., 'Performance Enhancements and Muscular Adaptations of a 16-week Recreational Football Intervention for Untrained Women'.
54. Bangsbo et al., 'Performance Enhancements and Muscular Adaptations of a 16-week Recreational Football Intervention for Untrained Women'.

55. Janssen et al., 'Body Mass Index and Waist Circumference Independently Contribute to the Prediction of, Abdominal Subcutaneous and Visceral Fat'.
56. Brown, 'Waist Circumference in Primary Care'; Egger and Dobson, 'Clinical Measures of Obesity and Weight Loss in Men'.
57. Jensky et al., 'The Association Between Abdominal Body Composition and Vascular Calcification'.
58. Czernichow et al., 'Body Mass Index, Waist Circumference and Waist–hip Ratio: Which is the Better Discriminator of Cardiovascular Disease Mortality Risk? Evidence from an Individual-participant Meta-analysis of 82 864 participants from nine cohort studies'.
59. Fujioka et al., 'Improvement of Glucose and Lipid Metabolism Associated with Selective Reduction Of Intra-Abdominal Visceral Fat in Premenopausal Women with Visceral Fat Obesity'.
60. Brown, 'Waist Circumference in Primary Care'; Egger and Dobson, 'Clinical Measures of Obesity and Weight Loss in Men'.
61. Brown, 'Waist Circumference in Primary Care'; Egger and Dobson, 'Clinical Measures of Obesity and Weight Loss in Men'.
62. Fujioka et al., 'Improvement of Glucose and Lipid Metabolism Associated with Selective Reduction of Intra-abdominal Visceral Fat in Premenopausal Women with Visceral Fat Obesity'.
63. Jolly et al., 'Comparison of Range of Commercial or Primary Care Led Weight Reduction Programmes with Minimal Intervention Control for Weight Loss in Obesity: Lighten Up Randomised Controlled Trial'.
64. Solway et al., 'A Qualitative Systematic Overview of the Measurement Properties of Functional Walk Tests Used in the Cardiorespiratory Domain'.
65. Solway et al., 'A Qualitative Systematic Overview of the Measurement Properties of Functional Walk Tests Used in the Cardiorespiratory Domain'.
66. Egger and Dobson, 'Clinical Measures of Obesity and Weight Loss in Men'.
67. Brown, 'Waist Circumference in Primary Care'; Egger and Dobson, 'Clinical Measures of Obesity and Weight Loss in Men'.
68. Gray et al., 'Football Fans in Training: The Development and Optimization of an Intervention Delivered Through Professional Sports Clubs to Help Men Lose Weight Become More Active and Adopt Healthier Eating Habits'; Pringle et al., 'Effect of a National Programme of Men's Health Delivered in English Premier League Football Clubs.'
69. Fitzgerald et al., 'Muscular Fitness and All-cause Mortality: Prospective Observations'.
70. Gray et al., 'Football Fans in Training: The Development and Optimization of an Intervention Delivered Through Professional Sports Clubs to Help Men Lose Weight Become More Active and Adopt Healthier Eating Habits'; Pringle et al., 'Effect of a National Programme of Men's Health Delivered in English Premier League Football Clubs'.
71. Pringle et al., 'Effect of a National Programme Of Men's Health Delivered in English Premier League Football Clubs.'
72. Sherry, '(Re)engaging Marginalized Groups Through Sport: The Homeless World Cup'.
73. Caudwell, 'Women's Experiences of Sexuality Within Football Contexts: A Particular and Located Footballing Epistemology'.
74. Scraton et al., 'It's Still a Man's Game?' The Experiences of Top Level European Women Footballers'; Butler, *Gender Trouble*.
75. Hunt et al., 'A Gender-sensitised Weight Loss and Healthy Living Programme for Overweight and Obese Men Delivered by Scottish Premier League Football Clubs (FFIT): A Pragmatic Randomised Controlled Trial'.

References

Anagnostopoulos, C., and D. Shilbury. 'Implementing Corporate Social Responsibility in English Football: Towards Multi-theoretical Integration'. *Sport, Business and Management: An International Journal* 3 (2013): 268–84.
Bangsbo, J., J.J. Nielsen, M. Mohr, M.B. Randers, B.R. Krustrup, J. Brito, L. Nybo, and P. Krustrup. 'Performance Enhancements and Muscular Adaptations of a 16-week Recreational Football Intervention for Untrained Women'. *Scandinavian Journal of Medicine & Science in Sports* 20 (2010): 24–30.

Bigaard, J., J. Christensen, A. Tjønneland, Birthe Lykke Thomsen, K. Overvad, and T.I.A. Sørensen. 'Influence of Lifestyle Aspects on the Association of Body Size and Shape with All-cause Mortality in Middle-aged Men and Women'. *Obesity Facts* 3 (2010): 252–60.

Bloyce, D., and A. Smith. *Sport Policy and Development: An Introduction*. London: Routledge, 2010.

Brady, A., C. Perry, D. Murdoch, and G. McKay. 'Sustained Benefits of a Health Project for Middle Aged Football Supporters at Glasgow Celtic and Glasgow Rangers Football Clubs'. *European Heart Journal* 24 (2010): 2696–98.

Brage, S., N. Wedderkopp, P.W. Franks, L.B. Andersen, and K. Froberg. 'Reexamination of Validity and Reliability of the CSA Monitor in Walking and Running'. *Medicine & Science in Sports & Exercise* 35 (2003): 1447–54.

Brown, P. 'Waist Circumference in Primary Care'. *Primary Care Diabetes* 3 (2009): 259–61.

Brown, W.D., D. McLaughlin, J. Leung, K. A. McCaul, L. Flicker, O. P. Almeida, G. J. Hankey, D. Lopez, and A. Dobson. 'Physical Activity and All-cause Mortality in Older Women and Men'. *British Journal of Sports Medicine* 46 (2012): 664–8.

Butler, J. *Gender Trouble*. New York: Routledge, 1990.

Caudwell, J. 'Women's Experiences of Sexuality within Football Contexts: A Particular and Located Footballing Epistemology'. *Football Studies* 5 (2002): 24–45.

Coalter, F. *Realising the Potential of Cultural Services: The Case for Sport*. London: LGA Publications, 2001.

Coalter, F. 'Sports Clubs, Social Capital and Social Regeneration: 'Ill-defined Interventions with Hard to Follow Outcomes'?' *Sport in Society* 10 (2007): 37–559.

Collins, M., and T. Kay. *Sport and Social Exclusion*. London: Routledge, 2003.

Conn, V., A. Hafdahl, and D. Mehr. 'Interventions to Increase Physical Activity among Healthy Adults: Meta-analysis of Outcomes'. *American Journal of Public Health* 101 (2011): 751–8.

Czernichow, S., A.-P. Kengne, E. Stamatakis, M. Hamer, and G.D. Batty. 'Body Mass Index, Waist Circumference and Waist–Hip Ratio: Which is the Better Discriminator of Cardiovascular Disease Mortality Risk? Evidence from an Individual-Participant Meta-Analysis of 82 864 Participants from Nine Cohort Studies'. *Obesity Reviews* 12 (2011): 680–7.

Dagan, S.S., S. Segev, I. Novikov, and R. Danker. 'Waist Circumference vs. Body Mass Index in Association with Cardiorespiratory Fitness in Healthy Men and Women: A Cross Sectional Analysis of 403 Subjects'. *Nutritional Journal* 12 (2013): 12–20.

Department for Culture, Media and Sport. *Report to the Social Exclusion Unit – Arts and Sports*. London: HMSO, 1999.

Egger, G., and A. Dobson 'Clinical Measures of Obesity and Weight Loss in Men'. *International Journal of Obesity* 24 (2000): 354–7.

Enright, P.L. 'The 6 Minute Walk Test'. *Respiratory Care* 48 (2003): 783–5.

Ezzati, M., A.D. Lopez, A. Rodgers, S. Vander Hoorn, and C.J. Murray. 'Selected Major Risk Factors and Global and Regional Burden of Disease'. *The Lancet* 360 (2002): 1347–60.

Fitzgerald, S.J., C.E. Barlow, J.B. Kampert, R.R. Morrow, A.W. Jackson, and S.N. Blair. 'Muscular Fitness and All-cause Mortality: Prospective Observations'. *Journal of Physical Activity & Health* 1 (2002): 7–18.

Foresight. *The Foresight Report, Tackling Obesities: Future Choices – Modelling Future Trends in Obesity and the Impact on Health*. London: Department for Innovation, Universities and Skills, 2007.

Freedson, P.S., E. Melanson, and J. Sirard. 'Calibration of the Computer Science and Applications, Inc. Accelerometer'. *Medicine & Science in Sports & Exercise* 30 (1998): 777–81.

Fujioka, S., Y. Matsuzawa, K. Tokunaga, T. Kawamoto, T. Kobatake, Y. Keno, K. Kotani, S. Yoshida, and S. Tarui. 'Improvement of Glucose and Lipid Metabolism Associated with Selective Reduction of Intra-abdominal Visceral Fat in Premenopausal Women with Visceral Fat Obesity'. *International Journal of Obesity* 15 (1991): 853–9.

Gortmaker, S., B.A. Swinburn, D. Levy, R. Carter, P.L. Mabry, D.T. Finegood, T. Huang, T. Marsh, and M.J. Moodie. 'Changing the Future of Obesity: Science, Policy, and Action'. *The Lancet* 378 (2011): 838–47.

Gray, C.M., K. Hunt, N. Mutrie, A.S. Anderson, J. Leishman, L. Dalgarno, and S. Wyke. 'Football Fans in Training: The Development and Optimization of an Intervention Delivered Through Professional Sports Clubs to Help Men Lose Weight, Become More Active and Adopt Healthier Eating Habits'. *BMC Public Health* 13 (2013): 232–49.

Haslam, D.W., and W.P. James. 'Obesity'. *The Lancet* 366 (2005): 1197–209.

Hindley, D., and D. Williamson. 'Measuring and Evaluating Community Sports Projects: Notts County Football in the Community'. In *Routledge Handbook of Sport and Corporate Social Responsibility*, ed. J.L. Paramio-Salcines, K. Babiak, and G. Walters. London: Routledge, 2013.

Hirt, E.R., and J.J. Clarkson. 'The Psychology of Fandom: Understanding the Etiology, Motives, and Implications of Fanship'. In *Consumer Behavior Knowledge for Effective Sports and Event Marketing*, ed. L.R. Kahle and A.G. Close, 59–85. New York: Routledge, 2010.

Hunt, K., S. Wyke, C.M. Gray, A.S. Anderson, A. Brady, C. Bunn, P.T. Donnan, et al. 'A Gender-sensitised Weight Loss and Healthy Living Programme for Overweight and Obese Men Delivered by Scottish Premier League Football Clubs (FFIT): A Pragmatic Randomised Controlled Trial'. *The Lancet* 383 (2014): 1211–21.

International Association for the Study of Obesity. *International Obesity Taskforce Prevalence Data*. IOFT. http://www.ioft.org/database/index.asp.

Janssen, I., S.B. Heymsfield, D.B. Allison, D.P. Kotler, and R. Ross. 'Body Mass Index and Waist Circumference Independently Contribute to the Prediction of Abdominal Subcutaneous and Visceral Fat'. *American Journal of Clinical Nutrition* 75 (2002): 683–8.

Jensky, N.E., M.H. Criqui, C.M. Wright, C.L. Wassel, J.E. Alcaraz, and M.A. Allison. 'The Association Between Abdominal Body Composition and Vascular Calcification'. *Obesity* 19 (2011): 2418–24.

Jolly, K., A. Lewis, J. Beach, J. Denley, P. Adab, J.J. Deeks, A. Daley, and P. Aveyard. 'Comparison of Range of Commercial or Primary Care Led Weight Reduction Programmes with Minimal Intervention Control for Weight Loss in Obesity: Lighten up Randomised Controlled Trial'. *British Medical Journal* (2011): 343–59.

Kahn, R., R.M. Robertson, R. Smith, and D. Eddy. 'The Impact of Prevention on Reducing the Burden of Cardiovascular Disease'. *Circulation* 118 (2008): 576–85.

Kopelman, P. 'Health Risks Associated with Overweight and Obesity'. *Obesity Reviews* 8, no. s1 (2007): 13–7.

Logue, J., L. Thompson, F. Romanes, D.C. Wilson, J. Thompson, and N. Sattar. 'Management of Obesity: Summary of SIGN Guideline'. *British Medical Journal* 340 (2010): c154.

Lohman, T.G., A.F. Roche, and R. Martorell, eds. *Anthropometric Standardization Reference Manual*. Champaign, IL: Human Kinetics, 1988. http://www.bmj.com/content/340/bmj.c154

McGuire, B., and R. Fenoglio. *Football in the Community: Resources and Opportunities*. Manchester Metropolitan University, Department of Exercise and Sport Science, 2004.

Mellor, G. '"The Janus-faced Sport": English Football, Community and the Legacy of the "Third Way"'. *Soccer & Society* 9 (2008): 313–24.

National Institute of Health and Clinical Excellence. *The Most Appropriate Means of Generic and Specific Interventions to Support Attitude Behavioural Change at Population and Community Levels*. London: National Institute of Health and Clinical Excellence, 2007.

Ness-Abramof, R., and C.M. Apovian. 'Waist Circumference Measurement in Clinical Practice'. *Nutrition in Clinical Practice* 23 (2008): 397–404.

NHS Information Centre. *Health Survey for England-2008 Trend Tables*. NHS. http://www.ic.nhs.uk/statistics-and-data-collections/health-and-lifestyles-related-surveys/health-survey-for-england/health-survey-for-england–2008-trend.

Nichols, G. *Sport and Crime Reduction: The Role of Sports in Tackling Youth Crime*. London: Routledge, 2007.

Nichols, J.F., C.G. Morgan, J.A. Sarkin, J.F. Sallis, and K.J. Calfas. 'Validity, Reliability, and Calibration of the Tritrac Accelerometer as a Measure of Physical Activity'. *Medicine & Science in Sports & Exercise* 31 (1999): 908–12.

Nottingham City Council. *Nottingham City JSNA Adult Obesity Chapter*. Nottingham City Council. http://www.nottinghaminsight.org.uk/insight/jsna/adults/jsna-adult-obesity.aspx.

Ottesen, L., R.S. Jeppesen, and B.R. Krustrup. 'The Development of Social Capital through Football and Running: Studying an Intervention Program for Inactive Women'. *Scandinavian Journal of Medicine & Science in Sports* 20 (2013): 118–31.

Parnell, D., G. Stratton, B. Drust, and D. Richardson. Implementing Monitoring and Evaluation' Techniques within a Premier League Football in the Community Programme: A Case Study Involving Everton in the Community. In *Routledge Handbook of Sport and Corporate Social Responsibility*, ed. J.L. Paramio-Salcines, K. Babiak, and G. Walters. London: Routledge, 2013.

Parnell, D., G. Stratton, B. Drust, and D. Richardson. 'Football in the Community Schemes: Exploring the Effectiveness of an Intervention in Promoting Healthful Behaviour Change'. *Soccer & Society* 14 (2013): 35–51.

Perkins, S. 'Exploring Future Relationships Between Football Clubs and Local Government'. In *The Future of Football: Challenges for the Twenty-first Century*, ed. J. Garland, D. Malcolm, and M. Rowe, 102–13. London: Frank Cass, 2000.

Priest, N.R. Armstrong, J. Doyle, and E. Waters. 'Interventions Implemented Through Sporting Organisations for Increasing Participation in Sport'. *Cochrane Database System Review* 3 (2008a) No.: CD004812. 1–17. doi:10.1002/14651858.CD004812.pub3.

Priest, N., R. Armstrong, J. Doyle, and E. Waters. 'Policy Interventions Implemented Through Sporting Organisations for Promoting Healthy Behaviour Change'. *Cochrane Database System Review* 3 (2008b) No.: CD004809. 1–18. doi:10.1002/14651858.CD004809.pub3.

Pringle, A. 'The Growing Role of Football as a Vehicle for Interventions in Mental Health Care'. *Journal of Psychiatric and Mental Health Nursing* 16 (2009): 553–7.

Pringle, A., J. McKenna, and S. Zwolinsky. 'Health Improvement and Professional Football: Players on the Same Side?' *Journal of Policy Research in Tourism, Leisure and Events* 5 (2013): 207–12.

Pringle, A., S. Zwolinsky, J. McKenna, A. Daly-Smith, S. Robertson, and A. White. 'Effect of a National Programme of Men's Health Delivered in English Premier League Football Clubs'. *Public Health* 127 (2013): 18–26.

Pringle, A., S. Zwolinsky, A. Smith, S. Robertson, J. McKenna, and A. White. 'The Pre-adoption Demographic and Health Profiles of Men Participating in a Programme of Men's Health Delivered in English Premier League Football Clubs'. *Public Health* 125 (2011): 411–6.

Randers, M.B., L. Nybo1, J. Petersen, J.J. Nielsen, L. Christiansen, M. Bendiksen, J. Brito1 et al. 'Activity Profile and Physiological Response to Football Training for Untrained Males and Females, Elderly and Youngsters: Influence of the Number of Players'. *Scandinavian Journal of Medicine Science and Sports* 20 (2010): S14–23.

Ross, R., T. Berentzen, A.J. Bradshaw, I. Janssen, H.S. Kahn, P.T. Katzmarzyk, J.L. Kuk, et al. 'Does the Relationship Between Waist Circumference, Morbidity and Mortality Depend on Measurement Protocol for Waist Circumference?' *Obesity Reviews* 9 (2008): 312–25.

Scraton, S., K. Fasting, G. Pfister, and A. Bunuel. '"It's Still A Man's Game?" The Experiences of Top-level European Women Footballers'. *International Review for the Sociology of Sport* 34 (1999): 99–111.

Seefeldt, V., R.M. Malina, and M.A. Clark. 'Factors Affecting Levels of Physical Activity in Adults'. *Sports Medicine* 32 (2002): 143–68.

Sherry, E. '(Re)engaging Marginalized Groups through Sport: The Homeless World Cup'. *International Review for the Sociology of Sport* 45 (2010): 59–71.

Solway, S., D. Brooks, Y. Lacasse, and S. Thomas. 'A Qualitative Systematic Overview of the Measurement Properties of Functional Walk Tests Used in the Cardiorespiratory Domain'. *Chest Journal* 119 (2001): 256–70.

Spaaij, R. 'The Social Impact of Sport: Diversities, Complexities and Contexts'. *Sport in Society* 12 (2009): 1109–17.

Tacon, R. 'Football and Social Inclusion: Evaluating Social Policy'. *Managing Leisure* 12 (2007): 1–23.

Trost, S.G., K.L. Mciver, and R.R. Pate. 'Conducting Accelerometer-based Activity Assessments in Field-based Research'. *Medicine & Science in Sports & Exercise* 37 (2005): S531–43.

Walters, G., and S. Chadwick. 'Corporate Citizenship in Football: Delivering Strategic Benefits through Stakeholder Engagement'. *Management Decision* 47 (2009): 51–66.

Wang, Y., K. McPherson, T. Marsh, S. Gortmaker, and M. Brown. 'Health and Economic Burden of the Projected Obesity Trends in the USA and the UK'. *The Lancet* 378 (2011): 815–25.

Welborn, T.A., and S.S. Dhaliwal. 'Preferred Clinical Measures of Central Obesity for Predicting Mortality'. *European Journal of Clinical Nutrition* 61 (2007): 1373–79.

Welk, G.J. 'Principles of Design and Analyses for the Calibration of Accelerometry-based Activity Monitors'. *Medicine & Science in Sports & Exercise* (2005): S501–11.

Wilcox, J., R. Doherty, and H. Thompson. *Evaluation of Healthy Change – A Telephone Based Behaviour Change Service to Address CVD Risk Factors*. London: PHE Annual Conference, 2013.

Witty, K., and A. White. *The Tackling Men's Health Evaluation Study*. Leeds: Centre for Men's Health, Leeds Metropolitan University, 2010.

World Health Organization. *Global Strategy on Diet, Physical Activity and Health*. Geneva: WHO, 2004.

Assessing the impact of football-based health improvement programmes: stay onside, avoid own goals and score with the evaluation!

Andy Pringle, Jackie Hargreaves, Lorena Lozano, Jim McKenna and Stephen Zwolinsky

Centre for Active Lifestyles, Leeds Metropolitan University, Leeds, UK

> Health improvement is an important strand of the Premier League's 'Creating Chances' strategy. Through community programmes, professional football clubs offer health-enhancing interventions for a number of different priority groups at risk from a range of lifestyle-related health conditions. However, while national guidance recommends evaluating health improvement interventions, concerns remain about how to do this most effectively. This study aims to investigate the popularity of football-based health improvement schemes and assess the challenges associated with their evaluation. Adapted from existing methodologies, a semi-structured questionnaire was administered to an 'expert' sample ($n = 3$) of football-led health evaluators. The sample was selected because of their experience and knowledge of performing evaluations of football-led health improvement programmes. Our 'experts' offered reasons for the popularity of football settings as channels for health improvement (including the reach of the club badge and the popularity of football), the justification for evaluating such schemes (including confirming effectiveness and efficiency) and the challenges of implementing evaluations (capacity, commitment and capability). Finally, a selection of key considerations for the evaluation of the impact of football-led health improvement programmes (obtaining expert guidance, building capacity and planning for evaluations) are discussed.

Introduction

The Chief Medical Officer's report confirms that participation in regular physical activity in line with the recommended guidelines can provide an array of substantial health benefits.[1] Yet fewer than 39% of men and 29% of women met the current recommendations for an active lifestyle.[2] Given these low levels of physical activity participation, concerns prevail over the health and well-being of the UK population, along with thoughts as to how best to intervene. Professional football clubs are being deployed as channels for connecting with communities over their health and physical activity[3] including those hard-to-engage groups, with health improvement schemes.[4] This extends to those individuals who encounter substantial barriers for engaging in health behaviour change and in doing so, do not/would not make use of traditional health care services.[5] Given the importance of deploying robust evaluation and monitoring approaches for identifying programme impact, anxieties remain over the extent to which football-based health improvement schemes are being evaluated.[6] Failing to evaluate the effect of such interventions raises the possibility that their impact on public health will be lost.

Between 2010 and 2022, it is estimated that the number of people presenting a 20% risk of developing cardio-vascular disease (CVD) in the UK is set to rise from 3.5 to 4.5 million people.[7] CVD and other inactivity-related conditions pose not only great personal costs to individual sufferers and their families through loss of functionality, livelihood and pain,[8] but also significant annual financial expense to UK health care services.[9] Indeed, the cost of inactivity-related conditions to the NHS was estimated to be in the region of £1b pa.[10] Moreover, the financial impact of inactivity-related conditions is set to continue rising; by £2b annually up to 2030.[11] Understanding that the NHS is already under extreme pressure to meet health needs, amidst sustained reductions in government funding,[12] efforts to facilitate positive changes in health behaviours[13] are an important component of effective and cost-effective health care strategies. The drive for better health at lower cost is clearly on.

Recognizing that a common suite of problematic health behaviours is at the heart of non-communicable diseases (NCDs),[14] Public Health is increasingly faced with the further problem of how best to intervene. Typically, large-scale health improvement schemes have had a limited effect on changes in health behaviours, and physical activity is no different with the majority of the population failing to meet guidelines.[15] This is because, there are few universal drivers of behaviour change, meaning that each community is likely to be distinctive for what prompts and sustains behaviour change.[16] One such distinctive community is made up of those who follow, attend and spectate on sporting and leisure events. Indeed, people interested in sport may be assumed to be uniquely responsive to attempts to promote lifestyle change, especially around physical activity. Either way, from a social perspective, sporting clubs represent important anchors and focal points of communities while their potential for promoting health deserves close consideration.[17]

From a Public Health perspective, sporting clubs can offer important channels for connecting with people regarding their health,[18] typically, although not exclusively, through sport and physical activity.[19] More specifically, professional football clubs have been identified as holding latent potential for making connections with individuals whose health issues remain unaffected by conventional provision.[20] This is especially important, as new ways of commissioning and providing health services will offer greater roles and responsibilities for non-NHS providers, including for-profit, not-for-profit and voluntary organizations; some of these providers may have little experience as health care providers in any, let alone unconventional, settings.

In the UK, a number of community health improvement services already operate within professional football clubs. Through their football-in-the-community (FitC) schemes, clubs have a track record of delivering interventions aimed at improving the health profiles of individuals and the groups they serve. From a strategic perspective, there is a strong resonance between the concerns of Public Health and the five strands of the Premier League's 'Creating Chances' programme especially in the specific 'Health' theme. Creating Chances uses positive associations with the football 'brand' to support the health improvement of individuals and communities.[21] Resources made available through the combined efforts of Creating Chances, local partners and the participating clubs, have all helped to deliver health improvement interventions for a number of different health priority groups and conditions. More generally, football-led health interventions have targeted children, adults and older adults.[22] Interventions have also been used to tackle behaviours linked to NCDs, such as substance use, obesity, CVD and mental health.[23]

In doing so, deliverers aspire to appeal to the interests of possible participants through the trappings of a popular, highly visible sport: football. For potential recruits entering into health improvements, this interest may not have been converted into actual playing of the game, or indeed, participation in any physical activity, but rather into other health-related activities. Importantly, football's powerful appeal helps to include groups that might otherwise be regarded as 'hard-to-engage'[24] and who are unlikely to attend conventional health promotion activities.[25] Indeed, football has also been used as a strategy for social inclusion by intentionally attempting to connect with those groups referred to as 'hard-to-engage' and 'unreached', including those not using health services.[26] These communities and groups are defined in this way, because they are impacted by factors which determine whether or not a connection can be made, as well as the intensity of those connections.[27]

Research suggests that these factors act *within* the expectations that programme planners typically consider in relation to age, gender, location, income, ethnicity and/or language.[28] Within each of these powerful factors are further elements that can overwhelm planners' expectations about how well their interventions will 'work'. Without careful consideration of what makes these groups hard-to-engage or what leaves them unreached, and by offering suitable programme modifications, physical activity provision is only likely to maintain the status quo.[29]

It is also important to appreciate that the designation of 'hard-to-engage' extends into many areas of daily life. Perhaps because of their restricted access to information that they trust, hard-to-engage individuals are often slow to hear about and take up new programmes, even when they are tailored to specific needs.[30] This converts into hard-to-engage groups being under-represented in figures for the uptake and use of services such as physical activity.[31] For instance, one of the largest English physical activity interventions was Walking the Way to Health and this specifically targeted those who took little regular activity and/or lived in areas of poor health and who faced barriers to engagement in regular exercise.[32] Yet, some walking interventions largely recruited relatively educated and affluent recruits.[33] Similar difficulties also exist with regard to particular groups securing access to health care provision.[34]

Whilst difficulties exist with the recruitment of such populations into interventions, once there, a different set of challenges emerge, especially around how to engage them in the evaluations of the programmes they populate.[35] More positively, a number of 'hard-to-engage' groups have been at the centre for football-based health improvement schemes with associated evaluations of their effectiveness.[36] This responsiveness is encouraging and indicates more that these groups are better described as 'unreached' rather than 'hard-to-reach'.[37]

Beyond establishing acceptable interventions, current thinking holds that it is not only important to identify which interventions work best, but also how these activities are implemented.[38] National guidance recommends that behavioural change interventions are effectively evaluated.[39] In spite of these directives, concerns remain over the extent to which rigorous, valid and acceptable evaluation is undertaken let alone to good effect.[40] With this understanding, it is easy to see why, on occasions, assessing the effect of health improvement programmes is not given greater priority.

More specifically, the challenges typically faced by those tasked with implementing evaluations will include personal and collective *commitment, capacity and capabilities* to undertake and complete this work.[41] These issues affect health improvement interventions delivered within community settings, including professional football clubs.[42] Given their backgrounds, education, training and organizational priorities, it will be no surprise that only a few deliverers are equipped to deploy the necessary resources, skills and expertise to undertake an evaluation on top of the pressure needed to deliver high-quality, responsive interventions.[43] In supporting evaluation, guidance is available from a number of sources.[44] At the same time, it is important to learn how to successfully undertake community-based evaluation, where these can be found.

Methodology and background
Purpose of the study
Given the rise of football-based health improvement programmes and the need to evaluate their impact, this paper explores three important objectives which we pose as questions. (I) Based on the increased need to assess their effectiveness, what are the challenges in monitoring and evaluating football-based health improvement interventions? (II) Assuming evaluation is integral to the implementation of football-based health improvement schemes, what are the key activities that deliverers should consider when evaluating their schemes? (III) What are the reasons for the apparent popularity of football-based health improvement interventions?

Study sampling
To investigate these key questions, methods and sampling have been adapted from an earlier published study with similar aspirations around identifying delivery factors, evaluating community health interventions and/or evaluating physical activity interventions.[45] In selecting our approach, we consider principles set out by Palys who suggests that 'there is no single 'best' sampling strategy because the 'best' strategy will depend on the context of the research and the research objectives'.[46] We then administered a semi-structured questionnaire with an 'expert sample' who were firmly linked to the purpose of the research. In our recruits, 'expertise' was linked to an advanced understanding of the evaluation of football-led health improvement schemes for a number of priority groups. Furthermore, Stake in Curtis has suggested that 'where qualitative research requires cases to be chosen, nothing is more important than making a proper selection of those cases'.[47] With this in mind, we identified our sample against two further criteria: (I) Impact: they demonstrate a commitment to informing policy and practice through their work. (II) Credibility: they share the results of their work both at the meetings of relevant professional bodies and agencies, and both nationally and/or internationally.

Methods of investigation
Instrumentation and data management
We used a semi-structured questionnaire adapted from previous research[48] and deployed this method to investigate the three study objectives previously reported.

Identified 'experts' were invited to participate by e-mail; this message also contained the questionnaire and instructions for completion. Participants were permitted 10 working days to complete and return their responses. Previous research has indicated that this would allow sufficient time for our volunteers to carefully consider and then offer a reflective response for each question, in around 200 words or less.[49] In this way, the questionnaires yielded qualitative data. Once questionnaires were returned, two researchers read and familiarized themselves with the responses and generated initial codes. Individually, each researcher then collated codes, with examples, into potential themes. To triangulate their codes, the researchers reviewed and refined the coding to confirm the dominant themes and how they were best defined. Given the importance of the context of the research we performed, we have elected to report participant responses verbatim.[50] This aspires to preserve the integrity, focus and context of their responses. In presenting the findings, we remained 'close' to the data. In doing so, have used our research objectives as an organizing framework to present, and manage the data.[51] In the Discussion, we offer interpretation/synthesis of the emergent themes according to (I) our research objectives, (II) key literature and guidance on delivering football-led health improvement schemes, and (III) advice and recommendations for evaluating community health and physical activity programmes based on the literature.[52] In doing so, we draw out the implications for evaluating football-led health improvement schemes, as this is an important element of future programme delivery.

Findings

Participants

With the lead authors posing the questions, our respondents were asked to respond to four key questions in turn. Prior to the first question, we asked our 'experts' (EX) to introduce themselves along with the scope of their current work.

> **EX 01:** is a practitioner involved in evaluating a number of football-led health improvement programmes delivered at Premier and Football League clubs. Most notably among these has been a national evaluation of men's health in 16 English Premier League and Championship football clubs. Expert 01 has also been involved in evaluating football-led interventions with older adults, as well as other community health interventions.
>
> **EX 02:** is a practitioner investigating the effect of commercial male-specific weight management interventions delivered on behalf of a local authority and in community venue in Northern England, United Kingdom. These interventions take place in football-related venues and deploy football as one of a suite of physical activities within the programme.
>
> **EX 03:** is a practitioner investigating the effects of football-led health improvement interventions aimed at (I) mental health promotion in adults and (II) health improvement in older adults. Both programmes are delivered in and by a professional football club located in English Football League. Interventions involve both sport and physical activity as modes of exercise.

We start with our first question, in what ways have you seen football and football-related settings being used to promote better health? Why is this approach suddenly so popular?

FOOTBALL, COMMUNITY AND SOCIAL INCLUSION

EX 01: There are many examples of football settings being used to promote better health, programme including 'It's a Goal', 'Extra Time' and 'Fit Fans'. I think these schemes have become so popular due to the interest generated by the clubs hosting the interventions and the opportunities they provide to mix with professional players at prestigious venues. This is a huge draw for many people, and the ability of such interventions to reach out to large numbers of individuals who don't traditionally engage with health promotion cannot be underestimated. A lot of interventions have actively listened to the needs of the participants and don't necessarily have a blanket offer of football – that may be off-putting to some groups – but instead promote a range of activity opportunities. For example, one of the 'Premier League Men's Health' interventions at Newcastle United offered a midnight badminton league designed to engage shift workers from the south Asian community. This also highlights how flexible clubs can be providing a desirable avenue activity alongside social interaction. One of the key draws of these programmes are the informal and non-clinical approaches to health promotion which help appeal to certain groups. Interventions have tended to avoid instructional or directive approaches linked to more clinical settings and as a result seen fantastic engagement and minimal attrition rates.

EX 03: I have seen football being used to promote better health through both professional football clubs and community groups. For instance, I have been involved in projects provided by professional football to improve the health of older adults, where a variety of physical activities were provided. Football as an activity was not offered, but a range of social and physical activities were provided and these were based at the football club. This appeared to be an accessible and acceptable setting for the participants to attend and importantly, for older adults, an opportunity to socialize. Furthermore, this particular project attracted females as well as males in equal measure, which other football interventions do not always achieve or indeed intend to achieve. I have also witnessed football being used for community dwelling adults with mental health problems, such as anxiety and depression. I have been involved in projects where football is provided by the clubs for people with mental health concerns, and also where football is provided by mental health community groups in community locations such as council run sports centres. I see these football-led approaches as popular because the game is seen by many as a normal and acceptable activity to participate in. It is a normalizing activity which encourages social interaction, which for both people with mental health problems and older adults can be limited by opportunities.

EX 02: I am currently involved in assessing the effect of football centred health improvement for a key health priority group. My work involves investigating men's experiences of weight problems before, during and after participating in a weight loss programme. The sessions in this programme include informative activities about healthy lifestyles and also exercise classes where football prevails as a team sport. My research differs somewhat, as interventions are not delivered by professional football clubs, but use football related settings to deliver health improvement activities. For a number of men, football as an activity is an ideal means to approach a captive audience and its success has been documented in the research. Yet, not all men like football. In some locations, football is not the dominant professional sport such as those towns where Rugby League or Union is king!

Is it really that important to assess the impact of football-led health improvement interventions?

EX 03: It is imperative that interventions are assessed so that we know if they are successful and if so, which parts of the intervention. Where feasible, objective measures of health status and/or behaviour should be used, alongside a qualitative exploration of the individual's voices. The objective measures are important to investigate what health outcomes did or did not improve, however, if this is not feasible subjective self-report measures could be implemented. Hearing an individual's voice is essential for the evaluation and to help us to understand not only what, but also how and why an intervention worked. This feedback is essential to the development of interventions. It is also important to evaluate health interventions for ethical purposes. If interventions are not evaluated they may be delivered with limited or no evidence-based practice to support their implementation. Therefore, if interventions are not evaluated there will be little evidence to implement new interventions. Consequently, interventions may be delivered which are poorly designed and may have no impact or a negative impact on the intended participants, which is an ethical consideration.

EX 01: Absolutely, if you don't measure it, you can't manage it, and if you can't manage it there are limited avenues for assessing impact. Ultimately, evidence on programme effects, or a lack of it, is an influential factor when it comes to allocating funding for health intervention. Therefore, evaluation is essential for championing the role of football-led health interventions. Nonetheless, assessing the impact of interventions can be seen as time consuming and even problematic in some circles taking a lower priority over service delivery and day to day running. It is important here to remember some advice from the World Health Organisation; recommending that practitioners allow resources for evaluation, somewhere in the region of 10–20% of total intervention costs. By doing this, assessment of impact and evaluations can potentially be outsourced to organisations who have experience in this field. They can act as impartial external evaluators adding validity and rigour, helping to shoulder the perceived burden of evaluations. However, outsourcing evaluations is not always an option and the evaluation has to be led by the intervention staff and appropriate to programme needs.

EX 02: Evaluation is essential; the expedience with which football-led health improvement interventions are being implemented underpins the need for a comprehensive assessment of both the positive and negative impact of these programmes. This approach would enable practitioners to ascertain that harm does not outweigh benefits, and if it does, the issue has to be addressed as soon as possible, before rolling it [the intervention] out more widely.

Given that our experts all agreed that evaluation was important, we asked them to identify the challenges of evaluating health improvement interventions delivered in the football-related settings they have worked in:

EX 01: There are many challenges associated with the evaluation of football based interventions, and health interventions in general. Many of these challenges will be dependent on the methodology, the type of evaluation being undertaken and the data collection tools. A sound evaluation framework, such as RE-AIM that incorporates process and impact measures would be a good starting point. If this is followed, it will help to ensure that data collection generates practice based evidence. The obvious problem stemming from the choice of a robust evaluation framework will be how to make it workable within the intervention itself. To make the evaluation workable, it needs to be an integral component of the intervention itself, from the outset. Further, interventions that incorporate outcome measures will require follow up data, which is notoriously difficult to collect and requires separate considerations. Follow up periods, collection methods and means of contacting participants to collect the data should be clearly defined and relayed to participants at the outset to avoid surprises, and allow for contingency planning.

EX 03: One of the main challenges of evaluating interventions is cost. Implementing evaluations can be expensive, especially if the 'gold standard' health measures are implemented. One way this challenge can be surmounted is to use less expensive subjective measures of assessment. A second challenge is obtaining suitably qualified personnel to evaluate the intervention. For instance, obtaining useful and in-depth information from qualitative methods requires skill from the individual conducting the interviews or focus groups. Finally, the challenge of performing the evaluation will also vary depending upon the experience of the individual conducting the evaluation with the population who are participating in the intervention. For example, evaluating a football-led health intervention for young healthy men would vary to evaluating an intervention for older women, especially if qualitative interviews were implemented. Therefore, the evaluator needs to be trained and have experience in the population of people who are participating in the intervention.

EX 02: The loss of pre and post-intervention data (before and or after) is a major challenge of evaluating physical activity programmes delivered in community settings. Some of the factors contributing to non completion rates include the inability of participants to understand what is being asked, in particular where language is a barrier to engagement meaning self-reports can be returned incomplete. While participant attrition from programmes and evaluations also contributes to data loss. To manage the effect of these issue's evaluators need to apportion sufficient time to each participant to accurately complete the data sets and provide guidance where needed. Where possible those participants dropping out should be followed up either by phone or emails so that evaluators can explore why they dropped out and any other valuable information. Last but not least, evaluators should work in partnership with deliverers as they know how the group works and how evaluation activities may dovetail with intervention activities. In partnership designs it must be ensured that deliverers do not coerce participants to take part in the evaluation.

Finally in attempting to help deliverers charged with evaluating football-led health improvement scheme, we asked our 'experts' to identify their 'top three' issues that practitioners should consider when creating effective/workable evaluations football-led health improvement interventions:

EX 01: The first thing to consider when creating an effective evaluation would be staff training. This should be a key component of any good evaluation. It is important to ensure that all staff, including those involved with oversight, service delivery and monitoring and evaluation are all working towards the same goals and are on the same page from the outset. This should be a recurring theme throughout the intervention, undertaken at regular intervals allowing for the sharing of best practice. This leads me on to the second issue to consider, piloting. Ideally this would be incorporated in to the training process. Potential measurement tools can be tested with individuals responsible for administering them, and once they have been suitably refined and deemed workable, they need piloting with potential participants. It's all well and good having great evaluation tools, however if they are not fit for purpose, and won't work in the 'real world', then they won't be effective. This requires a certain level of 'buy in' and ownership from both parties. Finally, given the current financial issues faced by the 'National Health Service', cost effectiveness should be part of any good evaluation. Comparative effectiveness research is a relatively new area of research and is designed to inform health-care decisions by providing evidence on the effectiveness, benefits, and harms of different treatment options. Evidence is generated from research studies that compare pharmacological treatments with community health evaluations for example. This provides an interesting avenue for football based interventions; can they be delivered in a package that is comparable to medicine?

EX 03: For me, the three issues to consider are as follows. Firstly the choice of assessment methods: What are the best evaluation measures and methods available within the budget of the intervention and are these appropriate for the population undertaking the intervention? Secondly, the experience of the evaluator: does the individual assessing the intervention understand the needs of the population and do they have the necessary skills to conduct all aspects of the evaluation? Thirdly, the knowledge of the participants: Are the participants informed about the evaluation and do they who the evaluators are? A consideration would be that the participants are familiar with the evaluators, especially if qualitative methods are being used. This may enable more in depth information to be obtained. Equally, the evaluators should not be over familiar with the population, as social desirable responding on self-report measures could be more likely.

EX 02: The top three issues that practitioners should consider when evaluating effective football-led health improvement interventions are: Firstly, the use of an evaluation framework to address both the behavioural outcomes of health interventions and the process(es) by which such outcomes were achieved is crucial to optimize the development of these football-led programmes. For instance, RE-AIM provides an effective approach to explore the key characteristics of public health interventions. Secondly, the external validity of the evaluation needs to be ensured by addressing representative samples of participants and settings. It is important that the views of a diverse range of constituents are captured, including those participants who shy away from health improvement programmes and associated evaluations. Thirdly, it is important to explore the views of both service deliverers and participants through qualitative approaches. Those who deliver the service have their own insights of what works and what does not work, however participants may perceive things differently. In particular, it is important to explore the views of those participants who elected to drop out of programmes.

Discussion

The appeal of locating health improvement schemes within football settings

Sports clubs and specifically, professional football has been highlighted as offering powerful levers and mechanisms for improving social and Public Health. In their own ways, our three 'experts' each acknowledge the inherent popularity of football and professional football clubs for reaching diverse priority groups identified in UK health policy.[53] Football as a sport has been referred to as a 'world game' reflecting its global popularity with individuals and communities. It is unsurprising that health promoters are capitalizing on this appeal by locating their programmes in football contexts. Contributing to the appeal of professional football is the reach of the 'club badge' where the complex interplay of factors impacts on recruitment to health interventions. Pringle, Zwolinsky, Smith et al. suggest this includes the *place* (football ground or training venue), *people* (the players and deliverers) and the *process of delivery* (programme, promotions and packaging); each of these factors has been shown to contribute to participant recruitment and acceptability.[54] To this end, all our experts provided examples of efforts undertaken by deliverers to meet and shape programme delivery around the needs of participants, including hard-to-engage populations using football. Efforts such as these remain an important ingredient in providing health improvement which is accessible, affordable and acceptable to participants. Despite the apparent popularity of delivering programmes through football channels, such physical activity and health programmes require appropriate evaluation.

The case for evaluating football-led health improvement programmes

All our experts endorsed the importance of evaluation, and collectively they make a strong case for investing in the evaluation of football-led health improvement programmes and this fits with recommended public health guidance.[55] The argument for evaluation made by our evaluators is constructed on four cornerstones. First, from an ethical position, implementing interventions without evidence of effectiveness potentially jeopardizes efforts to meet the needs of the key stakeholder- programme participants. If these programmes are to optimize Public Health, selection – including comparative assessment should be guided by the 'best' available evidence. Second, inventive and engaging types of formative evaluation offer deliverers an opportunity to gauge how well programmes are helping recruits to change and improve their health behaviours. Third, where programmes rarely work as anticipated, evaluation can take on a remedial role in helping to identify which parts of the intervention work less well and require further attention and subsequent rectification. Fourth, is sustainability, in a climate of reduced public funding and increased competition for resources, evaluations can help to secure evidence in which to make the case for sustainability once initial start-up investment has ceased.

Difficulties of and strategies for evaluating football-led health improvement schemes

While our experts make a powerful and contemporary case for investing in the evaluation of interventions, each highlights the difficulties they experienced during their implementation. Individually and collectively they have overcome a diverse range of challenges within their own research and evaluation activities. Their experiences are not unique and mirror many of the problems encountered in evaluating physical activity interventions including those in football settings.[56] In helping to handle these challenges, we asked our 'experts' to provide their guidance on factors that should be considered when evaluating football-led health improvement programmes. At this point, it is important to bear in mind that football-based research and evaluations range widely. There are randomized controlled trials, e.g. *Football Fans in Training,* running in the Scottish Premier League.[57] Others have deployed partnership evaluation designs[58] with a combination of specialist evaluators working alongside programme staff.[59] For in-house evaluations, football clubs provide their own bespoke evaluations. Our expert's experience was typically formed from their involvement of working in a partnership arrangement. They all endorsed the importance of clubs and/or deliverers working with individuals who have expertise in evaluation, a recommendation which was also endorsed by Public Health guidance[60] and physical activity promotion more generally.[61]

Linked to this was cost. Evaluation funding is often a barrier. Only occasionally are resources sufficiently plentiful to commission bespoke evaluations and/or involving specialist evaluators who perform all the evaluation duties. While commissioned approaches may be desirable, there are examples where football clubs and deliverers work in collaboration with evaluation specialists.[62] These specialists may come from commercial research companies, universities and/or individuals who work for local partners and who support health improvement programmes.[63] Guidance recommends appointing external evaluators prior to commencing of the programme, meaning experts are in place to advise on a host of evaluation considerations.[64] This recommendation, along with nine others, is included in a checklist of activities based on our experts experience (Table 1). While not exhaustive, these activities are in-line with guidance on general physical activity-led health improvement and delivered in at times, complex community settings.[65] More detailed guidance is available from a number of other sources although once again, this is not an exhaustive list and further guidance on evaluating public health interventions can be found elsewhere.[66]

Research shows that deliverers often express concerns about balancing the challenge of programme delivery against evaluation.[67] Their concerns are that evaluation diverts their attention away from what they see as their main business. This highlights one of the obvious benefits of working with external evaluators; they build capacity for evaluation while allowing delivery specialists to concentrate on programme implementation. In partnership designs, delivery staff can also perform evaluation duties such as data collection so in these instances it is important they receive appropriate training and education so they feel confident in such roles. From a validity perspective,[68] these deliverers-cum-evaluators risk having a biased stance; irrespective of their methods, they stand to be accused of 'having their own dog in the race'.

In contrast, external expertise can be neutral, while also helping with a host of other activities that may be beyond the capability of some deliverers. For instance, some deliverers do not hold a view that can formally integrate the purpose, focus and the scope of the evaluation. To this end, all our experts outlined the value of adopting evidence-based framework for shaping the parameters of evaluations in football-led health improvement programmes. One of these frameworks is RE-AIM.[69] While extensively used in the Public Health improvement literature, and is valued for providing useful forms of 'practice-based evidence', RE-AIM has recently been adopted into football-led health programme evaluations. Pringle, Zwolinsky, McKenna et al., claim *'REAIM not only provides a comprehensive structure for assessing the impact of interventions across the behavioural change continuum (Reach, Adoption and Maintenance), but also the process (Implementation) by which interventions are (Effective) when impacting on the behaviour of participants'* (717).[70]

Table 1. Key evaluation activities: checklist.

Key evaluation activities	Check (✔)
Secure specialist evaluators/evaluation or expertise/guidance	
Establish the evaluation purpose, aims, objectives and measures from the outset	
Select, pilot and review valid and reliable evaluation methodologies, processes and frameworks	
Build capacity for evaluation processes such as data collection	
In-build evaluation activities into the programme	
Train staff involved in evaluation processes, e.g. data collection and inputting	
Observe ethical standards in evaluation, participant needs, consent, data protection, storage report and ethical release	
Consider participant needs including fears, language and literacy issues	
In-build quality assurance activities from planning to reporting stage	
Maintain regular communication between stakeholders	

Such frameworks can be helpful when organizing the scope of the evaluation and, subsequently, the choice of evaluation outcomes and methods for their assessment. The decision to use self-report vs. objective methods and quantitative vs. qualitative measures or a combination of these approaches/techniques (multi-methods) is one best taken by those with expertise and experience in their application. These decisions are likely to be optimized following dialogue with important stakeholders on how such methods will be received by participants and how their application can be worked into programme delivery.[71] Crucially, from an ethical perspective, it is important that the evaluation does nothing to deter likely participants from engaging an intervention; little can be as harmful as to identifying intervention outcomes as beneficiaries who avoid completing follow-up measures, because of embarrassment about their low levels of literacy or through fear that their responses – or even their engagement with the intervention – will produce harmful consequences. Discussions about the 'participant burden' of evaluation are important in the planning phase.

Our experts also highlighted the importance of not only identifying what, but how and why football-led health programme effects are achieved and this is a fundamental facet of RE-AIM.[72] With process evaluation in mind, interviews and focus groups can be used to investigate the way in which participants experience behaviour change opportunities, such as those found in football-led interventions. These issues are important in gauging the impacts – intended and unintended – of health improvement programmes. Moreover, interview-led approaches are especially valuable when including those participants who express fears and anxieties around the completion of self-report evaluation owing to literacy, language and concerns over surveillance. These and other factors can impact on loss of data, a common occurrence in the evaluation of community physical activity[73] and football-led health improvement programmes.[74] With evaluations being assessed using intention-to-treat analysis, where the baseline scores are used also as follow-up outcomes or vice versa, this increases the likelihood of showing that interventions had no positive effects of behaviour. When an intervention is not powerful, this is fine, but it risks presenting powerful interventions as being 'weak'. Finally, the implementation of ethical processes is also an important consideration. This will include securing participant consent/assent, data protection, storage and transfer of data along with ethics release, where this is required. In our experience, these concerns are frequently reported within in-house evaluations, and this only limits the capacity to publish the outcomes of such interventions and share learning with a diverse audience.

Limitations and strengths of this research

Our research includes both limitations and strengths. Limitations relate to an 'expert' sample who had typically worked in partnership evaluation designs. Including constituents who had worked in other research and evaluation designs would provide a different perspective. Our 'expert's' practice was typically centred on adults, whereas including those participants who had worked with children and young people on football-led interventions would also provide different viewpoints. Strengths included an 'expert' sample with experience of evaluating football-led health improvement interventions who shared in detail, their rich experiences and informative accounts, along with a desire to improve evaluation practice. Moreover, these views were captured through the administration of research methods that had been used in public health and activity contexts previously.

Conclusion

To assess the Public Health value of football-led health improvement interventions, there is a need for appropriate evaluation. If football genuinely delivers the potential that many see in it, it is imperative that the effectiveness of these interventions is clarified, and indeed, compared. Our paper highlights the importance and challenges of performing evaluations, as reported by experts with direct recent experience in football clubs/football settings. Through their commentaries, we provide some key considerations for evaluating the impact of football-led health improvement programmes.

Notes

1. Department of Health, *Start Active, Stay Active*.
2. The Information Centre for Health and Social Care, *Statistics on Obesity*.
3. Parnell et al., 'Football in the Community Schemes'.
4. Dunn et al., 'Kicking the Habit'.
5. Pringle et al., 'An Even More Beautiful Game'.
6. Pringle et al., 'Health Improvement for Men and Hard-to-engage-men Delivered in English Premier League Football Clubs'; Pringle et al., 'Health Improvement and Professional Football: Players on the Same Side?'.
7. Hippisley-Cox et al., 'Predicting Cardiovascular Risk in England and Wales'.
8. Kahn et al., 'The Impact of Prevention on Reducing the Burden of Cardiovascular Disease'.
9. Scarborough et al., 'The Economic Burden of ill Health Due to Diet, Physical Inactivity, Smoking, Alcohol and Obesity in the UK'.
10. BHF, *Evidence Briefing. The Economic Costs of Physical Inactivity*.
11. Wang et al., 'Health and Economic Burden of the Projected Obesity Trends in the USA and the UK'.
12. Black, 'Can England's NHS Survive?'.
13. Clark et al., 'Effectiveness of a Lifestyle Intervention in Promoting the Well-being of independently Living Older People'; Pringle et al., 'Cost Effectiveness of Interventions to Improve Moderate Physical-activity'.
14. Khaw et al., 'Combined Impact of Health Behaviours and Mortality in Men and Women'.
15. The Information Centre for Health and Social Care, *Statistics on Obesity*.
16. Pringle et al., 'Effect of a National Programme of Men's Health Delivered in English Premier League Football Clubs'; Pringle et al., 'Cost Effectiveness of Interventions to Improve Moderate Physical-activity'.
17. Johnman et al., 'The Beautiful Game'.
18. Witty and White, 'Tackling Men's Health'.
19. Trivedy, 'Oral Health Through Sport'.
20. Gray et al., 'Can the Draw of Professional Football Clubs help promote Weight Loss in Overweight and Obese Men?'.
21. Premier League, *Creating Chances*.
22. Parnell et al., 'Football in the Community Schemes'; Hunt et al., 'You've Got to Run Before You Can Walk'; and Football Foundation, *Extra Time*.
23. Parnell et al., 'Football in the Community Schemes'; Brady et al., 'Sustained Benefits of a Health Project for Middle Aged Football Supporters at Glasgow Celtic and Rangers Football Clubs'; Pringle and Sayers, 'It's a Goal'; and Mason and Holt, 'A Role for Football in Mental Health'.
24. Gray et al., 'Football Fans in Training'.
25. Sinclair and Alexander, 'Using Outreach to Involve the Hard-to-reach in a Health Check'.
26. Zwolinsky et al., 'Optimizing Lifestyles for Men Regarded as "Hard-to-Reach" Through Top-flight Football/Soccer Clubs'.
27. Faugier and Sergeant, 'Sampling Hard-to-reach Populations'.

28. Curran, *Understanding the Barriers to, and Impact of Men's Engagement in Physical Activity and Health Related Behaviours* and Moffett, *Community engagement and Visible Manifestations of Conflict Programme.*
29. Withall et al., 'Why Some Do But Most Don't'.
30. Pringle et al., 'Cost Effectiveness of Interventions to Improve Moderate Physical-activity'.
31. Yancey et al., 'Dissemination of Physical Activity Promotion Interventions in Underserved Populations'.
32. Withall et al., 'Why Some Do But Most Don't'.
33. Dawson et al., 'Perceived Barriers to Walking in the Neighbourhood Environment and Change in Physical Activity Levels Over 12 months'; Withall et al., 'Why Some Do But Most Don't'.
34. Sinclair and Alexander, 'Using Outreach to Involve the Hard-to-reach in a Health Check'.
35. CRI, *National Evaluation of LEAP.*
36. Dunn et al., 'Kicking the Habit'; Parnell et al., 'Football in the Community Schemes'; Pringle and Sayers 'It's a Goal'; and Pringle et al., 'Effect of a National Programme of Men's Health Delivered in English Premier League Football Clubs'.
37. Robertson et al., 'It's Fun, Fitness, Football Really'.
38. Morgan et al., '12-Month Outcomes and Process Evaluation of the SHED-IT RCT'.
39. NICE, *Behaviour Change.*
40. Dugdill and Stratton, *Evaluating Sport and Physical Activity Interventions.*
41. Pringle et al., 'Qualitative Perspectives on Evaluability of Community Physical Activity Interventions'.
42. Curran, *Understanding the Barriers to, and Impact of Men's Engagement in Physical Activity and Health Related Behaviours* and Pringle et al., 'Health Improvement for Men and Hard-to-engage-men Delivered in English Premier League Football Clubs'.
43. McKenna et al., 'Scientists Within Community Research'.
44. Dugdill and Stratton, *Evaluating Sport and Physical Activity Interventions*; Glasgow et al., 'Evaluating the Impact of Public Health interventions: The REAIM framework'; MRC *Developing and Evaluating Complex Interventions*; and NOO, *Standard Evaluation Framework for Physical Activity Interventions* and Sport England *Learning from LEAP.*
45. McKenna et al., 'Scientists Within Community Research'.
46. Palys, *Purposive Sampling.*
47. Curtis et al., 'Approaches to Sampling and Case Selection in Qualitative Research: Examples in the Geography of Health'.
48. McKenna et al., 'Scientists Within Community Research'.
49. McKenna et al., 'Scientists Within Community Research'.
50. McKenna et al., 'Scientists Within Community Research'.
51. Janesick, 'The Choreography of Qualitative Research Design'.
52. Dugdill and Stratton, *Evaluating Sport and Physical Activity Interventions*; Glasgow et al., 'Evaluating the Impact of Public Health Interventions: The REAIM Framework'; MRC, *Developing and Evaluating Complex Interventions*; NOO, *Standard Evaluation Framework for Physical Activity Interventions* and Sport England *Learning from LEAP.*
53. Department of Health, *Start Active, Stay Active.*
54. Pringle, Zwolinsky, Smith et al., The pre-adoption, demographic and health profiles of men participating in a programme of men's health delivered in English Premier League Football clubs. Pringle et al., 'Effect of a National Programme of Men's Health Delivered in English Premier League Football Clubs'; Pringle et al., 'Delivering Men's Health Interventions in English Premier League Football Clubs: Key Design Characteristics'.
55. NICE, *Behaviour Change.*
56. Curran, *Understanding the Barriers to, and Impact of Men's Engagement in Physical Activity and Health Related Behaviours* and Parnell et al., 'Football in the Community Schemes'.
57. Hunt et al., 'A Gender-sensitised Weight Loss and Healthy Living Programme for Overweight and Obese Men Delivered by Scottish Premier League football clubs (FFIT)'.

58. South and Tilford, 'Perceptions of Research and Evaluation in Health Promotion Practice and Influences on Activity'.
59. Burton Albion Community Trust, *Golden Goal*; Pringle et al., 'Effect of a National Programme of Men's Health Delivered in English Premier League Football Clubs'.
60. NICE, *Behaviour Change*.
61. Dugdill and Stratton, *Evaluating Sport and Physical Activity Interventions*.
62. Burton Albion Community Trust. *Golden Goal*; Curran, *Understanding the Barriers to, and Impact of Men's Engagement in Physical Activity and Health Related Behaviours*; and Parnell et al., 'Football in the Community Schemes'.
63. McKenna et al., 'Scientists Within Community Research'.
64. Dugdill and Stratton, *Evaluating Sport and Physical Activity Interventions*. Sport England, Learning from LEAP.
65. McKenna et al., 'Scientists Within Community Research' and CRI, *National Evaluation of LEAP*.
66. Dugdill and Stratton, *Evaluating Sport and Physical Activity Interventions*; Glasgow et al., 'Evaluating the Impact of Public Health Interventions: The REAIM Framework'; MRC, *Developing and Evaluating Complex Interventions*; NOO, *Standard Evaluation Framework for Physical Activity Interventions*; and Sport England, *Learning from LEAP*.
67. CRI, *National Evaluation of LEAP*.
68. Dugdill and Stratton, *Evaluating Sport and Physical Activity Interventions*.
69. Glasgow et al., 'Evaluating the Impact of Public Health Interventions: The REAIM Framework'.
70. Pringle et al., 'Delivering Men's Health Interventions in English Premier League Football Clubs: Key Design Characteristics'.
71. CRI, *National Evaluation of LEAP*.
72. Glasgow et al., 'Evaluating the Impact of Public Health Interventions: The REAIM Framework'.
73. Wood et al., 'Comparison of Imputation and Modelling Methods in the Analysis of a Physical Activity Trial with missing Outcomes'.
74. Pringle et al., 'Effect of a National Programme of Men's Health Delivered in English Premier League Football Clubs'.

References

Black, N. 'Can England's NHS Survive?' *New England Journal of Medicine* 369 (2013): 1–3. http://www.nejm.org/doi/full/10.1056/NEJMp1305771 (accessed September 9, 2013).

Brady, A., C. Perry, D. Murdoch, and G. McKay. 'Sustained Benefits of a Health Project for Middle Aged Football Supporters at Glasgow Celtic and Rangers Football Clubs'. *European Heart Journal* 24 (2010): 2696–98.

British Heart Foundation National Centre Physical Activity and Health. *Evidence Briefing. The Economic Costs of Physical Inactivity*. 2013. http://www.bhfactive.org.uk/userfiles/Documents/eonomiccosts.pdf (accessed October 07, 2013).

Burton Albion Community Trust. *Golden Goal*, 2013. http://burtonalbioncommunitytrust.co.uk/courses/golden-goal-over-50s-activity-programme/ (accessed August 1, 2013).

Carnegie Research Institute (Leeds Metropolitan University) with Matrix RCL and Ipsos MORI. *National Evaluation of LEAP: A Final Report on the Local Exercise Action Pilots*. London: Department of Health, 2007. http://www.dh.gov.uk/en/Publicationsandstatistics/Publications/PublicationsPolicy-AndGuidance/DH_073600 (accessed September 24, 2013).

Clark, F., J. Jackson, M. Carlson, C.P. Chou, B. Cherry, M. Jordan-Marsh, B. Knight, et al. 'Effectiveness of a Lifestyle Intervention in Promoting the Well-being of Independently Living Older People: Results of the Well Elderly 2 Randomised Controlled Trial'. *Journal of Epidemiology & Community Health* 66 (2012): 782–90.

Curran, K. 'Understanding the Barriers to, and Impact of Men's Engagement in Physical Activity and Health Related Behaviours: An Examination of an English Premier League Football in the Community Men's Health Programme'. PhD thesis, Liverpool John Moores University, 2013.

Curtis, S., W. Gesler, G. Smith, and S. Washburn. 'Approaches to Sampling and Case Selection in Qualitative Research: Examples in the Geography of Health'. *Social Science & Medicine* 50 (2000): 1001–14.

Dawson, J., M. Hillsdon, I. Boller, and C. Foster. 'Perceived Barriers to Walking in the Neighbourhood Environment and Change in Physical Activity Levels over 12 Months'. *British Journal of Sports Medicine* 41 (2007): 562–8.

Department of Health. *Start Active, Stay Active: A Report on Physical Activity for Health from the Four Home Countries Chief Medical Officers*. London: Crown, 2011. http://www.dh.gov.uk/prod_consum_dh/groups/dh_digitalassets/documents/digitalasset/dh_128210.pdf (accessed September 24, 2013).

Dugdill, L., and G. Stratton. *Evaluating Sport and Physical Activity Interventions: A Guide for Practitioners*. University of Salford, 2013. http://usir.salford.ac.uk/3148/1/Dugdill_and_Stratton_2007.pdf (accessed September 24, 2013).

Dunn, K., B. Drust, D. Flower, and D. Richardson. 'Kicking the Habit; A Biopsychosocial Account of Engaging Men Recovering from Drug Misuse in Regular Recreational Football'. *Journal of Men's Health* 8 (2011): 233.

Faugier, J., and M. Sergeant. 'Sampling Hard to Reach Populations'. *Journal of Advanced Nursing* 26 (1997): 790–7.

Football Foundation. *Extra-time: Evaluation Summary Report*. 2011. http://www.footballfoundation.org.uk/our-schemes/extra-time/extra-time-summary-report/?assetdet240618=29315 (accessed August 1, 2013).

Glasgow, R., T. Vogt, and S. Boles. 'Evaluating the Impact of Public Health Interventions: The REAIM Framework'. *American Journal of Public Health* 89 (1999): 1323–27.

Gray, C., K. Hunt, N. Mutrie, A. Anderson, S. Treweek, and S. Wyke. 'Can the Draw of Professional Football Clubs Help Promote Weight Loss in Overweight and Obese Men? A Feasibility Study of the Football Fans in Training Programme Delivered through the Scottish Premier League'. *Journal of Epidemiology and Community Health* 65 (2011): A37–8. doi:10.1136/jech.2011.143586.84.

Gray, C., K. Hunt, N. Mutrie, A. Anderson, J. Leishman, L. Dalgarno, and S. Wyke. 'Football Fans in Training: The Development and Optimization of an Intervention Delivered through Professional Sports Clubs to Help Men Lose Weight, Become More Active and Adopt Healthier Eating Habits'. *BMC Public Health* 13 (2013): 232.

Hippisley-Cox, J., C. Coupland, Y. Vinogradova, J. Robson, R. Minhas, A. Sheikh, and P. Brindle. 'Predicting Cardiovascular Risk in England and Wales: Prospective Derivation and Validation of QRISK2'. *British Medical Journal* 336 (2008): 1475–82.

Hunt, K., C. McCann, C. Gray, N. Mutrie, and S. Wyke. '"You've Got to Walk before You Run": Positive Evaluations of a Walking Program as Part of a Gender-sensitized, Weight-management Program Delivered to Men through Professional Football Clubs'. *Health Psychology* 32 (2013): 57–65.

Hunt, K., S. Wyke, C. Gray, A. Anderson, A. Brady, C. Bunn, P. Donnan, et al. 'A Gender-sensitised Weight Loss and Healthy Living Programme for Overweight and Obese Men Delivered by Scottish Premier League Football Clubs (FFIT): A Pragmatic Randomised Controlled Trial'. *The Lancet* 383 (2014): 1211–21.

Janesick, V. 'The Choreography of Qualitative Research Design Minuets, Improvisations and Crystallisation'. In *Strategies of Qualitative Enquiry*, ed. N. Denzin and Y. Lincoln, 46–79, California: Sage, 2003. http://books.google.co.uk/books?hl=en&lr=&id=2Bvxli1d2a0C&oi=fnd&pg=PA46&dq=staying±close±to±the±data±janesick&ots=EG8porKmFT&sig=dmM4QZtMdTX-hgS_nZOHJZho-30#v=onepage&q&f=false (accessed February 19, 2014).

Johnman, C., P. Mackie, and F. Sim. 'The Beautiful Game'. *Public Health* 127 (2013): 697–8.

Kahn, R., R.M. Robertson, R. Smith, and D. Eddy. 'The Impact of Prevention on Reducing the Burden of Cardiovascular Disease'. *Circulation* 118 (2008): 576–85. http://circ.ahajournals.org/cgi/content/full/118/5/576 (accessed September 9, 2013).

Khaw, K., N. Wareham, S. Bingham, A. Welch, R. Luben, and N. Day. 'Combined Impact of Health Behaviours and Mortality in Men and Women: The EPIC-Norfolk Prospective Population Study'. *PLOS Med* 5 (2008): 39–47.

Mason, O., and R. Holt. 'A Role for Football in Mental Health: The Coping through Football Project'. *The Psychiatrist* 36 (2012): 290–3.

McKenna, J., M. Davis, and A. Pringle. 'Scientists Within Community Research'. *The Sport and Exercise Scientist* 4 (2005): 6–7.

Medical Research Council. *Developing and Evaluating Complex Interventions: New Guidance*. London: Medical Research Council, 2008. http://www.mrc.ac.uk/Utilities/Documentrecord/index.htm?d=MRC004871 (accessed October 7, 2013).

Moffett, L. *Community Engagement and Visible Manifestations of Conflict Programme: Extending Reach*. 2010. https://www.google.co.uk/search?q=Moffestt±community±engagement±and±visible±man&oq=Moffestt±community±engagement±and±visible±man&aqs=chrome..69i57.12899j0&sourceid=chrome&ie=UTF-8#q=Moffestt±community±engagement±and±visible± manifestations (accessed August 1, 2013).

Morgan, P., D. Lubans, C. Collins, J. Warren, and R. Callister. '12-Month Outcomes and Process Evaluation of the SHED-IT RCT: An Internet-based Weight Loss Program Targeting Men'. *Obesity* 19 (2010): 142–51. doi:10.1038/oby.2010.119.

National Institute of Health and Clinical Excellence. *The Most Appropriate Means of Generic and Specific Interventions to Support Attitude Behavioural Change at Population and Community Levels*. London: National Institute of Health and Clinical Excellence, 2007. http://www.nice.org.uk/PH6 (accessed September 24, 2013).

National Obesity Observatory. *Standard Evaluation Framework for Physical Activity Interventions*. London: National Obesity Observatory, 2012. http://www.noo.org.uk/uploads/doc/vid_16722_SEF_PA.pdf (accessed February 20, 2014).

Palys, T. *Purposive Sampling*. undated. http://www.sfu.ca/~palys/Purposive%20sampling.pdf (accessed January 30, 2014).

Parnell, D., G. Stratton, B. Drust, and D. Richardson. 'Football in the Community Schemes: Exploring the Effectiveness of an Intervention in Promoting Healthful Behaviour Change'. *Soccer & Society* 14 (2013): 35–51.

Premier League. *Creating Chances*. London: Premier League, 2011. http://addison.ceros.com/premier-league/creating-chances-2011/page/1 (accessed January 25, 2013).

Pringle, A., and P. Sayers. 'It's a Goal: Basing a Community Psychiatric Nursing Service in a Local Football Stadium'. *The Journal of the Royal Society for the Promotion of Health* 124 (2004): 234–8.

Pringle, A., J. McKenna, E. Whatley, and N. Gilson. 'Qualitative Perspectives on Evaluability of Community Physical Activity Interventions'. From Education to Application: Sport, Exercise and Health Proceedings of the British Association of Sport & Exercise Science Meeting, Wolverhampton University, Leeds, UK, British Association of Sport & Exercise Science, September 11–13, 2006.

Pringle, A., C. Cooke, N. Gilson, K. Marsh, and J. McKenna. 'Cost-effectiveness of Interventions to Improve Moderate Physical Activity: A Study in Nine UK Sites'. *Health Education Journal* 69 (2010): 211–24.

Pringle, A., S. Zwolinsky, A. Smith, S. Robertson, J. McKenna, and A. White. 'The pre-adoption, demographic and health profiles of men participating in a programme of men's health delivered in English Premier League Football clubs'. *Public Health* 125 (2011): 411–16.

Pringle, A., J. McKenna, and S. Zwolinsky. 'An Even More Beautiful Game'. *Public Health* 127 (2013): 1143–4.

Pringle, A., J. McKenna, and S. Zwolinsky. 'Health Improvement and Professional Football: Players on the Same Side?' *Journal of Policy Research in Tourism, Leisure and Events* 5 (2013): 207–12.

Pringle, A., S. Zwolinsky, J. McKenna, A. Daly-Smith, S. Robertson, and A. White. 'Effect of a National Programme of Men's Health Delivered in English Premier League Football Clubs'. *Public Health* 127 (2013): 18–26.

Pringle, A., S. Zwolinsky, J. McKenna, A. Daly-Smith, S. Robertson, and A. White. 'Delivering Men's Health Interventions in English Premier League Football Clubs: Key Design Characteristics'. *Public Health* 127 (2013): 717–26.

Pringle, A., S. Zwolinsky, J. McKenna, A. Daly-Smith, S. Robertson, and A. White 'Health Improvement for Men and Hard-to-engage-men Delivered in English Premier League Football Clubs'. *Health Education Research* 29 (2014): 503–20.

Robertson, S., S. Zwolinsky, A. Pringle, J. McKenna, A. Daly-Smith, and A. White. '"It is Fun, Fitness and Football Really": A Process Evaluation of a Football-based Health Intervention for Men'. *Qualitative Research in Sport, Exercise and Health* 5 (2013): 419–39.

Scarborough, P., P. Bhatnagar, K. Wickramasinghe, S. Allender, C. Foster, and M. Rayner. 'The Economic Burden of Ill Health due to Diet, Physical Inactivity, Smoking, Alcohol and Obesity in the UK: An Update to 2006–07 NHS Costs'. *Journal of Public Health* 33 (2011): 527–35.

Sinclair, A., and H. Alexander. 'Using Outreach to Involve the Hard-to-reach in a Health Check: What Difference Does It Make?' *Public Health* 126 (2012): 87–95.

South, J., and S. Tilford. 'Perceptions of Research and Evaluation in Health Promotion Practice and Influences on Activity'. *Health Education Research* 15 (2000): 729–41.

Sport England. *Learning from LEAP*. London: Sport England, 2006.

The Information Centre for Health and Social Care. *Statistics on Obesity, Physical Activity and Diet in England 2010*. London: The Information Centre for Health and Social Care, 2010. http://www.ic.nhs.uk/webfiles/publications/opad10/Statistics_on_Obesity_Physical_Activity_and_Diet_England_2010.pdf (accessed February 20, 2013).

Trivedy, C. 'Oral Health through Sport'. *British Dental Journal* 210 (2011): 150.

Wang, Y., K. McPherson, T. Marsh, S. Gortmaker, and M. Brown. 'Health and Economic Burden of the Projected Obesity Trends in the USA and the UK'. *The Lancet* 378 (2011): 815–25.

Withall, J., R. Jago, and K. Fox. 'Why Some Do but Most Don't. Barriers and Enablers to Engaging Low-income Groups in Physical Activity Programmes: A Mixed Methods Study'. *BMC Public Health* 11 (2011): 507. http://www.biomedcentral.com/1471-2458/11/507 (accessed September 24, 2013).

Witty, K., and A. White. 'Tackling Men's Health: Implementation of a Male Health Service in a Rugby Stadium'. *Community Practitioner* 84 (2011): 29–32.

Wood, I., I. White, M. Hillsdon, and J. Carpenter. 'Comparison of Imputation and Modelling Methods in the Analysis of a Physical Activity Trial with Missing Outcomes'. *International Journal of Epidemiology* 34 (2005): 89–99.

Yancey, A., M. Ory, and S. Davis 'Dissemination of Physical Activity Promotion Interventions in Underserved Populations'. *American Journal of Preventive Medicine* 31 (2006): 82–91.

Zwolinsky, S., J. McKenna, A. Pringle, A. Daly-Smith, S. Robertson, and A. White. 'Optimizing Lifestyles for Men Regarded as "Hard-to-Reach" Through Top-flight Football/Soccer Clubs'. *Health Education Research* 28 (2013): 405–13.

Index

6 Minute Walk Test 134–9

account of men's health themed match day events 97–111
activism 26
activities of Fit Fans programme 62–5; data analysis and representation 65; participants 62–3; programme 63–5
Adab, P. 137
adoption profiles 88–9
age 42–96, 129–47; older adults 80–96; older fans 42–60; older men 61–79
Age UK 62
Ahtonen, A. 48
aims of FitC delivery 137–9
Alcaraz, J.E. 138
alcohol awareness 97, 100, 113
Allison, Eric 31
Allison, M.A. 138
Americans with Disabilities 2010 5
Anagnostopoulos, C. 7
Anderson, A. 120, 133, 139
ANOVA measures 135
appeal of football 2
appeal of football settings 156
Apprenticeships 31, 34–6
appropriate evaluation 160
Arsenal 45
assessing football-based health programmes 148–65; conclusion 160; discussion 156–9; findings 152–6; introduction 148–51; methodology 151–2
attendance profile 87–8
attendance social composition 49–51
austerity 25
autonomy 17
Aveyard, P. 137
avoidance 102–3
avoiding own goals 148–65
'Award for All' scheme 84

Babiak, K. 14, 19
BACT *see* Burton Albion Community Trust

Baker, P. 98, 106
Bangsbo, J. 137–8
Bayern Munich 45
Beach, J. 137
behaviours of men 97–9
Bendiksen, M. 137
benefits of health intervention programmes 148–51
Berentzen, T. 134
Berry, R. 121
best practice 2
'Big Society' 25–41; *see also* Little United and Big Society
Blackshaw, T. 13
Blond, Philip 27, 39
BMI *see* body mass index
body mass index 63–4, 81–2, 97, 129–31, 134–7
Bogdan-Lovis, E. 122
Bolton Immigration Integration Group 33–4
boycotting 29–30
Bradshaw, A.J. 134
Brady, A. 139
Brammer, S. 6, 10
branded freebies 103–4
branding football 1–2, 118–20
Brazil 1; World Cup 2014 1
Brighton & Hove Albion FC 35
Britol, J. 137–8
Brown, A. 13
Bundesliga 45–7, 49–52
Bunn, C. 139
Burton Albion 80–96
Burton Albion Community Trust 83–4
business case for inclusivity 46
Business in the Community 113

CAFÉ *see* Centre for Access to Football in Europe
Camp Nou 51
cancer 97, 100, 103–5, 130
cardiac risk 64
cardiometabolic risk 134

INDEX

cardiovascular risk factors 81–2, 97, 129–47, 149–50
Carmichael, J. 99, 101, 117
centralized funding 17–18
Centre for Access to Football in Europe 47–9
challenges of research 123
Championship football clubs 82, 160
charitable model 17, 25
Chief Medical Officer 148–51
Christiansen, L. 137
chronic conditions 80–83
club strip 34–5, 104
co-morbidity 130
coaching 121–2
Coalter, F. 130
cognitive decline 81, 83
community empowerment 29
Community Mark 113
community rights 28
community share scheme 30, 36
Community Sports Trust 6–7
Conservative Party 26–7
'construction site of knowledge' 31
consumer spending 52
content analysis 65
contextual factors for pressure 13–15
control theory 63
cooperative triangulation 101
corporate misbehaviour 9
corporate social responsibility 2, 6–24, 43, 45, 50; conclusion 18–20; findings 11–18; introduction 6–8; methods 10–11; and social partnerships 8–10
Courtney, W. 98
Crabbe, T. 13
'Creating Chances' brand 16, 149–50
creating inclusivity 46
crime reduction 2, 30
Criqui, M.H. 138
CSR *see* corporate social responsibility
CST *see* Community Sports Trust
cultural 'capital' 34–5
cultural inclusion 30
culture of football 1

Daley, A. 137
Dalgarno, L. 133
Daly-Smith, A. 106, 121
data analysis 65, 84, 101–2, 117–18
data management 151–2
DCLG *see* Department for COmmunities and Local Government
De Sousa, B. 97–8

De Visser, R. 97–8
Deeks, J.J. 137
degree of leverage 13
dementia 83
demographic trends 47–9, 84–5, 87–8; in GG programme 87–8
Denley, J. 137
Department for Communities and Local Government 28
Department for Culture, Media and Sport 13–14
Department of Work and Pensions 47
dependencies 17, 35
deportation 37
depression 120, 130
deprivation 83, 112–14, 134
design of Fit Fans programme 73–5; participant needs 73–4; practitioner's role 74–5
design of interventions 88–9
Deutsche Football League 50–52
DFL *see* Deutsche Football League
Dhaliwal, S.S. 134
diabetes 61, 73, 97, 130, 134
difficulties for evaluating football-led schemes 157–9
disabilities 42–60
disability liaison officers 46–7
disadvantaged communities 30–31
Dobson, A. 138–9
Donaldson, T. 9
Donnan, P.T. 139
Downs, Phil 45, 47, 53
dysfunctional affiliation 7, 19

EAFC *see* Everton Active Family Centre
economic relevance of older fans 42–60
economic sclerosis 26–7
effect of delivered weight loss programme 129–47
effect of health-improvement pilot programme 61–96; conclusion 90–91; discussion 87–90; introduction 80–83; method 83–4; results 84–7
Egger, G. 138–9
EitC *see* Everton in the Community
elite clubs 25, 29
empathy 73–4
employment enhancement 36–7
enabling football clubs 25–31; FC United 29–31; legislative context 2010–2013 26–7; public service reform 27–9
engagement with health on match days 102–6; avoidance 102–3; branded freebies 103–4;

INDEX

engagement 'inside' stadium 104–5; take-home message 106
engagement with health service staff 102–3
engagement 'inside' stadium 104–5
engaging 'at risk' populations 124
England 1–2, 43, 49–51; attendance levels 49–51
entering old age 81, 87
environmentalism 9
EQ 5D questionnaire 84–7
escalation of obesity 129–31
esteem 28, 31, 34–5
ethics 19, 63, 84, 131
ethnographic engagement 112–28; conclusion 124; data analysis and representation 117–18; football club brand 118–20; future for FitC 122–3; introduction 112–15; limitations and strengths 123; method 115–16; practitioner skill base 121–2; research design 116–17; researcher role 123; results 118
European football industry 42–60
Eurostat 47–8
evaluating football-led programmes 157
evaluating impact of health improvement programmes 151–2; investigation methods 151–2; purpose 151; study sampling 152
events on match days 100
Everton Active Family Centre 62–4, 112–28
Everton in the Community 112–17
Everton Football Club 62–3, 99–101, 112–28
evidence on impact on health 106–7
Evo-Stick Premier division 26
exer-gaming 83, 116
expert samples 159
exploring inclusivity 46–7
Extra Time programme 82–3, 120, 153

FaaF see Fit as a Fiddle programme
fans with disabilities 42–60; club policies for 52; European demographic trends 47–8; spending power of 51; sport/leisure interests 48–9
FC Barcelona 51
FC United of Manchester 25–41; see also Little United and Big Society
FC United Youth Forum 31, 34–5
FCUM see FC United of Manchester
Federal Statistics Office 47–8
FFIT see Football Fans in Training intervention
FIFA 1
Fit Fans 3, 61–79, 153; conclusions 75; discussion 73–5; introduction 61–2; methods 62–5; participants' needs 67–73; results 65–7
Fit as a Fiddle programme 62

FitC see Football in the Community
FJF see Future Jobs Fund
FL see Football League
focus on CSR 10–11
focus groups 31–2
football club brand 104, 118–20, 122–3
football clubs and their communities 29–31
Football in the Community 2, 10, 61–2, 98–9, 107, 112–47, 149–50; effect of delivered weight loss programme 129–47; ethnographic engagement 112–28
Football Fans in Training intervention 133, 157
Football Foundation 30
football governing bodies 3–4, 52–4; managerial implications 52–4
Football League 2, 7–8, 16–17, 80–82, 87
Football Pools 98
Football Task Force 2
Football World Cup 1–3
football as world game 1–5
football-based health programmes 148–65
Foresight programme 129–30
frailty 81
Freedson, P.S. 134
FTF see Football Task Force
Fujioka, S. 138
Future Jobs Fund 31, 33–4, 36
future research on health 107

Germany 1, 43, 47–51; social composition of attendance 49–51; World Cup 2006 1
GG see Golden Goal programme
Gilbourne, D. 117
Glazer, Malcolm 29
global awareness 1–3
global epidemic 129–31
goals 65–7
Golden Goal programme 83–4; data analysis 84; ethics 84; intervention context 83–4
'good neighbourliness' 15
Goodison Park Stadium 63, 99, 114, 118–19
Gough, B. 98
government intervention 2
Graafland, J. 9
Grady, J. 48
Gray, C. 120, 133, 139
Greenhouse–Geisser correction factors 135
growing the game 42–60; building case for inclusivity 46; club policies 52; conclusion 52–4; findings 47–9; introduction 42–3; levels of attendance 49–51; methods 46–7; spending power 51; understanding football stadia 43–6

INDEX

Hamil, S. 13
hard-to-engage groups 90, 138, 148–51, 156
Harrison, J. 98
having 'politics' 37–8
HCPC *see* Health and Care Professions Council
Health and Care Professions Council 3
health improvement programmes 61–96, 148–65
health needs 65
health profiles 88
Health Survey for England 2008 81
Healthy People, Healthy Lives 98
heritage of football 1
high accessibility 1
history of FitC 112–15
Hogston, R. 97–8
homogenization 6, 20, 30
hooliganism 2, 7, 112
Hunt 133
Hunt, K. 120, 139

identifying customer profile 42–3
immersion in football culture 64–5, 100–101
impact on adoption profiles 88–9
impact of football-based health programmes 148–65
impact of Golden Goal programme 87–90; attendance profiles 87–8; health profiles 88; impact of adoption profiles 88–9; limitations of study 90; physical activity promotion 89–90
implications for practice 107
importance of partnerships 11–18; contextual factors 13–15; dependencies 17; primary interest 12–13; source of problem definition 15–16; time-frame 17–18
inclusive weight loss interventions 140
inclusivity 43–6
increasing circle of life 81, 87
independent living 81–2
innovative weight loss interventions 140
instrumentation 84, 151–2
Inter Mancunia 31, 36–7
interdependency 14, 17
intervention context 83–4, 131–4
investigation methods 151–2; instrumentation 151–2

Jackson, G. 6, 10
Janssen, I. 134
Janus-faced sport 25–6
Jeffares, S. 27
Jensky, N.E. 138
Jolly, K. 137

Kahn, H.S. 134
Katzmarzyk, P.T. 134
Kawamoto, T. 138
Keno, Y. 138
key questions on health improvement 152–6; participants 152–6
Keynesian–Monetarist split 26
Kobatake, T. 138
Kramer, M. 15
Krustrup, B.R. 137–8
Krustrup, P. 137–8
Kuk, J.L. 134
Kvale, S. 31

La Santiago Bernabeu 50
lack of engagement 102–3
Lancet 3
Lee, R. 123
Leeds Metropolitan University 4, 84
legislative context of Big Society 26–7
Leishman, J. 133
Level Playing Field 45, 47, 50–51
levels of attendance 49–51
Lewis, A. 137
life expectancy 61–2, 73, 83–4, 97, 113, 130
Liga de Fútbol Professional 49–52
limited resources 33–4
Little United and Big Society 25–41; conclusion 38–9; findings 32–8; introduction 25–31; methods 31–2
Liverpool FC 28, 34
Liverpool John Moores University 4, 63, 74–5, 99, 101, 113–14
LJMU *see* Liverpool John Moores University
Local Enterprise Partnership 29
Localism Act 2011 26–8
locating health schemes in football settings 156
Lord Kitchener 26
Loudon, Jenny 31, 36–7
loyalty 130
LPF *see* Level Playing Field
Luker, R. 46

McKee, M. 97–8
McKenna, J. 106, 121, 158
Madsen, S. 97–8
Makara, P. 97–8
making activity choices 81
male role socialization 98
management of data 151–2
managerial implications for clubs 52–4
Manchester City FC 34, 45
Manchester Metropolitan Football 4

INDEX

Manchester United FC 28–30, 34, 45, 47, 50, 53
Mann–Whitney U tests 84
marginalization 98–9
Marginson, Karl 34
masculine identity 98–9
match attendance levels 49–51
match day events 97–111
match day ritual 107
Matsuzawa, Y. 138
Matten, D. 6, 10
meaning of 'Big Society' 32–8; employment enhancement 36–7; esteem factors 34–5; having 'politics' 37–8; as resource 33–4; structures of real engagement 35–6
measurements from FitC programme 63–5; immersion/observation 64–5; physiological 64
measurements from Motivate programme 134–5
Melanson, E. 134
Mellor, G. 13
men's health themed match day events 97–111; conclusion 107; data analysis and representation 101–2; discussion 106–7; implications for practice 107; introduction 97–9; methods 100; research design 100–101; researcher profile 99; results 102–6
metabolic health 81
Miller, K. 99, 101, 117
mobilization 37–8
moderate-to-vigorous physical activity 132–4, 137, 139–40; *see also* physical activity
Moeykens, B. 100
Mohr, M. 137–8
Moloney, T. 100
morbidity 81
Morrow, S. 13
motivation 129–47; conclusion 140; discussion 137–9; introduction 129–31; limitations and strengths 139–40; methods 131–5; results 135–7
Motive programme 131–4
multiple health problems 75
Mutrie, N. 120, 133
MVPA *see* moderate-to-vigorous physical activity

NADS *see* National Association of Disabled Supporters
national Association of Disabled Supporters 45
National Football Museum 29
National Health Service 63, 81, 120, 131, 149–50
NCDs *see* non-communicable diseases

NCFIT *see* Notts County Football in the Community
NEETs *see* 'not in education, employment or training'
negotiating gaps between football and social inclusion 25–41
neighbourhood communities 30
New Labour 2, 9, 14, 16, 30, 112–13
'new old market' 46
NICE guidance 133
Nielsen, J.J. 137–8
non-communicable diseases 97, 115, 149–50
Norman, Jesse 27, 39
'not in education, employment or training' 38
Nottingham Trent University 131
Notts County Football in the Community 131–5; intervention context 131–4; procedures 134–5; statistical analysis 135
NVQ training 31
Nybol, L. 137–8

obesity 61–2, 73, 97, 113, 129–31, 134–7, 150
objectives of research 151
observation 64–5
Office for Disability Issues 47, 51
Office for National Statistics 47
Old Trafford Stadium 45, 47, 50
older fans 42–60, 80–96, 129–47; club policies for 52; effect of weight loss programme 129–47; European demographic trends 47–8; health-improvement pilot programme 80–96; increasing economic/social relevance of 42–60; spending power of 51; sport/leisure interests 48–9
older men's health promotion 61–79
Open Public Services Act 2012 27
opportunities for football 27–9
organizational collaboration 8
outcomes of GG programme 90–91
outcomes of inclusivity research 47–9; demographic trends 47–8; sports/leisure interests 48–9

PA *see* physical activity
Palazzo, G. 9–10
Paramio Salcines, J.L. 48
Pardo, R. 48
Parker, B. 7–12, 18–19
participant burden 159
participants' needs 65–73
participation in physical activity programmes 115–16
peer mentoring 82

171

INDEX

Perkins, S. 130
perspective 65–7
Petersen, J. 137
philanthropy 9, 19
physical activity 61–79, 100, 114–15, 129–47
physiological measurements 64–5
pilot Golden Goal 84–7; demographic profile 84–5; EQ 5D questionnaire profiles 85–7; pre-intervention health screening profiles 85
Pirelli Stadium 83, 89
Platini, Michael 42
Playing for Success 14
'politics' 37–8
Porter, M. 15
Positive Futures 14
powerful lever for improving public health 156–9; appeal of football settings 156; evaluating football-led health programmes 157; research limitations 159; strategies for evaluating health programmes 157–9
practitioner perspectives on older men's health 61–79
practitioner skills base 121–2
practitioner–researcher role 99
pre-intervention health screening 85
premature death 97–8
Premier League 7, 16, 25, 45–7, 49–52, 62–3, 80–82, 97–128, 149–50; ethnographic engagement 112–28; health themed match day events 97–111; Scotland 3
Premier League Men's Health programme 82, 89
Preston, L.E. 9
primary interest in collaboration 12–13
Primera Liga 46–7, 49–50
principles of ethnography 116–17
Pringle, A. 106, 121, 156, 158
problem definition 15–16
process of creating reality 20
professional football 6–24, 52, 80–96; club policies 52; corporate social responsibility and 6–24; health promotion programmes 80–96
Professional Footballers' Association 2, 130
promotion of physical activity with OAs 89–90
public health guidance 81–9
public service reform 27029

quality of life 81

raising health awareness 2–3
Randers, M.B. 137–8
rapport 72, 74

RE-AIM framework 158–9
real engagement structures 35–6
Real Madrid 50
reality check 71–3
Refugee and Asylum Seekers 31
regeneration 30
relevance of older fans 42–60
representation of data 65, 101–2, 117–18
reputation of football 2
resource transfer 38
resources 33–4
ResPublica 27
results of Fit Fans programme 65–7; health needs 65; participant goals 65–7
Richardson, D. 117
richness of data 123
risk factor scores 135–7
Robertson, S. 98, 106, 121
Rochdale FC 35
role of practitioner 74–5
role of researcher 123
Ross, R. 134
Rudd, R. 100
Ryan, A. 8

Scherer, A.G. 9–10
Scott, W.R. 20
Scott-Parker, S. 45–6, 53
Scottish Premier League 3, 13, 62, 120, 133, 157
Scudamore, Richard 49
Seitanidi, M.M. 8
self-confidence 134
self-efficacy 81–2
self-help 26–7, 73–4
self-identity 28
self-interest 12, 18–19
self-sufficiency 28
Selsky, J.W. 7–12, 18–19
semi-structured interviews 10
separation of social inclusion 25–41
settings for research 131
Shapiro–Wilk test 135
Sheth, H. 19
Shilbury, D. 7
Sirard, J. 134
skills shortages 3
Sky-ification of football 2
Skype 47
Smith, A. 156
smoking cessation 100, 113
social cognitive theory 63
social composition of attendance 49–51

INDEX

social good 1–4, 112
social isolation 81–2
social partnerships 6–24
social problem communities 30
social relevance of older fans 42–60
social role of football 4
source of problem definition 15–16
Sousa, A. 122
South Africa 1; World Cup 2010 1
space for development 38–9
Spain 43, 47, 49–51
Spanish Statistics Office 48
spending power 51
sport/leisure interests 48–9
Sports Council 2
Spotlight of Cheetham Hill 33–4
State of Men's Health in Europe 97–8
statistical analysis 135
Statistical Package for Social Science 84
staying onside 148–65
Stone, C. 13
Stone, S. 46
strategic motivations 7–8, 10–11, 19
strategies for evaluating football-led schemes 157–9
strong synergies 19
structures of real engagement 35–6
study sampling 151
subliminal messages 103–4
suicide 97
supporters 42–60
sustainability 16

t-testing 84
Tackling Men's Health intervention 98–9, 106, 120
take-home messages 90, 106–7
Taking Part 48
Taylor, P. 48, 113
Thatcher, Margaret 28
Third Way 2
time frame 17–18
Tokunaga, K. 138
Tottenham Hotspurs 13
Treweek, S. 120

Trojan horse 39
types of social partnership 6

UEFA 42, 47–8, 122
underlying analytic platforms 8–10
understanding football stadia 43–6
understanding impact of Fit Fans intervention 67–73; reality check 71–3
understanding participant health needs 61–79
understanding social partnerships 18–20
United States 45, 51
universal accessibility 52–3
US Department of Justice 51
use of limited resources 33–4

van de Ven, B. 9
VIP experience 43
volunteering 27, 31, 36–7
vulnerability 98

walking schemes 82–3, 116, 150
Walking the Way to Health 150
Walsh, Andy 31–3, 35, 38
Walsh, D. 100
Wassel, C.L. 138
watching the match 97–111
ways forward for FitC 122–3
weight loss interventions 129–47
Welborn, T.A. 134
White, A. 97–9, 106, 120–21
WHO *see* World Health Organization
Wilcoxon signed rank tests 84
Wilkins, D. 98, 106
Witty, K. 98–9, 106, 120
Wolfe, R. 14
World Cup 1, 3
World Health Organization 129–31, 134
Wright, C.M. 138
Wyke, S. 120, 133, 139

Yo-Yo test 138
young-older men 73–5

Zadek, S. 45–6, 53
Zwolinsky, S. 106, 121, 156, 158